Making IT
LEAN

Applying Lean Practices to the Work of **IT**

Howard Williams • Rebecca Duray

Making IT
LEAN

Applying Lean Practices to the Work of **IT**

CRC Press
Taylor & Francis Group
Boca Raton   London   New York

CRC Press is an imprint of the
Taylor & Francis Group, an **informa** business

Trademark Notice: Product or corporate names may be trademarks or registered trademarks, and are used only for identification and explanation without the intent to infringe.

ITIL is a registered trademark of the Cabinet Office.

CRC Press
Taylor & Francis Group
6000 Broken Sound Parkway NW, Suite 300
Boca Raton, FL 33487-2742

© 2013 by Taylor & Francis Group, LLC
CRC Press is an imprint of Taylor & Francis Group, an Informa business

No claim to original U.S. Government works

Printed in the United States of America on acid-free paper
Version Date: 20121004

International Standard Book Number: 978-1-4398-7602-2 (Paperback)

Library of Congress Cataloging-in-Publication Data

Williams, Howard.
  Making IT lean : applying lean practices to the work of IT / Howard Williams and Rebecca Duray.
    p. cm.
  Includes bibliographical references and index.
  ISBN 978-1-4398-7602-2
  1. Software engineering--Management. 2. Information technology--Management. 3. Electronic data processing departments--Management. 4. Computer software--Development--Cost control. 5. Lean manufacturing. I. Duray, Rebecca. II. Title.

QA76.758.W535 2013
005.1068--dc23
                                                                          2012022422

Visit the Taylor & Francis Web site at
http://www.taylorandfrancis.com

and the CRC Press Web site at
http://www.crcpress.com

Contents

Preface ix

1 Introduction 1
    Lean 2
    Lean Improvement Model 4
    Narrative of the Book 6
        A Word about our References 9
    References 9

2 The Work of IT 11
    The IT View of IT 11
    IT Work as Process-Based Work 13
    People–Process–Technology 14
    IT as Service-Based Work 17
    Business–IT Alignment 18
    IT Operations 21
    Lean IT 22
    Making IT Lean 24
    Summary 26
    References 26

3 The OM Perspective 27
    Process Types 28
    Process Types in IT Work 31
    Customer Contact Workflow Model 35
    Workflow Concepts 38
        Volume, Variety, and Variation 38
        Concepts of Flow 41
        Waiting in Line 42
        Capacity 44

Looking at the IT Factory 45
Process Analysis 45
Process Improvement 51
Quality Improvement 53
Summary 55
References 55

4 The Lean Improvement Model 57
Lean Thinking 59
  Customer Value 59
  Value Stream Flow 60
  Elimination of Waste 61
  Continuous Improvement 63
Lean Learning 63
  A3 Thinking 64
  Plan–Do–Check–Act 66
Lean Problem-Solving 71
Lean Tools 71
Lean Enablers 73
Summary 74
Appendix: Examples of Waste in IT Work 74
References 77

**5 Lean Problem-Solving: Identifying and Understanding
Problems 79**
Identifying Waste 79
Stumbling on Waste from Pain Points 81
  Tool: Process Mapping 83
  Tool: Swim-Lane Diagram 85
  Tool: RACI Chart 86
  More on Process Mapping 87
  Root Cause Analysis (RCA) 90
  Tool: Cause and Effect Diagram 91
Identifying Waste in Clearly Identified Workflows 95
  Tool: Value Stream Map 97
  Tool: 5 Whys 104
  Tool: Pareto Chart 106
Clarifying Difficult-to-Identify Workflows 107
  Tool: Go-and-See (Gemba) 109
Surfacing Waste and Exposing Problems 113

Tool: Removal of Work-in-Progress (WIP)................................114
Tool: 5S 117
    Sort 118
    Straighten 118
    Shine 118
    Standardize 118
    Sustain...119
Tool: Visual Management..120
Tool: A3 Reports 121
Summary 121
References 122

6 Lean Problem-Solving: Identifying and Managing Solutions ..123
Starting with Root Causes..123
Identifying Solutions 124
    Tool: Brainstorming...125
Planning, Implementing, and Improving Solutions 128
Tool: PDCA..129
    Tool: Checklists 130
    Tool: Mistake Proofing 131
Creating Flow 132
    Tool: Pull (versus Push)...135
    Tool: One-Piece Flow (versus Batch)............................138
    Tool: Rapid Changeover 138
    Tool: Work Cell Optimization 139
Automation of IT Operations 140
Improving Nonlinear Processes...141
Continuous Improvement 141
    Kaizen..142
    Tool: Rapid Improvement Events.................................143
Summary 144
References 144

7 Lean IT Service Management..147
IT Infrastructure Library (ITIL)...147
Incident Management 150
Problem Management 154
Service Request Fulfillment 155
Service Desk..157
    External View of the Service Desk.................................158

Internal View of the Service Desk...160
Lean Service Desk 164
Applying Lean to Other ITSM Processes...166
Availability Management 166
Event Management 166
Change Management...167
Implementing Lean ITSM..168
Summary 171
References 171

8   **Implementing and Sustaining Lean IT Improvements 173**
Continuous Improvement 174
Rapid Improvement Events 175
Lean Enablers..178
Dealing with Obstacles 182
Tool: 5 Questions 186
Lean Culture..187
Metrics and Measurement..188
Lean IT at Work 191
Lean IT in a Healthcare Company...191
Lean IT at a Health Insurance Company 196
Lean IT in a Hospital 200
Summary 205
References 206

9   **Looking at Lean IT 207**
Future Drivers of IT Work 207
The Role of Lean..208
References 210

Index 211

Preface

This book has its origins in an independent study course taken by one of the authors (Howard), at that time a student in the MBA program at University of Colorado at Colorado Springs (UCCS), under the direction of the second author (Rebecca), who is a professor of Operations Management at UCCS. The focus of the independent study, Applications of Lean to IT (Information Technology), was an outgrowth of a more general class on Lean taken by Howard and taught by Rebecca in the previous semester.

We thought the topic would be well-covered in the literature, so our intention was to read what was written, summarize the content, and use the findings for our respective purposes. For Howard, this meant applying Lean practices within IT, where he worked, and, for Rebecca, this would mean adding to her body of knowledge on applications of Lean in various disciplines.

Our surprise was that not much had been written at that time on the subject. This led to a more detailed line of inquiry that extended well beyond the timeframe of the course, and, in fact, beyond Howard's completion of his MBA. What began as a student–professor affiliation evolved into a true research collaboration that eventually led to publication of this book.

By the time we had outlined the general scope of the book, we were delighted to find that there had been other books published on the subject, and this naturally led to consideration of the best niche on which to concentrate. What we finally decided was that there might be value in offering a book for IT practitioners who had limited exposure to Lean, and also make it appropriate for Lean practitioners who had not yet had the opportunity to look at IT as a domain of application. There is a bit more focus on the first audience, if only because the presentation of Lean practices is simplified for the demands and challenges that often characterize IT work. So, for example, we have deliberately simplified many of the Lean tools so that they can be utilized fairly quickly by IT practitioners. We are hopeful that Lean practitioners who have a more sophisticated understanding of tools and practices will appreciate the intent behind this presentation, and also will gain something from a deeper understanding of IT operational work.

Our intention is to bring a practitioner's orientation to the subject. For the Lean practitioner, as well as the IT practitioner, we provide a starting point for doing real-world applications of Lean IT. In fact, our aim is to present material in such a way that practitioners can consider how to *immediately* apply the concepts. We believe that Lean is that intuitive and that easy to use.

As a product of collaboration, there are others who have helped us along the way, and we wish to give credit to these individuals for the time and effort they have spent on our behalf.

For review of draft content, critical feedback, and suggestions, as well as shared knowledge and experience, we would like to thank the following individuals: Judy Gerber (Accenture), John Toth (Hewlett-Packard), Ann Hickey (University of Colorado at Colorado Springs), Bob Grinsell (Blue Cross Blue Shield of Minnesota), Dan Lafever (Franciscan Alliance), and Glenn Coleman (Merck & Co.).

For improvement of many of the operational workflow models used throughout the book, Howard would like to thank two of his colleagues at Microsoft, Amy Hariharan and Michael Wheatfill, who generously shared their knowledge and experience.

For patient rendering of all the figures and models in the book, we would also like to thank Kayla Ross of University of Colorado at Colorado Springs.

Finally, for guiding us through the process of publishing this, our first book, we would like to thank Michael Sinocchi, Amber Donley, Theresa Delforn, Jay Margolis, and Sophie Kirkwood of Productivity Press.

On a personal note, Howard would like to thank his wife, Linda, whose contribution goes well beyond merely tolerating the time spent at work on the book. Her role included not only active ongoing encouragement, but, in fact, she can take much of the responsibility for my embarking on this effort by encouraging me to write a book in the first place, and before then, by encouraging me to get my MBA. I thank Linda with all my heart.

Rebecca would like to thank her husband, Jim Zerefos, for his continual support in all her endeavors, her daughter, Kate, for sharing her weekends with Mom's book, and all her students who shared their process improvement journeys.

Chapter 1

Introduction

This book is based on the simple, but powerful, idea that a set of process and quality improvement practices that have historically been associated with advanced manufacturing operations can be usefully applied to the operational work of IT. It is, in short, about the application of *Lean* practices to the work of *IT*.

We will introduce these topics, Lean and IT, in a somewhat deliberate manner, but it's possible to quickly identify the critical intersect between them by way of the following example.

Consider an IT project that's behind schedule. What else is new, you might say! There is a lot of pressure on the team to meet the current deadline, and everyone is working late to do so. Everyone is tired. There aren't enough resources anyway, and everyone knows this, but we are all grateful for our jobs, so we do the best we can without complaint (well, some grumbling, maybe). A critical application update needs to be installed, so this represents operational work that the project depends on. In other words, there is a team (call it the Apps Support team) that does this sort of work all of the time, and now they are going to do it as part of the project's critical path of tasks. Because of the demand on this team for many other assignments, including other projects and ongoing operations support, we have identified the best window in which this work should happen, and we have scheduled it through Change Management. The update should take four hours, and the update window starts at 10 p.m. Work commences, when suddenly something happens—we don't know what—but there is an outage in the production environment. As it turns out, it takes a full 24 hours to resolve it, and this not only puts the project behind schedule, but, during that time, we had business users who couldn't access critical business applications. Another consequence is that all of the other work that the Apps Support team had in its queue is now delayed as well.

We could carry the example further, but this is probably sufficient to make the point. Another day in the life of IT perhaps, but there is a decidedly operational interpretation of events that makes this completely similar to problems we might confront on a production line in a factory. We have "products" in the form of projects and tasks being pushed down the line. We have volume and schedule demands being placed on resources. Most importantly, for our purposes here, we have delays in getting products completed, we have backlogs and bottlenecks at points along the production line, and, finally, we have defects in the product itself.

Delays, bottlenecks, backlogs, and defects. This is a not uncommon profile for work in IT, and, even if the results are not always catastrophic, they are often critical enough in our day-to-day life to occupy significant amounts of time in their prevention or remediation. These symptoms of underlying problems (for that is what they really are) also are precisely in the ballpark of Lean improvement and Lean solutions.

Lean

So what is Lean? For right now, let's just say it's an approach to solving problems that emphasizes quality and efficiency in operations, especially for the processes that underlie these operations. In other words, all the world of operational process, regardless of domain, serves as the stage for Lean application. That means IT, too.

That is not much of a definition, but we think that the question is almost like asking "What is yoga?" We can define it upfront, but it's probably better to just try it out. Here our philosophy is that we can address the question "What is Lean?" from multiple perspectives (which we will throughout this book), but it also makes sense for the reader to get real experience with Lean along the way, if for no other reason than that doing reinforces learning, and learning Lean is what this book is about. To this end, we will be using simple examples of various Lean tools throughout this book, in the hope that this will help the learning process.

Ironically, even though Lean has its origins in manufacturing, we won't have a lot to say about this area of application. One of the main reasons is that there have been many good books written on the subject, and many other books on Lean applications in other domains include introductions to the history of Lean.[1,2] When we consider the application of Lean to other disciplines, particularly those with administrative- or service-based orientations, we believe there is a fairly close connection to the work of IT. This suggests that the benefits gained in use of Lean in these other disciplines might equally be realized within IT.

One Lean author and consultant, Jeanne Cunningham,[3] has suggested that within many businesses there is a natural evolution of Lean applications from manufacturing (where it all began) to essential business functions, such as purchasing or sales support, before we see evidence of its use within IT. This makes sense when we think about the primacy of business processes in support of business objectives. As every IT practitioner knows, it is in support of the business where IT value is perceived and provided, and IT neglects this relationship at its peril. More pertinent to our argument here is, if the business process is inefficient and wasteful, it is hard to see how any IT solution can do much more than compensate for these inefficiencies. Overall then, we might view applications of Lean to IT as an indicator of a company's maturity in use of quality management practices generally.

One of our contentions throughout this book is that the benefits of using Lean are gained chiefly by looking at the world of work from a Lean perspective. This is much more than applying a set of tools that have conventionally been associated with Lean. It is about looking at things in a way that is somewhat different than many of us are used to. The Lean orientation that helps in seeing the world differently is what is sometimes called Lean Thinking. The notion of Lean Thinking was popularized by Womack and Jones in their book by the same name,[4] and in that book they highlight a number of concepts, such as emphasis on customer value, flow through a value stream, elimination of waste, and continuous improvement. We will spend some time with these concepts throughout the book because we believe they are fundamentally important in order to appreciate the value of Lean and also to understand how best to apply these notions to the work of IT.

We purposefully adopt a broad definition of Lean throughout the book, and this definition will actually accommodate a variety of practices that are related to Lean but have different names, such as Six Sigma. In fact, many of these practices that we might call Lean, in some cases could be viewed as good common sense applied to problems. We will argue that this broad definition is consistent with the notions of Lean Thinking and is helpful to the practitioner because it allows for great flexibility and creativity in applying these notions to real work. Consistent with this orientation, we also will argue that Lean is much more than a set of tools, but is really about a larger set of practices that, taken together, can be associated with what we refer to as Lean Culture.

Lean is fundamentally about the improvement of process-based work, and, as we shall see, processes are ubiquitous within the domain of IT work. In fact, processes are actually evident everywhere we look, regardless of the domain under consideration, and it is for this reason that we find potential applications of Lean both widespread and potentially far-reaching in their impact. We can easily observe the flip side of Lean, namely inefficiency and waste, in a great many places, and even though we may not think of it in these terms, the likely culprits for what we observe are very often process-based and just as often amenable to correction through application of Lean practices. We can think of these instances of waste and inefficiency as *un-Lean* indeed, and with an increased understanding of Lean concepts it is possible to identify the causes of inefficiency and waste, and then do something about it.

One of the benefits of Lean, and of Lean Thinking specifically, is that it can serve as a lens through which we view the world of process-based work. It helps to clarify the nature of the work (*how* it works) and helps to understand the underlying causes of inefficiencies and waste that often characterize work. Finally, it helps by providing a set of tools that can assist not only in solving problems, but in identifying problems in the first place.

Lean Improvement Model

Most books on Lean include models that capture the authors' sense of what Lean is all about, and below is ours. We will use this as a reference point throughout the book and, in fact, will devote an entire chapter to its description (Figure 1.1).

We introduce the model here so the reader can gain a toe-hold on our principal themes and topics right at the start. In the model, we provide some direction on things we think are important (Do This Work, and Think This Way, and Use These Tools, and Enable Everything, and Learn to Improve). While prescriptive in tone, we do not want to suggest

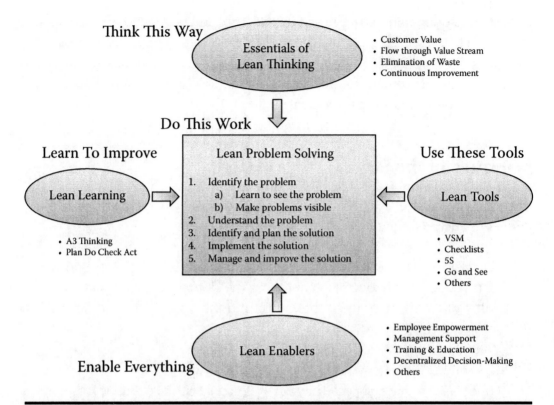

Figure 1.1 Lean Improvement Model.

that Lean is a cookbook and all you have to do is follow the recipe. It is more like a way of seeing things in the world around us, and once this orientation is adopted (by choice and through hard work), it allows us to see opportunities for improvement where previously we might only have seen obstacles.

Doing the Work is central and this is all about Lean problem-solving, which, as we will see, is really not much different than good, sound problem-solving that any other methodology for improvement might employ. What makes it Lean is how it is done, and the *how* of it is characterized by Lean Thinking, which is a distillation of essential principles we find in many Lean solutions, and Lean Learning, which is an approach to problem-solving that is not unlike scientific reasoning applied to process-based work.

We have devised the Lean Improvement Model so that it is hopefully easy to comprehend. It would be great if the reader looked at the model and said something like: "That's simple enough." We would like that because we believe that much of Lean is, or should be, quite simple. We will have plenty of time to discuss what is challenging about Lean, but as we will see, it's almost exactly parallel to the situation one encounters when learning a new skill, such as playing the piano. The early lessons are actually quite simple. The hard part is practicing. The fundamental idea is that by making small, incremental improvement frequently, over a period of time, significant gains in skill and performance can be achieved.

Narrative of the Book

Briefly, the narrative (Figure 1.2) that we will explore throughout this book addresses the following topics:

1. *The Work of IT*: We will start by looking at the work of IT from an IT practitioner perspective, identifying the domain of work that we will work with throughout this book, and then consider what Lean IT means in this context.
2. *The OM Perspective*: We will then look at the work of IT from an Operations Management (OM) perspective, showing how many of the concepts that have successfully been applied within manufacturing and services can be applied to IT. The purpose of this chapter is to help complement conventional IT interpretations of problems and issues that we confront in the work of IT with notions that are common across other operational domains.
3. *The Lean Improvement Model*: Here we will look at the concepts and practices that we refer to as Lean, and present in detail our model for Lean improvement.
4. *Lean Problem-Solving (Identifying and Understanding Problems)*: In this chapter, we will look in detail at operational work in IT and apply Lean concepts and practices related to problem identification and root cause analysis.
5. *Lean Problem-Solving (Identifying and Managing Solutions)*: We use good problem identification as the basis for identifying good solutions and then discuss how solutions, once implemented, are managed and improved.
6. *Lean IT Service Management*: We will extend the discussion begun in the previous two chapters and take a somewhat different focus by looking at IT work from an IT Service Management (ITSM) perspective, using the ITIL[5] framework as a guide.

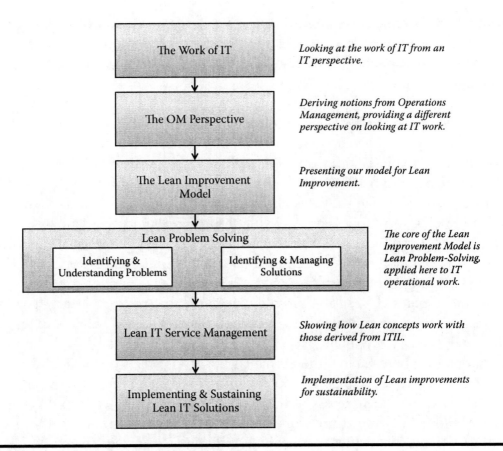

Figure 1.2   Narrative structure for the book.

7. *Implementing and Sustaining Lean IT Improvements:* Our final topic will look at what it means to implement Lean IT improvements, and particularly, how these improvements can be sustained over time. Within this chapter, we will include case experiences that provide demonstration of many concepts discussed throughout the book.

We used the analogy of piano playing above and, perhaps the reader can find an activity, hobby, or interest of his or her own that seems intuitive and relevant as an analogy for this notion of incremental skill development. We would like to suggest that any activity that requires skill and practice is a good one. Sometimes in IT we have a tendency to think that any improvements can only be gained by starting a program (or at least a project) and investing in a long timeline to do the work that leads—hopefully—to some desired improvement. Alas, this is often not the case, as the work often gets complicated by hundreds of everyday interruptions and obstacles, and the planned improvements seem further and further from sight. We think Lean provides a better way of looking at this. To come back to our piano playing, rather than spend a lot of time working out how to play the piano, we would like to turn focus on just practicing, first with simple lessons, and then increasing the degree of challenge over time.

We have designed the book and introduction of concepts within it in such a way that you can take away small bits at a time and apply the notions within your IT operation. We really want you to try out these ideas. We also happen to believe that there is no *one* right way of doing so. We think it's okay to make mistakes and we think that sincerity and the right effort in doing work in a Lean way will ensure, over time, that you are doing what is right for your organization. Coupled with that is our belief that any IT organization can benefit from Lean, so we think that the opportunity space for Lean improvements is practically endless.

Another expected response from the reader is that you might say, in looking at various ideas and practices: "We already do that." We would expect that, and, actually, we might expect that you have this response without even knowing perhaps that the particular notion or practice is related to Lean. If that's the case, then the book can be helpful in positioning what you already do in the context of what it means to do Lean. For those who might think that Lean cannot work in their particular environments, the counterpoint is that you are probably already doing it in some way or another, so it will be helpful to recognize where you have these Lean practices so you can further build on them.

In other cases, you might say something like: "Well, we do that, but not very well," or "We don't do that at all." These responses will suggest areas of potential improvement within the overall scheme of implementing Lean solutions. Hopefully, seeing how various Lean ideas and practices relate to your current environment (as a form of gap analysis) and to a desired future environment (as a design activity) can help in accelerating improvements and in sustaining them over time.

The practical orientation of this book is reinforced by the way in which we have used models throughout. The reader will notice that some of them are not particularly sophisticated in use of modeling conventions, and we have done that on purpose so that we can emphasize the purpose behind various features of the models. We want to provide the reader with enough modeling tools so that you can start your Lean experience right away, and, with that objective, we have provided examples that are simple and straightforward in their derivation and representation.

Finally, we would like to say that we see this book as complementary to other, very good books on the same subject.[6,7,8] There are also numerous books on Lean applications in other disciplines[9,10] that, as we shall see, also can be related to applications in IT. Our particular focus is on creating a beginner's guide to Lean IT, not by simplifying the work of IT (which is hard to do), but by showing how much of the complexity of IT work can be penetrated and influenced by Lean Thinking.

Lean practitioners often regard themselves as being on a journey of sorts, and that metaphor carries with it various notions, an important one being that it is the journey that is important, and not the destination. Not to sound too philosophical, but in this sense, the journey *is* the destination. It's how we get there that counts, and as we will see, getting there is accomplished in small, measured steps that over time will introduce efficiency into your IT operations. It's never-ending and it's continuous, and that is the point.

With this as our introduction then, let's start the Lean Journey.

A Word about our References

Lean practitioners are avid learners, borrowing from other disciplines and resources to develop their own knowledge over time. Our lists of references at the end of each chapter are not just intended as supplemental, nice-to-know sources, but rather, in some respects, *required* reading. No single book will tell it all, so it helps to gain different perspectives on Lean concepts and practices.

References

1. Liker, J. K. 2004. *The Toyota way*. New York: McGraw-Hill.
2. Womack, J. P., D. T. Jones, and D. Roos. 1990. *The machine that changed the world*. New York: Simon & Schuster..
3. Cunningham, J. 2012. Are lean IT and agile compatible? Online at: http:// www. jeancunninghamconsulting.com/ (accessed July 15, 2012).
4. Womack, J. P. and D. T. Jones. 2003. *Lean thinking*. New York: Simon & Schuster.
5. ITIL® and IT Infrastructure Library® are registered trademarks of the U.K. Government Cabinet Office. See the official ITIL® web site for information on intellectual property rights (http://www.itil-officialsite.com) Information in this book that is derived from the IT Infrastructure Library® is noted with

acknowledgment and in compliance with intellectual property guidelines. Diagrams based on the ITIL® content are original works of the authors and are not representations from the Library. Unless otherwise noted, content is derived from Verizon 3 of the IT Infrastructure Library® (2007).

6. Cunningham, J. and D. Jones. 2007. *Easier, simpler, faster: Systems strategy for Lean IT*. New York: Productivity Press.
7. Bell, S. C. and M. A. Orzen. 2011. *Lean IT: Enabling and sustaining your Lean transformation*. New York: Productivity Press.
8. Plenert, G. J. 2011. *Lean management principles for Information Technology*. New York: Productivity Press; Plenert, G. J. 2011. Lean management principles for Information Technology. New York: Productivity Press.
9. Graban, M. 2009. *Lean hospitals*. New York: Productivity Press.
10. Huber, J. J. 2011. *Lean library management*. New York: Neal-Schuman.

Chapter 2

The Work of IT

In this chapter, we are going to look at the operational work of IT (Information Technology) first from the perspective of an IT practitioner, and then set the stage for looking at this same work from a Lean perspective. When we look at IT from the point of view of someone who works in IT, we will often find a rather technology-focused perspective. This is understandable given the primary importance of technology within IT, and is probably reinforced by the attraction that technology has for individuals who choose this profession. By the same token, even with a technology bias, IT is obviously not just about technology. Most IT practitioners would acknowledge that there is an equally strong influence by both people and process that underlies much of the work that they do. When we consider IT work from a process perspective, we can begin to identify the domain of influence for Lean applications.

The IT View of IT

When IT practitioners look at the world around them, they see the demand to respond to rapid business change against a landscape of changing technology, and the requirement to deliver high-quality services while managing resources under tremendous cost constraints. They can take satisfaction in the successes they have achieved in balancing many competing demands. With a more critical lens, many practitioners may see opportunities for further improvement to services and operations. In some cases, they might even observe low-quality service delivery, inefficient or ineffective processes and operations, strained resources, low productivity, and, in a word, lots of *waste*.

Despite the motivation to identify and implement improvements based on these observations (or in IT parlance, despite the clear identification of pain points as a driver of change), we often observe that the IT practitioner is too busy or too distracted, or has insufficient resources to address solutions in a deliberate, focused way. Within his or her world of work, the immediate needs often take precedence and systemic issues often fade into the background. These immediate needs can be seen throughout the apparent jumble of activities that characterize day-to-day operational work of IT, and include such things as:

- Rolling out new technology to support mobile computing needs of users
- Managing increasingly complex networks (internal, external, Internet)
- Upgrading servers without loss of business functionality
- Responding to pressures from the business side of the organization to release new applications to support business needs
- Ensuring that security measures are implemented to prevent compromise to internal systems from both known and unknown threats
- Keeping critical business functions, such as email, operable and supported around the clock

This is just a short list of concerns that makes up the daily life of the IT practitioner, and despite the attention that these activities get, there are still things that can fall through the cracks. Ask a CIO (Chief Information Officer) what keeps him or her up at night and it's often the anxiety of not knowing what they don't (but should) know.

If we look at this jumble of operational work from a somewhat more structured perspective, but one which is still aligned with the IT viewpoint, we might categorize the work of IT according to the functions identified below:

- IT Operations (e.g., server provisioning, tape backups, job scheduling)
- Technical Management (e.g., network management, messaging, middleware)
- Applications Management (e.g., software development, testing)
- IT Project Management (project management for IT projects)
- IT Service Management (IT as a provider of services)

There are other ways to characterize the world of IT work, but we want to present this scheme as a somewhat familiar structure within many IT organizations. While individuals may play multiple roles across the boundaries of these functions, they still represent distinct areas of responsibility, and are in fact, often reflected in the organizational structures within IT. What they have in common, however, is that they are all inherently process-based.

IT Work as Process-Based Work

A process is an activity or set of activities that transform inputs into outputs. That simple, classical definition of a process suffices to argue that process-based work is pervasive in IT (as it is practically everywhere, we might add). It is especially easy to identify processes when work is sequential and repetitive, but even when it is not, it is still possible to identify the essential components of inputs, outputs, and transformational activities. The real question is not whether processes characterize the world of IT work, but rather how we should view and understand and work *with* these processes. For this, we want to adopt a view of processes that position them relative to current and future states, and also with a distinction between how they are designed and how they actually work in practice (Figure 2.1).

We have shown processes here as having three definable states. First, there is the Current State—*as designed*. This *"as-we-designed-it"* process is often mentioned when practitioners are asked how a particular process works. In other words, it's often how the process is represented by practitioner stakeholders, even though it is not usually how the process is actually

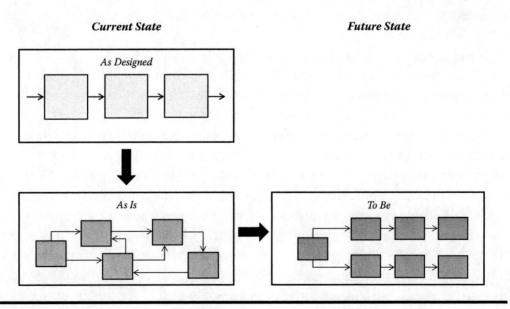

Figure 2.1   States of process-based IT work.

performed. Practitioners will often qualify this *as-designed* state by saying something like: "Well, at least that's how it's supposed to work." What we find, however, is that the *as-designed* process is often quite different from the actual process in its everyday *as-is* state.

The Current *as-is* State is the important starting point for process improvement. We will be spending time in this book talking about how an accurate representation of the Current *as-is* State can be derived and also about the importance of validating the *as-is* state through observation. It won't be sufficient to just ask someone how the process works. You need to verify how it works, because it is too easy (and common) for the *as-designed* state to substitute for the *as-is* state. Most importantly, it is the Current *as-is* State where the causes of many common problems, such as delays, bottlenecks, backlogs, and defects occur. Therefore, it is the starting point for considering Lean applications.

In addition, we also have a defined or implied Future *to-be* State, which is the desired state of the process based on process improvements to the Current State. What this suggests is that we will quite often be thinking in terms of moving from the Current State to the Future State. This idea of transformation is commonplace in IT, even if only in casual expression, as when we lament the current state of affairs and hope that someday things might be different. Unfortunately, the demands of day-to-day activities, putting out fires, and dealing with crises often keep the IT practitioner from improving the process.

People–Process–Technology

If we adopt a conventional IT abstraction for looking at IT work, we might, as suggested earlier, look at the work from a *People–Process–Technology* perspective. That is to say, regardless of whether we are looking at work associated with procurement, provisioning, network management, or software development, we can look at the work with respect to the *People* who perform the work (their roles, their skills, their morale, or even the organizational structures in which they reside). We also can look at the work with respect to the *Processes* that characterize the work (those pervasive, yet sometimes invisible streams of activities that determine how and how well work gets done, sometimes expressed as procedures, and often recognized as enablers or constraints on how people behave, e.g., "This is how we do it here."). Finally, we can look at the work with respect to *Technology*, which, as we said earlier, is often in the foreground and perhaps of primary interest to the IT practitioner.

This is sometimes represented as a three-legged stool, with one leg each for People, Process, and Technology—the idea being that we need to attend to all three in order to have a stable platform. This three-legged stool model often helps as a tool to communicate the importance of People and Process issues to practitioners who may think of the world predominantly in terms of Technology. It serves in this sense as a conversation piece, but it really does not do justice to the overriding importance of People and Process. In other words, People and Process issues are actually more important than this picture suggests. It might actually be more accurate to convey the relationship as seen in Figure 2.2.

In this representation, technology is wrapped in process, suggesting that technology supports the process and that technology, when implemented, often has its own process constraints. For example, we might design support activities (processes) for the IT Help Desk, and then support them with tool/technology solutions (Help Desk applications). However, these tool/technology solutions typically have their own constraints in how they work that impose their own processes on those who use them. Finally, we note that people design, use, participate in, and sometimes work against the processes that characterize their work. Above all, we like to think we can design processes that make the work of people easier and simpler.

Adopting the People–Process–Technology perspective, we can isolate each dimension and consider the work of IT from that particular vantage point. If we consider the work of a team that provides database management support, for example, we can look at the People and ask whether there are enough of them to do the work, whether they have the right skills, or

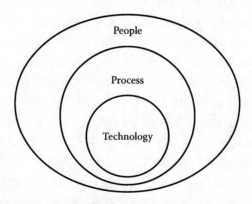

Figure 2.2 People, Process, and Technology.

whether they are adequately supported by their management team. There is, in fact, a very long list of potential considerations we might find by simply looking at their work from this perspective.

Likewise, a Process orientation will reveal much to the discerning eye. We might find uncoordinated work among team members, perhaps experienced as inadequate handoffs of information between shifts, or recognition that not all team members are using the same tools to perform certain routine maintenance procedures, or the simple observation that the work is not getting done well or on time. We also might observe finger-pointing by staff who may only partially appreciate that they do not have adequate process to support the work they do.

We have suggested that the Technology viewpoint may actually conceal some of the process work underlying the use of technology, and, in fact, we often find that technologists require some education in order to appreciate this parallel universe of concerns. But, of course, Technology has its own legitimate place in the overall perspective we are identifying here, and there is an ample amount of complexity to justify the distraction that Technology often provides.

What can we do with this People–Process–Technology perspective when we look at the categories of IT work we identified above? Simplistically, we can view it as a matrix by which we can undertake assessments within IT organizations. Likewise, it might be used for diagnostic purposes by asking the general question: "What's not working well here?" Finally, we might use the matrix as the basis for identifying specific opportunities for improvement. As such, it serves as a tool for a gap analysis ("What does it take to get from our current state to a desired future state?"). Table 2.1 is a matrix with this structure, including some sample questions.

One observation from using this matrix is that it's difficult to ask People and Technology questions without taking at least *some* Process considerations into account, suggesting that process issues are often lurking in the background when we look at the other dimensions. For example, when we ask whether the organizational structures might prevent us from getting work done quickly, it might be because the organization is structured around vertical "silos" and it's hard to work across boundaries, or it might be because there has been no attention to the processes that traverse these boundaries. Likewise, when we ask about component failure, it might be a purely technical issue at play or it could be the result of inadequate procurement or installation. These are all processes that could be documented and improved.

Table 2.1 People–Process–Technology Matrix

	People	*Process*	*Technology*
Assessment	• How much staff is needed to do a certain activity or job? • What's the current skill level of our workforce? • How is morale?	• What are the current audit procedures? • How long does it take to complete a server build? • To whom do I give this report?	• What's the capacity of our current email servers? • What's the availability of our email service? • What's our network load?
Diagnostics	• Is our organizational structure preventing us from getting work done quickly? • Why is staff reluctant to commit to project deadlines?	• Why does it take so long to build these servers? • Why was the Problem Manager not on the escalation call?	• Why is our component failure rate so high? • Did processor speed have anything to do with last night's outage?
Opportunities	• Can we do the same work with fewer people? • Can we do more work with the same people? • What are the required roles?	• Can we streamline this process so it can be done faster? • How can we prevent mistakes from happening when implementing changes?	• Will our new upgrades allow us to meet our service level targets? • What do we need to provide real-time performance data?

IT as Service-Based Work

Currently, there is a growing trend within IT to view IT as a service provider. As a service provider, IT's goals and objectives are the same as those of any service provider. That is, IT has motivation to define its work from the point of view of its customers, to ensure that IT delivers services that provide value to customers, and to provide these services in a cost-effective way. As with any service provider, if IT is unable to deliver cost-effective service that is valued by its customers, it is at risk of becoming obsolete.

However, the notion of service provision goes deeper than this. It means that IT views all of its work from a service perspective, defines it accordingly, and markets services to its customers. It can mean as well that it broadens the concept of customer to include not just the end user of its services or the customer who ultimately pays for the service, but any role in the supply chain of activities that comprise IT's work. Each IT service provider can be a customer to another IT service provider. When the Network team works with the Directory team, for example, each of these groups can view the other as a customer. By adopting this orientation, and viewing all its work as service-based, IT elevates its role from a reactive provider to a proactive one, because the only way to provide good service is to plan for it and design supporting processes to ensure its effectiveness.

Business–IT Alignment

If business success is the ultimate goal of IT, then any conversation regarding the work of IT and its successful implementation must begin with a good understanding of what it means for the business to be successful. When IT practitioners talk about business–IT alignment, they are referring to this level of understanding. This is a considerable challenge, because in some IT environments IT is viewed as a support function or cost center, its work is defined by solely administrative objectives ("keep email running"), and it seldom or never has a seat at the table with business owners. There was a time in IT when this more often than not characterized the business-as-usual situation in which IT practitioners operated. With the growing recognition that IT could have *strategic* value for the business, it became more critical for IT to take its seat at the table and figure out exactly what it meant to support the business.

Another way of looking at this is to look at the business from *its* point of view. The value of anything from the business perspective is realized by the achievement of objectives that are related to the business processes that effectively drive the business. Here we can think of processes, such as sales, marketing, logistics, order processing, accounts receivable, and so forth. These are processes that are *owned* by the business. They are directly related to goals of the business. If these processes function effectively (as designed), the business succeeds. If they do not, the business struggles.

Within these business processes are activities that are supported by people and technology, both of which play a role in the successful implementation of these business process activities. To the degree to which these roles directly contribute to the needs of the business process, they are aligned with the business process.

What if these supporting roles are not performed in a way that directly contributes to the needs of the business? In that case, we can say that the supporting functions (IT, for example) are not aligned, and their demonstration of value to the business will be correspondingly muted. What if the business process itself is not effectively designed or is operating very inefficiently? If there are problems, disconnects, or defects in the work at the *business* process level, then it is difficult if not impossible for the supporting roles to do much more than compensate for these inefficiencies. More often than not, they do essentially nothing of value and may even exacerbate the problems.

It's easy to see how crazy this can become. If the business does not have a well-defined set of processes to do its work and/or these processes are not operating effectively or efficiently, and the supporting functions (again, think IT) have trouble positioning their roles in support of the business in the first place, their contribution is not likely to be strategic in support of business goals. It is impossible under these circumstances to find the value derived from either the business process or the supporting process role that underpin it. It's fairly straightforward to see that the single most important priority of the business, under these circumstances, is to improve its business processes. Once that is done, then the supporting roles can be more clearly defined relative to the contribution they make.

Viewed in this context, we can begin to set the stage for how Lean applies to IT. We can see business process from a top-down perspective and IT from a bottom-up perspective. There is also a mediating role that is typically served by business services or business applications. These are directly utilized by the business to support its business requirements and are directly supported by IT.

We might think of this model as an end-to-end view of IT support of the business, or as a Business–IT Value Chain (Figure 2.3). We can begin with business processes, deconstruct them (decompose them into good faith representations of the Current *as-is* State) and consider their efficiency (or lack of it) from that point of view. This is the starting point for considering the improvements that need to be made to the business process, and for that, we will use Lean.

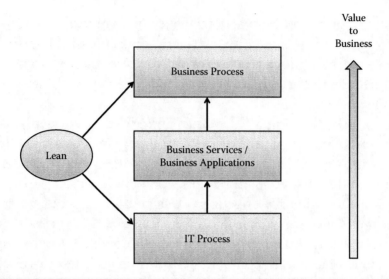

Figure 2.3 How Lean applies to the Business–IT value chain.

Similarly, we can look at IT processes, deconstruct them in a similar way, and also consider opportunities for improvement based on identified inefficiencies. These inefficiencies represent waste. For example, we can ask where there are sources of delays that might be attributed to IT, e.g., a change to a system that results in an outage. When we consider opportunities for improvement, again using Lean, we really are beginning to make a distinction between the Current *as-is* State and a Future *to-be* State.

Viewed altogether, we can see where inefficiencies in the business process trump all in priority, and must be addressed before it makes sense to look at the role of IT. But even with improvements to the business process, it is, of course, also possible that inefficiencies in the IT process can have impacts on the business, as with our errant change example above.

One of the reasons that IT process improvement efforts fail is because they do not take into account the full implications suggested by this model. Specifically, improvements within the IT realm are difficult enough, but when they are compromised or muted by inefficiencies in the business process itself, then it is challenging, if not impossible, to make the value connection between IT work and the business processes it supports. It's like making improvements to steering and braking on a car when the wheels are not balanced.

We have addressed the issue of Business–IT Alignment in some detail for two reasons. First, it is very important for IT to understand and address its relationship to the business. Second, it is the very best starting point for thinking about Lean applications. Because IT is often involved in the automation of business processes, adopting a Lean Approach will mean that IT needs to first simplify the process (Lean it) as a precondition to automation. In addition, we can Lean IT itself, because in so doing, it helps to eliminate sources of inefficiency and defects that may otherwise impact the business processes it supports.

IT Operations

The domain of IT Operations work is quite broad, and while it is not the intention here to provide an overview of the work itself, we will provide some top-down orientation in order to clarify our topic of discussion. For this, we adopt the framework for operational work as described within the IT Infrastructure Library (ITIL®).[1] ITIL is a framework of best practices that focuses on the provision of quality IT services. ITIL is widely used among IT practitioners and has become an increasingly popular reference model for implementation of both process and technical solutions within IT. In support of that, ITIL identifies core processes to support IT service operations, as well as the recommended workflows for many of these processes.

In ITIL, IT Operations includes operational work that is aligned with formal process areas (e.g., Access Management, Capacity Management, Security Management), as well as work that is conventionally associated with IT Operations, such as Network Management, Server Management, Storage and Archive, Database Administration, Directory Services Management, Desktop Support, and End-User Computing.

We might at this point say, and so forth, because the list of operational activities is seemingly endless in most IT Operations environments. We would like the reader to consider those operational activities that characterize his or her environment. The key takeaway is that *any* of these operational activities may be characterized from a People–Process–Technology perspective, and all of the processes can be represented in their Current *as-is* State (as long as they are in practice and not just in design). In addition, all of these processes may have problems of one sort or another (delays, backlogs, bottlenecks, defects), and therefore, any of them may be subject to Lean improvements.

Problems with processes in IT operational work will occupy the central focus of this book. We will look at these problems for what they are (using the Lean lexicon)—examples of waste. We will argue that waste is widespread and pervasive across IT operations. Rather than view this as simply a problem statement, we will talk about how these problems really represent opportunities for improvement. We also will argue that their occurrence is neither surprising nor blameworthy; that is, they should not be viewed as evidence of something wrong, but rather as the natural outcome of evolving processes that have not yet been subjected to Lean inquiry.

Lean IT

When we talk about Lean IT, we find that the term itself actually has two different interpretations, which reflect two complementary perspectives. One refers to the application of IT to support Lean business processes. For example, if the logistics operation in a business is improved through use of Lean practices, we may identify an opportunity for an IT service or solution to provide support for the improved operation. We refer to this meaning of the term as *IT for Lean*. On the other hand, we also can apply Lean practices to the work of IT itself, and we refer to this as *Lean for IT*.[2]

These two perspectives are represented in Figure 2.4. This model also looks at the larger domain of IT and serves as a framework for addressing the variety of potential applications.

IT for Lean means that the supporting role of IT is identified after and in direct contribution to the work and objectives of the improved *Lean* business process. The degree to which IT supports the improvement of a Lean business process means that IT is providing a *service* in support of the Lean business. Not only does IT support the business and its objectives, so does Lean. For that reason, we find many examples where business processes have been improved using Lean. These processes are evident not just in manufacturing, but could be processes in Human Resources (HR), Accounting, Sales, and so forth. At the end of the day, IT will always have a role in the modern organization, and almost every business process, once simplified, will have a role that requires IT skills and capabilities.

The view of process-based work corresponding to *Lean for IT* applications in this model shows a couple of different perspectives. One of these, the Service Lifecycle, is based on the ITIL framework for service-based IT improvement and corresponds with best practice guidance contained within ITIL Version 3. In addition, we have identified where the domain of IT

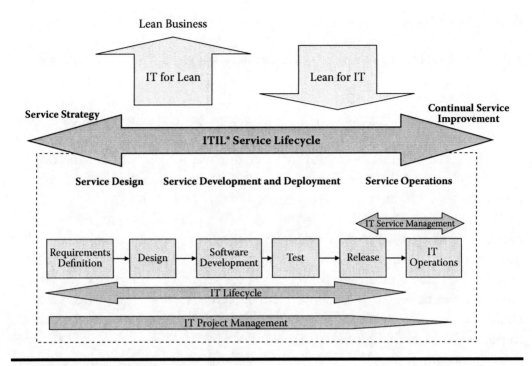

Figure 2.4   The domain of Lean IT.

Service Management applies, and this is conventionally associated with ITIL Version 2. (These distinctions are discussed in detail in Chapter 7.) The more conventional IT Lifecycle is also represented at the bottom of the diagram and it shows various clusters of IT work that most IT practitioners will find familiar. Finally, IT Project Management is identified as a parallel lifecycle underlying the work of the IT Lifecycle. Again, this work is process-based, so Lean inquiry applies.

This model of Lean IT serves as the framework for many of our discussions throughout the book and also provides quite a bit of material for us to work with. We can isolate any particular part of the model and consider the application of Lean concepts and practices within that area. In some cases, there is considerable experience in the use of Lean (e.g., Lean Project Management,[3,4] Lean Software Development[5,6]), and in other cases, we find only limited use of Lean. One of our arguments throughout the book is that Lean has not yet penetrated IT organizations in ways that parallel many other disciplines. Evidence of its limited use is, in our view, justification for identifying potential uses of Lean where we might not otherwise think of them.

Making IT Lean

For the IT practitioner, adoption of Lean may very well be a new and foreign way of looking at his or her world of work, although aspects should seem somewhat familiar. For example, we will look at IT work from a process perspective and, especially for practitioners of ITIL, this will be straightforward. For others, it will be helpful to first learn to see how process-based work pervades IT, and then with that perspective, also see where inefficiencies and waste can be found. As we will see, it is practically everywhere, providing us with many opportunities for improvement of IT work.

We believe that many Lean practices can be initiated without extensive planning and even, in some cases, without the support of management. This may seem like a surprising assertion, given that management support is conventionally viewed as a critical success factor for any IT improvement effort. However, we believe that grassroots efforts have been shown to be quite successful and we think this underscores the relative ease with which Lean improvements can be applied to IT. We will discuss this point in more detail throughout the book.

The reader may well ask, why, if Lean improvements are so relatively easy to apply and we know that they are commonly employed in manufacturing and in many service domains, we do not see more evidence of their use in IT. One possible explanation is that there are, in fact, examples of Lean IT applications but they don't get identified as Lean, either because the practitioner is not aware of the connection, or else they seem so simple and obvious that they do not warrant any particular categorization. In a sense, any time we make an efficiency improvement, we are very likely employing Lean concepts. As we will discover, Lean practices are sometimes very simple, and while they reflect the common and obvious origins of the practices themselves, they do not outwardly show the formalism that Lean provides. As an example, consider the pervasive application of what we formally call Plan–Do–Check–Act (sometimes referred to as the Deming Cycle). In some respects, we use PDCA everyday (although often not very well), but regardless of results, we are often unaware of its application.

A second reason why Lean practices may be less evident than might be expected has to do with where many companies are on the quality management maturity cycle. As mentioned earlier, many organizations do not show evidence of use of Lean practices until other Lean applications have been implemented (e.g., in support of critical business functions). So, while apparently obvious in their potential application, we believe that many IT practitioners do not use Lean more extensively simply because they are not generally aware of what the tools have to offer.

Another reason we may not see many examples of Lean in our day-to-day IT work is because it requires the ability to see problems and the symptoms of problems, namely waste, in a different way. That is, we see problems, but not through the Lean lens, and the consequence is that we have difficulty identifying the underlying root cause of these problems. In turn, it makes it difficult to apply Lean solutions if problems are not correctly identified and understood. Lean practitioners refer to this as "learning to see," and we will cover this topic more in Chapter 5. A related example reflects the way that many IT practitioners view their IT work, namely as project-based. This encourages them to view the entirety of their work as unique, or as one-off solutions, when there really is a lot of underlying common and repeatable work, and seeing this is a precondition for applying Lean solutions. But again, first you have to see it this way.

Finally, we also can say that Lean practices may not be more widely deployed, because while the practices themselves are straightforward to implement, making improvements *sustainable* over time is quite difficult. What this means is that the use of Lean tools and techniques is, in the long term, less important than how the tools are used and the underpinnings or enablers of Lean success. Here we can say that management support is a factor, although by no means the only factor. This enabling orientation is, we believe, reinforced by success in implementing Lean solutions in the first place, and together they help support the development of a Lean Culture as the direct result of incremental efforts that build on each other over time. They may begin as grassroots or bottom-up endeavors, but when viewed over the long term, they are the foundation of a Lean Culture.

When we talk about making IT Lean, we are not just talking about applying Lean concepts and practices for the sake of it, but we are talking about fixing real and common problems within the work of IT. In this respect, we can think of our objective in this book as providing resources to help the IT practitioner in identifying causes of common problems and finding solutions to address them. We believe that it is very common for IT practitioners to get so used to problems in their day-to-day work that it is easy to merely accommodate them, rather than to figure out how to get rid of them. In this sense, we can make the general assertion that, while process-based IT work does not, apparently, naturally evolve to a state of efficiency, it is the case that IT workers naturally learn to tolerate these inefficiencies as a matter of course. Why? Because they are distracted perhaps, but more importantly, because they do not in many cases have the tools to identify the problems in the first place, and then to understand the diagnostics behind them. For this reason, we will spend time in this book on identifying waste and its root causes.

In order to set the stage for looking at Lean applications, we want to first take a somewhat different view of IT work to complement the view we have just taken. For this, we will look at IT through the lens of Operations Management, the general field of study which includes Lean.

Summary

Our intention in this chapter was to present a somewhat conventional view of the work of IT operations and then show how several of its important elements can be considered from a Lean perspective. In this respect, our objective was to demonstrate that the issues and concerns of IT practitioners lend themselves quite readily to Lean interpretations. At the same time, however, we also have suggested that the conventional approach that IT practitioners have toward these issues and concerns may be somewhat different from that of a Lean practitioner. In this sense, our scheme was to begin the chapter in the conventional IT world and then end up in a slightly different place. From here, we want to provide what may be a *very* different way of looking at IT work, and this will provide the context for looking at what Lean is all about.

References

1. Office of Government Commerce. 2007. *Service Operation*. ITIL Version 3. Norwich, UK: TSO.
2. Bell, S. C. and M. A. Orzen. 2011. *Lean IT: Enabling and sustaining your Lean transformation*. New York: Productivity Press.
3. Poppendieck, M., and T. Poppendieck. 2007. *Implementing Lean software development: From concept to cash*. Boston: Addison-Wesley
4. Middleston, P., and J. Sutton. 2005. *Lean software strategies: Proven techniques for managers and developers*. New York: Productivity Press.
5. Chin, G. 2004. *Agile project management: How to succeed in the face of changing project requirements*. New York: AMACOM.
6. Leach, L. L. 2005. *Lean project management: Eight principles for success*. Boise: Advanced Projects.

Chapter 3

The OM Perspective

Now, we want to look at IT work from the perspective of Operations Management (OM). As a field of academic study, OM is concerned with the design, operation, and improvement of *systems* that produce and deliver products and services.[1] The OM definition of the term *system* quickly sets us apart from the conventional IT perspective because, unlike in IT, where system typically refers to automation or a technical solution, in OM, a system includes People, Process, and Technology, i.e., it includes everything that surrounds the use of automation.

OM has its origins in manufacturing but has been extended into many areas, including Administration and Services, both of which have relevance to the work of IT. In fact, Service Management is a topic of study within the larger OM domain, and its relationship to *IT* Service Management is not just semantic. Other topics of interest within OM include process design and development, process improvement, and quality management. Specific methodologies for process and quality management are directly relevant to the OM field of inquiry, including Lean. There has been a substantial amount of research in development of OM models that can help explain how process-based systems work for either manufacturing or services. We are including this view of process-based work because it represents the conceptual foundation for Lean and also provides the language that we will use throughout the book.

That introduction may sound dry and academic, but let us personalize this a bit. One of the authors, Howard, thought he knew something about IT process management from his work over many years in IT. However, then he took a course in Operations Management from the other author, Rebecca, who has a background in manufacturing consulting. The first revelation was that OM practitioners had very deep and extensive experience in complex process environments (such as making cars). The second revelation was that this process knowledge could be applied to the work of IT, although the language and practices of OM were not commonly employed, or even particularly evident. His eyes opened up to a whole new world, which later set the stage for understanding the specific contributions of Lean as an OM practice to the work of IT.

For many readers who may have had prior exposure to OM, the concepts and notions in this chapter may seem straightforward and obvious, in which case it will represent a quick review to set the stage for later chapters. For other readers who may not have had this exposure, our hope is that you will be able to absorb some language and tools that will not only add insight into looking at IT work in its own right, but also provide context for a better understanding of the role of Lean.

Process Types

Processes are the fundamental unit of work in Operations Management. A process is any activity that transforms an input into an output. Using a variety of established textbook definitions of process,[2] five process types are seen in manufacturing operations, some of which can be applied in service operations (and, as we discussed in the previous chapter, IT is a service operation). The five process types include:

■ Project
■ Job Shop
■ Batch
■ Line
■ Continuous Flow

These process types represent a spectrum of activities based on the variety and volume of the output of the process. *Volume* refers to the number of items being produced, while *variety* signifies the number of different types of items, each type requiring different ways of processing. For example, let's say you produce 10,000 units of *something* per month (e.g., bicycles parts, donuts, or computer components). If you produce 1000 *different* items (each item requiring different process handling) in batches of 10, you have high

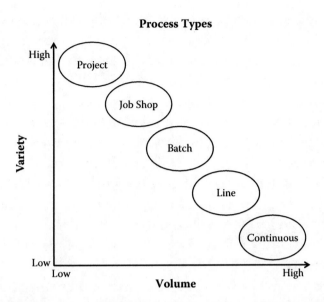

Figure 3.1   Process types.

variety (1000) and low volume (10). If you produce five different items with 2000 of each item, you have lower variety and higher volume. Figure 3.1 matches process types against the variables of volume and variety. Both ends of the spectrum have process types that require different management tools and techniques. The last mode of production, Continuous Flow, applies only to products that are not discrete and move without interruption. An example is electricity or water flowing to our homes in nonidentifiable units available continuously. This process type does not apply to IT, so we are really only interested in the other four process types.

Projects have unique one-of-a-kind outputs with low volumes. This textbook definition of projects refers to one-time-only work structures where each project is truly unique. Although in practice many people may believe they work on unique projects in a project-based organization, most project-based organizations do not have truly unique output with unique workflows. Typical IT projects, for example, may have customized outputs, but the work steps taken are well defined and repeated from project to project. In addition, they include work steps that are operational practices that are not one-of-a-kind. There are industry-wide practices for software development, for example, ensuring some level of consistency and standardization through software projects. These types of projects may have high variety customized output with low volumes of output, but because some of the work steps are standard and repeated from project to project, the type of process would be better characterized as a Job Shop, Batch, or Line process.

Job Shops respond to the demands of individual customers for customized products or services. An example might be a bicycle repair shop or a custom furniture operation. Because they provide customized solutions, they may generate a wide variety of products/services, and by the same token, typically will handle only low-to-moderate volumes of production. Sometimes we refer to the type of work that characterizes job shops as a *jumbled flow.* For example, many urgent care clinics have identified fixed location departments, such as triage area, imaging, blood lab, examination rooms, pharmacy, and so forth. Each patient arrives with a unique demand that may be serviced by jumbled flow between departments. A patient with the flu may start at triage, move to an exam room, then to the pharmacy. A patient with an arm injury may move to triage, then imaging, then the exam room, then pharmacy. A patient for a routine exam may move to labs prior to the exam room. Although this is a simplistic example, it captures the nature of jumbled flow: Fixed workstations with products/customers moving from workstation to workstation in a unique pattern. The individuals working in each area have freedom to perform their tasks as they see fit, but there also tend to be commonly held practices.

Sometimes job shops are best understood by following people around, or otherwise seeing how they move from place to place to get work done. When this is represented in a picture (sometimes called a spaghetti diagram), we can identify the paths, and more importantly identify paths that are traveled frequently. These frequently traversed paths suggest the existence of repeatable work, which may qualify as a different type of process, referred to as a *line.*

Lines are organized around a more limited set of activities than we find in job shops. They are set up to produce higher volumes of similar products or services (less variety with less customization). Repetitive activities are at the core of line processes, and the process steps that characterize these activities are relatively fixed, repeated, and sequential (and, therefore, standardized). There is typically more use of specialized tools that meet the specific needs of each step. As all product/customers proceed sequentially, there is little or no tool setup time between the orders. The linear workflow may be automated and/or each workstation will have a standard amount of time to perform its task before the product moves to the next workstation. In contrast to the job shop, line processes engage in a *linear flow,* suggesting the sequential, repeatable nature of the work. Very often, the movement of products/customers is highly automated.

Batch processes reside between job shops and line processes. With batch process, products are produced as a group or batch. Batch processes have higher volume of output, but still maintain some level of variety, although a vastly reduced variety than we find in a job shop. So using a batch process for cookie making, for example, we might make chocolate chip cookies and oatmeal raisin cookies, while in a job shop, we might make a "special order" oatmeal chocolate chip cookie. In job shops, products have unique orders with unique work steps. In batch processes, products may be reproduced with more regularity. Batch processes often work from a stated list of products. Batch processes can exhibit either a jumbled or sequential line flow. With a jumbled flow, each product has a designated series of work steps and its unique flow, but the flow is repeated when the product is ordered again. The jumbled nature comes from the variety of product utilizing different flow patterns. With linear flow batches, all products tend to follow through the same work stations, but the actual steps of each process may differ. In a bakery, for example, cookies might be made in batches of two dozen cookies per batch. The cookie dough is mixed, spooned onto a tray holding 24 cookies each, and then baked in the oven. Multiple types of cookies can be processed using the same work steps, but the work stations remain the same. This is an example of a linear flow batch process. If some cookies require decoration prior to baking and some cookies are decorated with icing after baking and cooling, these two cookie types would have different routes through the workstations, thereby exhibiting a jumbled flow batch process.

By the way, even though batch processing is a common notion in IT and also could serve as an example of the characteristics of batch processes as we are describing them here, please keep in mind that we are talking about *IT work,* involving people, process, and tools, and not just about a computational activity.

Process Types in IT Work

If the chief characteristics of job shops are customization and nonroutine processes, and for line processes, they are standardized production and routine, highly repetitive processes, it's possible to view IT operations as utilizing both process types. For example, we can view the following types of operations as aligned with line process characteristics:

- Routine handling of incidents, services requests, or changes
- Server hardware processing (e.g., "rack and stack" installations)
- Routine database maintenance activities
- Manual or automated activities associated with scheduled jobs
- Operational responses to nonevent monitoring alerts

By the same token, the following examples can be viewed as consistent with job shop, jumbled flow characteristics:

- Nonroutine handling of problems or exceptions
- Processing of unusual or unexpected service requests
- Meeting the customized requirements of special user groups (e.g., executives)
- Responses to unplanned or unanticipated outages
- Ad hoc nonprocedural responses to monitoring alerts

By viewing IT operations from the perspective of process models, it's possible to test whether the correct mode of production has been matched to the requirements of the activities themselves. For example, many IT operations will perform routine (linear flow) activities as if they were a customized job shop (jumbled flow) operation. When we have a routine repeatable work order, such as a request for a routine change to a server configuration, but the responding worker needs to first determine the sequence of steps to be taken (perhaps consulting with colleagues or gathering required information from multiple sources before proceeding), even though the request is executed often, we are treating a linear flow like a jumbled flow. When we look at the environment more closely, we might find that highly skilled individuals who otherwise have the ability to work with complex jumbled flows may be used to perform routine standardized work, and in so doing, they apply personalized routines or combine them with other work on their plate. Or, we might find that each individual on a team essentially responds to routine requests using a variety of ad hoc procedures because everybody figures out for themselves how to do the work. We can sometimes see this in IT operations where there is no standard procedure in place to handle routine processes. It also can happen that the routine work is not even recognized as such, and this reinforces the use of the wrong model for delivery of services.

Not long ago, one of the authors had reason to call an IT help desk in order to fix a problem with access to a particular application. As it turned out later, it was a relatively simple configuration issue that prevented normal access. However, this diagnostic was not gained through the help desk, but through trial-and-error later on. The help desk agent walked through his own diagnostic script and quickly identified something completely different as the cause of the access issue, for which he sent a checklist of tasks he suggested be performed on the system. Now, notwithstanding the fact that the diagnosis was wrong, and, therefore, the remedy was inappropriate, the point to be noted here was that the task checklist he sent was ad hoc, pieced together on the fly, and clearly the product of a job shop operation, when in fact, simple scrutiny of the tasks would suggest that it should be off-the-shelf and produced as sequential tasks. The Help Desk agent treated linear flow work as if it were jumbled flow.

It can happen as well that activities that qualify as job shop operations are treated as if they were line processes. An example would be the Problem Management process. In the ITIL® (IT Infrastructure Library) framework, Problem Management is focused on deliberate determination of root cause of incidents or service failures, and, therefore, requires special process handling depending on the nature of the investigation. In other words, it's the work of a job shop. The problems all require unique investigation that most often requires a jumbled flow. However, if problems are handled as if they can be pushed through a production line, with goals and metrics that would be more appropriate for sequential task activities rather than special handling (e.g., all problems resolved within 24 hours or a target number of problems resolved per day), it can encourage speed at the expense of quality. When work that should exhibit flexibility and customization in its performance gets handled as a homogenous product, solutions or outcomes are ineffective, incomplete, and often short-sighted.

Another example is a customer calling a service vendor and interacting with a phone tree, which is set up as sequential tasks and decision points. The customer may have to walk through all the standard steps without a problem resolution. It is not uncommon for individuals to get "stuck" in the process, whereas it might better be handled as an interaction with an individual who can address needs based on unique considerations of the customer.

One of the interesting extensions of these ideas is how we can standardize work so that it is transformed from a jumbled flow to a linear flow. The impetus for doing this is simply to gain efficiencies in operations. The ability to identify the repeatable component of a service operation has its legacy in the work of Levitt.[3] In this seminal work, he outlined how repeatable operations within services could be managed in a way not unlike the production line in a factory.

What this suggests for IT service operations is that many of the activities that are organized as job shops with jumbled flow activities may have line flow characteristics, and if organized as such, can lead to improvements in process efficiency. For example, sometimes escalation procedures with vendors are handled as a jumbled flow, principally because the requirements for doing these escalations are minimal (they happen from time to time). Consequently, each time the escalation is required, somebody engages in a jumbled flow. They dig through files perhaps to find the right vendor contact, or go find somebody who knows who that contact is. They try to reach them by phone, only to find out that that individual is no longer the contact person for this type of escalation. There may be some additional disconnect that relates to the type of support contract in place with the vendor and the vendor's own internal process for handling types of escalations. The bottom line is that the process is jumbled (and takes time, by the way). In fact, however, the tasks that need to be engaged in are predictable, sequential, and repeatable, and therefore, could be handled as what they are, namely, a linear flow.

An interesting example of how standardized work can be identified from a jumbled flow to great advantage is the use of preoperative checklists in surgery environments. One might assume that all surgeries are unique, but there has been recent evidence of surprisingly beneficial results obtained from their use simply by identifying standardized, repeatable procedures and using them as a checklist.[4] In the preliminary test of 4000 surgeries, for example, a simple presurgical checklist accounted for saving 27 lives and preventing complications in 150 individuals. Complications from surgery went down 36%, deaths decreased by 47%, and returns to surgeries decreased by 25%. One observation from this is that opportunities for standardization exist even in complex, highly skilled, customized workplaces.

IT projects are a common mode of delivering IT services, but as we suggested above, we want at first to think of them not as something completely different, but as a set of work activities that has characteristics of both job shops and linear flows, which comprise a batch process. The latter is particularly important because many project managers often think of their work more as a jumbled flow than as a linear flow. In fact, the conventional definition of a project as a short-term effort to create a unique product or service[5] strongly suggests the custom characteristics of any single project. However, there often is a significant amount of sequential, repeatable work within and between projects. These repeatable batch linear flows can be the steps in the project or activities within the steps. The correct classification here may be batch processes with linear flows and a batch size of one project.

Think of a project, for example, that is about server upgrades. The project manager may treat the upgrade as a "one-off" project (something that is not repeated or reproduced), but the work itself has been done many times before. In fact, the project planning activity itself has most certainly been done many times before. If the work has been done before (more than once or twice) and the variation on the work activities is minimal, then it is repeatable and, most likely, sequential as well. Within projects then, we are interested in which part of the work is sequential and repeatable, and which part warrants the separate designation as a job shop operation. In addition, we draw attention to this here because project plans, as it turns out, are often a good source for identifying operational work. Many of the issues that plague projects (delays, for instance) can often be attributed to inefficiencies in the operational work that is required for project completion. In other words, the problem is not with the project, it is with the operational practices that underlie project work.

Here is a summary observation that we will have reason to revisit in later chapters. Many IT operations are not only run as jumbled flow job shops when they might have unidentified or underutilized linear flows within them, but the job shop operations themselves are not very efficient either. In other words, the jumbled flows are more jumbled than they need to be. They are in this sense disorganized job shops and they will benefit from efficiency improvements even if they are not managed as line operations. As we shall see, this is an important observation because it directly translates into visible and often painful signs of inefficiency, such as backlogs of work, bottlenecks, delays, and defects.

Customer Contact Workflow Model

Another OM model of interest is based on a Customer Contact Workflow Model where the process characteristics of the service operation are positioned against characteristics of the customer interaction.[6] With this matrix, we can identify *Front Office* operations, characterized by generally flexible flows of activities and often complex work with multiple exceptions, where there is high interaction with the customer and provision of highly customized services. At the other extreme are *Back Office* operations, characterized often by routine work (flows) subject to high degrees of standardization, where customer interaction is relatively low and there are fewer customized (more standardized) services.

In other words, the front office is handled like a job shop (jumbled flow), while the back office is handled like a line process (linear flow). While this is not always true (e.g., there may be flow characteristics in some front office operations or jumbled flows in back office operations), it provides a useful reference for understanding desirable characteristics of each part of the operation. A good example is the difference in a library between the front desk (circulation desk or reference desk) and the back room operations where book processing takes place. If all the staff in a library were working in the back room (e.g., because the processes are very inefficient and they need a lot of people to compensate for that), then there are very few workers at the front desk taking care of customers.

Figure 3.2 positions front office and back office activities relative to two different dimensions, one based on process type and the other based on degree of customer interaction.

Using this model, we can see where IT service operations may be positioned. For example, Service Desks (or Help Desks) have a significant front office component of their operations. In fact, any IT service or operation that is characterized by a high degree of customer interaction is a candidate as a front office operation. Using this model, many IT operations will

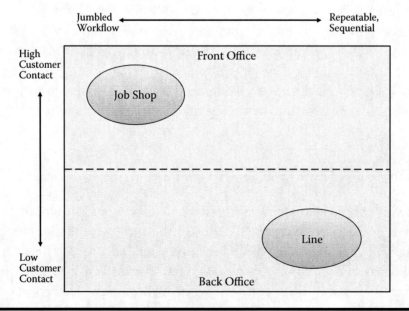

Figure 3.2   Customer Contact Workflow Model.

appropriately be viewed as back office activities, even if, in practice, they are not treated as such. For example, we might find back office workers (e.g., database administrators) who are interrupted by customers to perform ad hoc requests. Here the back office is being treated like a front office with high customer contact. This can happen when IT operations impose constraints on the customer interaction (e.g., by forcing them to use complex or very restricted options on their Help Desk call tree or voicemail scripts). Under these circumstances, the customer will often work around the front office and go directly to the needed resources in the back office.

One of the compelling demands on IT is that its work (both front and back office) be done with fewer resources and at lower cost. At the same time, one of the essential criteria for good service delivery is that there be good customer service and this begins with customer interaction (in the front office). It is where the needs of customers are identified, and where delivery of services is enabled. Most importantly, it is also where the value of services is realized by customers. One outcome of adopting an OM orientation is to see where it's desirable to shift resources from back to front, or front to back, depending on the nature of the work and the nature of customer requirements. Quite often, however, these resource deployment decisions are not really made in a planned fashion, but more or less happen over time, according to immediate circumstances. In others words, it is done reactively and not proactively, and the consequence is that the work in both front office and back office is not very efficient.

It's not uncommon, of course, to have resources deployed in *both* the front office and the back office. This also can lead to inefficiency because, in practice, we typically leave it to the individual to figure out how to balance work associated with each role. Invariably, they will find the optimal balance around their own individual needs, and this may be quite different from what makes sense for the organization as a whole.

The Customer Contact Workflow Model has wide application in Service Management and represents a conventional way that service providers think about their work. They will, for example, think of their back office operations as the place where efficiency gains can best be realized and, therefore, will be where we think first and foremost about applying Lean techniques. Conversely, the front office is where the customer communicates and experiences value in the interaction. Therefore, there is compelling reason for the service provider to shift resources from the back office to the front office, letting the front office handle interactions with the customer and letting the back office get the behind-the-scenes work done. Later in the book, we will discuss Service Desk or Help Desk operations and consider these front-end and back-end components in more detail. In order to set the stage for that discussion, we want to introduce some additional workflow concepts, so for that, let's look at a Help Desk ticketing system.

Workflow Concepts

From a process perspective, Help Desk activities are fairly straightforward. A customer calls on the phone (or emails, or interacts through a portal), a ticket is opened, some record is made of the interaction for a request or to report an issue (which we refer to as an *incident*), the ticket is put in a queue, an agent picks up the ticket, some level of attention is provided by the agent who picks up the ticket, who then works to resolve the issue or meet the request (often through handoffs to other service providers), and, finally, in a successful interaction, the ticket is resolved. This simple sequence of activities can be represented as a workflow (Figure 3.3).

Volume, Variety, and Variation

This workflow roughly maps to the ITIL workflow for Incident Management, but we have intentionally simplified it to introduce concepts that can assist in addressing effectiveness and efficiency issues. For example, we can view

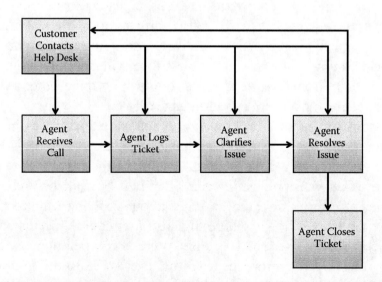

Figure 3.3   Help Desk workflow.

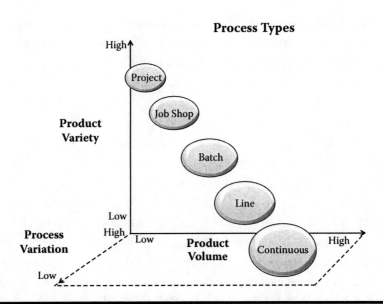

Figure 3.4   Volume, Variety, Variation Model.

the process workflow from the point of view of *product volume* (number of tickets), *product variety* (different types of tickets), and *process variation* (different ways of handling different types of tickets). Figure 3.4 builds on the Process Type model introduced earlier (Figure 3.1), but includes the additional dimension of variation.

In an ideal world, if the volume is even over time, variety is at a minimum, and the variations of the process are few, then it would be possible to manage the Help Desk as a linear flow with a steady rate of completion (presumably fast) that would not be unlike a factory line. However, in the real world, of course, volume is not even, variety is abundant, and there are (intentionally or not) many variations on the product/process itself.

It is possible to design processes to produce product variety without much process variation. Subway® restaurants, for example, use a linear process to produce assemble-to-order, customized sandwiches. The customer flow is linear with selections at each station, from choice of bread, meat and cheese, toppings (lettuce, tomato, etc.), and dressing. The product configurations (product variety) can be made using an assemble-to-order line flow with little or no process variation.

We sometimes think of process variation as deliberate (we want to have these variations in process in order to address the requirements of different types of requests), but there are also natural variations in how work gets done. These are essentially random variations that are inherent in all processes, and in this sense, we can think of them as natural occurrences in the process. While we could design processes with little or no natural variation of this sort (using tight product specifications, for instance), they would be extremely expensive and often would not meet the price point or value equation of the customer. We will refer generally to this sort of normal variation as *variability* to distinguish it from process variation that we build into our processes.

Often there is variability in a process that shows a pattern and is not random in nature. This type of variability is said to have an assignable cause. In this case, some outside event changed the process so that it is no longer operating as designed. This could be a single event or general erosion of the process over time. This is often seen as individuals add or delete something from a process to fit their individual preferences or work types, and over time the process gradually changes completely without any thought or design. One consequence of this is that other individuals are forced to make adjustments in how they interact with the "changed" process, and this, in turn, introduces more variability.

There are many potential causes of variability in process-based operations, and the Lean approach will provide direct assistance in identifying these. One source of variability may be in how the process work is done. Think, for example, of the effect of changing resources within an operational team. Perhaps the person who used to do a certain task was knowledgeable and experienced and the new resource (e.g., a lower cost, outsourced resource) may have less knowledge and experience. This will very likely introduce variability in how the task is done. Another source of variability may be in the customer interaction itself, and these can be attributed to different modes of interaction related to arrival, request, capability, effort, and subjective preference.[7] For example, changes in arrival rate (when the customer makes a request) can be difficult to predict, and so will be a source of variability, unless you have enough resources to match any rate of arrival.

As an example of how these variables interact, consider a call center where there is a lot of pressure to handle large volumes of standard items, such as routine in-bound sales calls. Although variety is relatively low, occasional items require exception handling that may consume resources in unplanned ways (people work longer hours, more staff is required, etc.). In this environment, it is not uncommon to have levels of stress increase, and under these circumstances, it is more likely mistakes will be made, which requires rework that adds to the workload. Negative feedback from management, as a response to mistakes, can lead to more pressure as well as attempts to "fix" the process, both of which introduce more variability. If you add more volume to this already over-stressed environment, it's easy to see how a crisis spiral is created as things get worse and worse.

While routinely subjected to high levels of standardization and automation, these call center (and Help Desk or Service Desk) operations are nevertheless frequently characterized by workflow problems such as backlogs, bottlenecks, and defects that are best understood from an OM point of view, rather than as a unique set of conditions that only affect IT. Many of these workflow problems represent what we can only refer to as *waste*. Examples include queue backlogs, misrouted tickets, unnecessary escalations, etc. When diagnosing these workflow problems, there are some additional OM concepts that are useful.

Concepts of Flow

Throughput is a measure of the output rate of a process. Throughput is routinely reflected in Help Desk metrics (e.g., number of incidents resolved per day), and can be viewed in terms of both Current State and desired Future State dimensions, the latter which may or may not be achievable. We may have a good understanding of our actual throughput without knowing what may be achievable with attention to various process improvements.

Another concept helpful in this analysis is that of **throughput time**. In a line process, throughput time is the average time it takes to complete one cycle through a process (in our example, the time it takes to process—from initiation to closure—a single ticket). Throughput time is a useful concept because it can serve as a measurement unit when we begin to do process modeling. However, be aware, throughput time is the *average* processing time. It is a great measure for standardized line flow processes, but if a process has variation or variability, the process throughput time may be significantly longer or shorter for some items. To find the Current *as-is* State, you may want to look at the minimum and maximum processing times.

Understanding the relationship between these variables provides the basis for looking at how process performance is impacted. One negative impact on performance is the existence of **bottlenecks**, which refers to any activity that limits throughput of the entire process. In a linear flow process, a bottleneck occurs at the station with the longest process time. In a batch operation with jumbled flow, we often find that the bottleneck moves. The bottleneck is the slowest step in a process. Bottlenecks are very common in IT operations, although they are often undiagnosed or merely accepted as business-as-usual. Help Desk bottlenecks occur when too much volume and variety overloads the capacity of the system. Where there are bottlenecks, there are also likely to be **backlogs**. In a Help Desk, these are represented as queues, and while queue management is customary and accepted in most every IT shop, the OM perspective encourages us to ask the question: "Why are there any queues at all?" The Lean Approach, as we shall see, is even simpler in its interpretation. Backlogs are waste, so we need to diagnose their cause and eliminate them. Clearly this is a tall order, but we introduce this somewhat radical idea here because it is a natural outcome of adopting an OM and, specifically, a Lean orientation toward this common phenomenon.

Waiting in Line

In OM there is a focus of study that leverages these concepts called *waiting line analysis*. Here, we can systematically consider various factors that influence time spent waiting. These include length of the line (queue), the number of lines, and the rules of conduct that determine how and when customers get attended to in the queue.[8]

Not long ago, one of the authors was standing in line at a fast food restaurant at an airport. There was quite a bit of confusion behind the counter and also in front. Customers were standing in what looked like a line waiting to place their orders, but, it turned out, after a short while waiting in this queue, that this was actually the line waiting to get food after already having placed an order. Meanwhile, the manager was trying to get things sorted out behind the counter and at one point exhorted his team by saying: "Spread 'em out, move 'em on." In other words, he wanted the staff to take orders from all available registers (four servers in total), thereby forcing customers to spread themselves across all of them (four queues, one for each server). His theory (we presume) was that by spreading out the customers, he could even out the workload among them, and thereby have faster throughput. The problem was that he still had confusion on the customer side, with nobody knowing where to stand in the line in the first place.

As a general rule, a single line or queue with multiple servers (such as in a bank) processes customers quicker with higher throughput than multiple lines for each of the multiple servers (as in a grocery store). In addition, it is very common for customers to feel that they "picked the wrong line." It's fairly easy to see how confusing this can become, on both the customer and server side of the equation.

Does this type of behavior happen at the Help Desk? Of course. Help Desks often get into situations where unusual spikes in volume (often with accompanying increase in variety) compel it to operate in what amounts to a panic mode. All hands on deck, and the backlog is hopefully quieted over time, until the next crisis occurs. During these episodes, just like the manager at the fast food restaurant, Help Desk managers exhort and experiment with different ways of handling the volume and variety, and the consequence is that necessary process variation often becomes amplified, introducing unnecessary variability. Notice, too, that it is not uncommon for those working at the Help Desk to develop normal reactions to the overload, perhaps represented by working exceptionally long hours, for example. This introduces additional variability (fatigue, anger, etc.), and even in the best of circumstances, it is extremely difficult to maintain a customer service orientation.

Waiting line analysis provides a scientific way to study this phenomenon, but, in fact, even the general concepts are sufficient to provide new tools for the IT practitioner in trying to diagnose and fix problems at the Help Desk. If the customer arrival intervals match the time it takes to perform the service, the process is perfectly balanced and no waiting lines will materialize. Unfortunately, this isn't the way of the world. Customers arrive at different intervals, introducing variability in the arrival rate. In general, the time to perform a service for each customer also will vary, introducing variability in the service rate. It may be possible to provide more servers than are needed under normal conditions of volume and variety in anticipation of erratic customer arrival behavior, but this solution can be prohibitively expensive. While waiting line formulation can help find the "right" number of servers for the anticipated customer arrival times, it is the rare Help Desk environment that has flexibility in deploying its resources.

Some of the strategies that address waiting line problems include changing demand or arrival patterns, such as offloading at the front end (through more use of customer self-service, for example), changing the server rates through systematic use of tools that reduce the time of resolution (diagnostic scripts, checklists, etc.), or changing the process through better categorization of tickets into groups (minimizing the process variation within a group) in order to route tickets more precisely and, therefore, reduce the burden on the front desk operation. Notice that these solutions are not unlike what we find in many Help Desk operations. By positioning these within the framework of OM, we are trying to widen the lens for IT practitioners to consider other reasonable solutions. For example, we can ask the question: "What else can we do to change the customer arrival rate or to change the server rate?" Asking these questions in a systematic and proactive way is at the heart of Operations Management problem-solving.

Capacity

One final concept that relates to others we have just discussed is that of **capacity**. Capacity refers to the capability of a process with reference to its available resources.[9] In one sense, capacity represents the achievable dimension of throughput with various dependencies. For example, how many tickets can be processed in a shift may be dependent on the number of workers available. In another sense, it refers specifically to the resources available to achieve certain levels of throughput. We may not typically think in terms of the capacity of a Help Desk process, but if we accept the notion that some of its work can be handled as a line operation, for example, then its capacity is a relevant concept. Many Help Desk operations may have performance targets that agents are expected to achieve, such as time to process a ticket, but these are very often completely detached from an understanding of the actual capacity requirements of the operation.

Capacity utilization is often used as a performance measure for process efficiency. Capacity utilization refers to that part of a resource that is actually used. High capacity utilization is expected in linear flow standardized work where work is readily available. In jumbled workflows where process times are variable, lower capacity utilization should be expected. If customer arrival rates are variable, capacity utilization also is lower, even in standardized line flows. Capacity utilization provides a cushion to have capacity available when needed, thereby increasing customer satisfaction. High utilization of Help Desk capacity would show an efficient process, but may be gained at the expense of long customer wait times. Therefore, capacity utilization measure should be used in the context of the type and goals of the process.

Considering these various concepts and their specific application to the Help Desk provides a new and different language for the IT practitioner, but what else does it do? The assumption throughout this book is that by applying concepts and solutions borrowed from OM we are drawing on a wider variety of tools to address process effectiveness and efficiency issues within IT. It is not commonplace to hear IT practitioners use this language, and we believe this represents an opportunity to leverage the OM body of knowledge to improve IT operational work. We will have reason to use these concepts when we drill down into Lean applications, and there we will explore specific practices that can be applied to IT.

Looking at the IT Factory

Looking beyond the Help Desk to the larger IT "factory" consisting of all operational elements across multiple processes, we can explore the parallels with manufacturing and stretch the analogy to its fullest. In one part of the factory we have incidents within the Help Desk workflow. In another, we have Requests for Change within a Change Management workflow. In yet another, we have products and services sourced from outside suppliers that are utilized in various places throughout our internal operations. This is really no different than a manufacturing environment with multiple product flows and a supporting supply chain. In many of these manufacturing environments they have solved problems of backlogs and bottlenecks by applying OM tools. It is not unreasonable to assume that these same tools might be used in order to address issues within the IT factory. The analysis we just provided for the Help Desk could really be applied across all of IT.

We probably don't want to push the factory analogy too far because, after all, we are talking about a service operation. However, the basic concepts still apply. One outcome of this approach is to identify linear flows within IT work so that this work can be made more efficient. Very often the way this happens is by analyzing an existing process, at first glance apparently a jumbled flow, and clarifying the activities within the process so that the potential ("hidden") linear flows within it can be made visible, and then optimized for efficiency. We will spend time later discussing this in more detail, but to help get us there we need to understand more about looking at IT work from a process perspective.

Process Analysis

Much of the work in IT operations can be viewed as process-based work. When we talk about Network Management, for example, we can identify more specific work that falls within this general category, such as planning of network components, installation of network components, assigning IP (Internet protocol) addresses, or network monitoring.

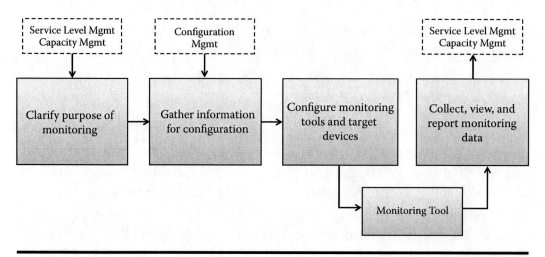

Figure 3.5 Network monitoring workflow (general).

Each of these activities is functionally aligned with the general category of work we call Network Management, and each is also process-based. For example, there is a process (or several, more likely) that comprises the work associated with network monitoring. There also are tools that support this process, and in most cases we will find, as this work is represented in practice, that there will be a corresponding set of procedures or work instructions associated with use of these tools.

The processes associated with IT operational work can be represented from a top-down perspective at a high level of abstraction (e.g., Network Management), and then at increasingly more detailed and tangible levels of representation. Under network monitoring, for instance, it would be possible to represent this work somewhat generically, as in the diagram in Figure 3.5.

While this model is perhaps helpful as the basis for an introductory tutorial on network monitoring, it does not correspond to a level of representation that characterizes real work. It is not possible, for instance, to implement this process as it is represented here. For that purpose, we might find a better representation in the procedural level workflows that are part of a tool-specific network monitoring solution. Alternatively, we could identify an appropriate process for network monitoring that is specific to an environment and serves as the workflow context for identifying tool requirements and integrating tool solutions. An example of this level of process description can be seen in Figure 3.6.

Note that this process workflow is still somewhat general, but contains more specificity than the previous model. In this particular case, we have

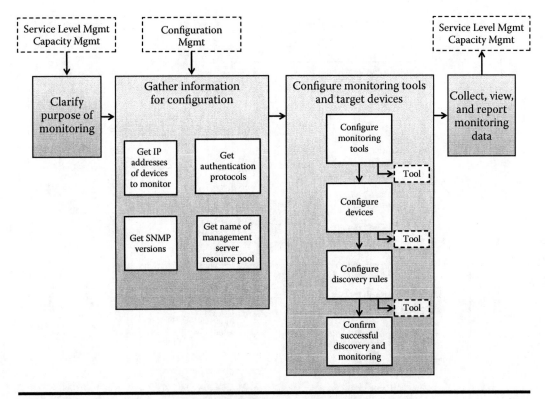

Figure 3.6 Network monitoring workflow (more specific).

identified some subactivities within activities for "Gather information for configuration" and "Configure monitoring tools and network devices." This representation suggests that the former is managed as a jumbled flow, while the latter is sequenced as a linear flow. "Configure monitoring tools and target devices" has sequential tasks listed, while "Gather information for configuration" shows tasks without any precedence relationship. Note also the important tool dimension for the actual configuration activities, suggesting that we might very well find procedures or work instructions associated with use of specific tools. This would be represented at the next level *down* in representation (not shown here).

As we drill down through levels of abstraction, the process workflows become more detailed and more tangible, until at some point they correspond to "real work." The reader will recall our discussion of IT processes in Chapter 2, where we made the distinction between process *as-we-designed-it* and process *as-it-actually-is*. The former is *intended* to be detailed and tangible and, as it is named, falls within the province of design work. The latter, in fact, is detailed and tangible and represents, for our purposes, the level of process description that is of interest for Lean application. In this

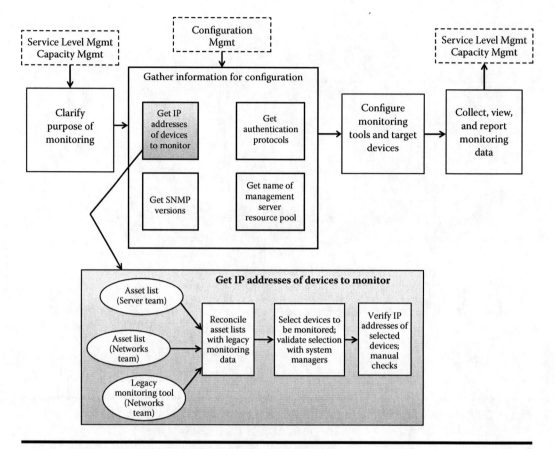

Figure 3.7   Network monitoring workflow (real work).

respect, one might say that the designed process is uncomplicated and untested, while the *as-is* process is very likely complex and messy.

The reason that we are drawing attention to these distinctions is so we can firmly root our level of interest in the here-and-now, *as-is* state of a process. In contrast to the other levels of representation, this one might look as shown in Figure 3.7.

Here, we have drilled down from the subactivity called "Get IP address of devices to monitor" and identified a sequence of activities that, while linear in representation, actually suggests tasks that may be more like a jumbled flow in the way the work is done. For instance, the first task for "Reconcile asset lists with legacy monitoring data" has three different inputs and the work for reconciliation may be in practice entirely manual. It could consume quite a bit of time. We have not noted the duration for the task itself, but let's say it takes three days, and that seems to stakeholders to be a long time (*too long*, in fact). We don't know why it takes that long right now, but it is reasonable to surmise that this is *too long* from the point of view of completing this task relative to the overall work for getting IP addresses of devices to monitor. If it is *too long*, we can identify this as a bottleneck that represents a source of delay. Later, we will talk about how we get to that type of conclusion, but for now, the main takeaway is that this level of representation corresponds to real work and, therefore, allows us to conduct analysis that is pertinent to how the work *really* gets done.

When we look at processes at this level of representation, there are characteristics that we frequently find in them, including:

- All of them share features of both jumbled flows and linear flows.
- Routine work in these areas is often sequential and repetitive (or could be).
- Many of them, in practical application, display evidence of problems, such as backlogs, bottlenecks, or defects (i.e., inefficiency and waste).
- Many sources of inefficiency and waste occur at customer interfaces or at handoffs, or may be related to excessively manual procedures where a great deal of process variation is introduced (lots of exception handling, information acquisition, information normalization, etc.).

The various levels of process abstraction that we have been describing are represented in Figure 3.8.

Any of these process layers can be further decomposed into what are conventionally referred to as levels (L0 for the top level, L1 below, etc.). That is, we can depict a sequence of activities in L0, and then subactivities in L1, and so forth. This decomposition is helpful because it allows us to isolate portions of a workflow for attention without losing the context in which this workflow exists. Using layers and levels allows us to identify and also construct workflow models that pertain to any of the possible abstractions of work that we may find relevant to address. Principally, for OM analysis, and especially for Lean, we are interested in the layer of work process that corresponds to real work.

We've been using the example of network monitoring, but it might be helpful to broaden the lens somewhat at this point so the reader can establish some basis for identifying with these observations. Please consider other IT operational processes that pertain to some of the following and think through the process characteristics just described.

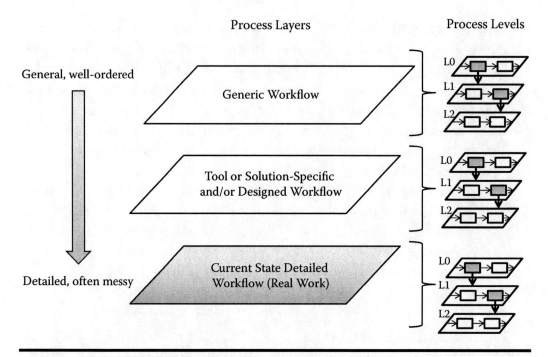

Figure 3.8 Layers and levels of process abstraction.

- ■ Job scheduling
- ■ Backup and restore operations
- ■ Database maintenance
- ■ Server management
- ■ Operating system support
- ■ License management
- ■ Patch management
- ■ Asset management
- ■ Security management
- ■ Application management
- ■ Capacity management

We have purposely identified these at various levels of abstraction, but the really important thing is to think about these processes as they are implemented within real-world environments (yours, for instance.). A very simple way of clarifying the workflows for "real work" is to simply ask the people who do the work, using very basic questions, such as: "How do you do backups?" or "How do you do restores?" It will be necessary to validate the answers we get, of course, but this is a useful starting point. It allows us to begin to identify the Current *as-is* State. We will have more to say about observation of work and validation of testimony, using data, later in the book.

Once we identify the process layer for real work, we can begin a further level of analysis that is influenced by OM and the Lean Approach. Specifically, it is possible to identify problems in terms of locations (where do we see them, e.g., at customer interface or at handoff points), symptoms of problems (which are the effects resulting from causes), and the underlying causes themselves (root cause). We might, as suggested above, find examples where the wrong process model is imposed on an operational activity, for instance. By the same token, this level of analysis also will help to identify strengths or core competencies. It is just as common to find these in operational work and we don't want to either disregard them or dismiss them in devising solutions to problems that we do find.

Process Improvement

One of the ways that OM tools help to improve process-based work is to simply analyze problems in the Current State and then identify remedies that we design and will use to characterize the Future State. This notion of moving from the Current State to Future State is enabled through a quality management concept called Plan–Do–Check–Act (PDCA) (Figure 3.9).

One of the reasons we emphasize the distinction between Current State and Future State is because it is very common to discuss both at the same time and/or to confuse them. For example, we often find conversations that are focused on solutions to problems (implied Future State) to be as much about Current State (how does it work now). Both are important, but it also is not uncommon to have discussions carry on almost indefinitely because there is no clear distinction and the conversation seems to go round and

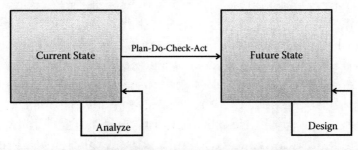

Figure 3.9   Current State to Future State and PDCA.

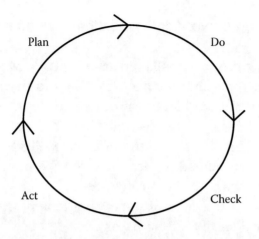

Figure 3.10   Plan, Do, Check, Act (PDCA).

round with indefinite resolution of either Current State or Future State. The Lean Approach will encourage us to maintain these distinctions and do good analysis of Current State *before* doing design of Future State.

The PDCA cycle (Figure 3.10), sometimes referred to as the Deming Cycle, is based on the premise that improvements are achieved through application of knowledge. As such, it is a learning cycle, and knowledge is systematically acquired through the process of learning. Applications of PDCA are practically universal, so it serves as a strong foundation for process improvement. It is grounded in OM, central to Lean, and is also strongly aligned with ITIL's notion of Continual Service Improvement. As such, it serves as a powerful tool for thinking about improvement of IT work. PDCA can be thought of as the underlying engine for all process improvement. We will have more to say about PDCA in the next chapter.

Another foundational concept that can be applied to process improvement is the notion of **process control**. As previously discussed, all processes have normal variation or variability. A process is in control when it exhibits only natural variation. A process is no longer in control when outside forces introduce assignable cause variations. A process is in control when selected process output measures fall predictably within predefined limits that are considered acceptable and normal and that represent the process "in control," i.e., expected within these limits. While outside factors may occasionally be a cause of instability, natural causes of instability are factored into the defined measurement limits and, in this sense, are treated as normal characteristics of a stable process. These concepts underlie the set of techniques referred to as Statistical Process Control and are also fundamental to Six Sigma.

All processes have some sources of variation within them. For example, with newly trained Service Desk employees, we might expect to see longer resolution times for incidents. While this might be expected normal behavior, we would probably be concerned if our Incident Management measurements showed changes over time and we were unable to attribute these to any known causes. Something is making the process unstable and we are not sure what it is. This may be a signal that the process has slowly changed over time as the "standard" was moved ever so slightly, day-by-day, in one direction. In the extreme, unstable processes can lead to processes that are "out of control" and this is usually experienced as a significant but unidentified change in the underlying process. Work feels stuck, there are too many crises, people are confused as to their roles, morale is low; all these are symptoms of unstable process. A fundamental principle that derives from this line of thinking is that a process must first be stable before it can be improved. This principle is frequently violated in practice and is one of the reasons why process improvement efforts seem to frequently fail.

It also should be noted that implementation of ITIL best practice does not in itself guarantee process stability. It most certainly improves the likelihood of stability, but as suggested above, stability is achieved through rigorous measurement and attention to causes of instability. This is the reason why, in ITIL, services are designed with the full lifecycle in mind (including attention to Continual Service Improvement). As noted, from the OM perspective, this same notion is captured within PDCA.

Quality Improvement

Many of the process improvement concepts and tools discussed above also apply to quality improvement. Within ITIL, specific quality systems are identified in the context of Continual Service Improvement (CSI). Concepts and practices associated with CSI are exactly the same as what is referred to as Continuous Improvement in the Quality Management field, and is expressed through specific methodologies and approaches such as Total Quality Management (TQM), Six Sigma, and Lean.

There has been a considerable amount of attention within OM and Services Management on quality in services. Notwithstanding the differences between quality definition and measures in manufacturing as opposed to services, there is nevertheless a strong culture of quality control practices within services. Some common quality characteristics in services include waiting time and delivery time, as well as indicators of conformance to quality expectations. In our previous example of the Help Desk, this might include timely restoration of normal operations (anything less will be perceived as a defect in service delivery).

All quality systems begin with some notion of customer value, since this provides the context for identifying indicators of quality, and is expressed through concepts generally referred to as Voice of the Customer (VOC). There are a variety of quality tools that serve the purpose of capturing customer value requirements. These can then be factored into service design using identified Critical-to-Quality requirements (CTQ), and the processes that underlie service operations then can be implemented with quality control considerations.[10]

Quality, as a designed outcome, addresses the natural tendency of systems to introduce defects, which is directly related to the notions of process variation and variability discussed above. As such, process improvement and quality improvement are closely intertwined, with the same objectives and the same underlying approaches. As a quality system, Lean emphasizes certain concepts that are represented in what we have been referring to as Lean Thinking, with some distinctive characteristics such as *flow through, value stream,* and *elimination of waste.* However, it is notable that two concepts of Lean Thinking (*customer value* and *continuous improvement*) are shared with other quality systems, reinforcing the shared origins and objectives.

Six Sigma is also a quality system with its own distinctive characteristics, reflected in the methodological framework called DMAIC (Define–Measure–Analyze–Improve–Control). Similar to Lean, Six Sigma focuses on problem-solving, with special attention to identifying and eliminating sources of errors and a strong emphasis on statistical analysis and control techniques.[11] From our perspective, we should view these as completely complementary with Lean and, while we will not be using Six Sigma tools in our discussion of Lean, many Six Sigma tools may be found in the Lean toolbox (and vice versa). All this is underscored by the emergence of hybrid approaches referred to frequently as *Lean Six Sigma.*[12]

Summary

In this chapter, we introduced a number of concepts as well as a language for description, borrowed from the discipline of Operations Management (OM). OM provides the underpinnings for process analysis and process improvement and, specifically, provides the foundation for Lean. We believe this OM perspective provides a good lens through which to look at IT work, in part because it allows IT to leverage a wider set of tools and practices than are typically used to solve problems. Specifically, it positions IT as an operations and service management practice that shares many of the same underlying dynamics as we find in many other domains of work, such as hospitals, office administration, insurance, accounting, or libraries, where OM practices have been applied successfully in the past. Finally, it sets the stage for looking more closely at IT work through a Lean lens. In the next chapter, we will do just that by exploring the Lean Improvement Model.

References

1. Chase, R. B., F. R. Jacobs, and N. J. Aquilano. 2006. *Operations management for competitive advantage,* 11th ed. New York: McGraw-Hill.
2. Ibid.
3. Levitt, T. 1972. Production-line approach to service. *Harvard Business Review* Sept–Oct., 41–52.
4. Gawande, A. 2011. *The checklist manifesto: How to get things right.* New York: Picador.
5. Project Management Institute. 2008. *A guide to the Project Management Book of Knowledge,* 4th ed. Newtown Square, PA: PMI.
6. Krajewski, L. J., L. P. Ritzman, and M. K. Malhotra. 2007. *Operations management: Processes and value chains,* 8th ed. Upper Saddle River, NJ: Pearson Education.
7. Chase, R. B., F. R. Jacobs, and N. J. Aquilano. 2006. *Operations management for competitive advantage,* 11th ed. New York: McGraw-Hill.
8. Ibid.
9. Schroeder, R. G. 2007. *Operations management: Contemporary concepts and cases,* 3rd ed. New York: McGraw-Hill.
10. Gygi, C., N. DeCarlo, and B. Williams. 2005. *Six Sigma for dummies.* Hoboken, NJ: John Wiley & Sons.
11. Ibid.
12. George, M. L. 2003. *Lean Six Sigma for services.* New York: McGraw-Hill.

Chapter 4

The Lean Improvement Model

In Chapter 3, we introduced some of the basic concepts of Operations Management (OM) and indicated that this provided a context for understanding Lean. Now, we would like to provide a more detailed look at Lean concepts, as well as background and some of the distinguishing characteristics of what is sometimes referred to as the Lean Approach.

The elements of the Lean Approach, which we will discuss in this chapter, can be brought together within what we call the *Lean Improvement Model*. This is our shorthand way of referring to a somewhat prescriptive representation of the Lean Approach, and in a sense, is our way of answering the question: "What is Lean?"

As discussed in the Introduction, the Lean Improvement Model provides a framework for presentation of essential concepts and ideas. We will use this model throughout the book as the reference point for many of our discussions on application of Lean to the work of IT. It is sometimes said that models are neither right nor wrong, but what really matters is how useful they are. We hope that the reader will find the model useful as a way of understanding and using Lean concepts.

In order to use the Lean Improvement Model (Figure 4.1), we believe it really doesn't matter where one begins or even *how* one begins. The point is to begin the journey. In general, we believe that if the IT practitioner is focusing on Lean Thinking, and Lean Learning addressing problems or opportunities using A3 and PDCA (Plan–Do–Check–Act), judiciously using Lean tools, or leveraging the Lean Enablers, that he or she is in the Lean ballpark. In other words, it's the right place to begin the Lean journey.

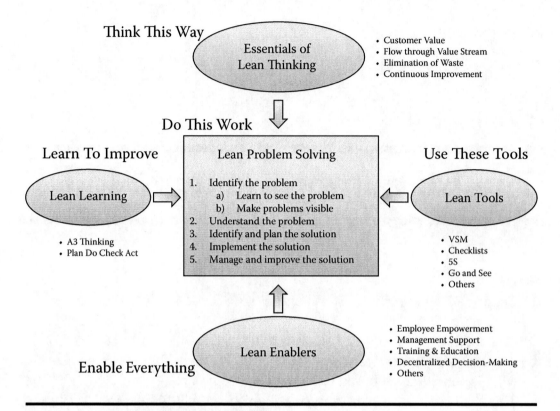

Figure 4.1   The Lean Improvement Model.

The really important thing is that the Lean orientation is adopted when considering the use of specific Lean practices.

We mentioned (in the Introduction) as an analogy for practicing a skill playing the piano or some other practice of interest to the reader, and we believe that these are *simple but strong* analogies (the best kind) to what IT practitioners should be trying to do. You will read books, you will do training, you will perhaps get a coach, but we think that, above all, you should start to practice Lean in the context of your workplace. Start small, build on success, learn more, and then extend the scope of Lean applications.

As you read through this chapter, we suggest that you refer back to the model itself so you can maintain context for each section. We will begin with Lean Thinking and then walk through the other components of the model. As we have suggested, it is in working all the pieces together that will add value over time.

Lean Thinking

While most of the general principles and objectives of the Lean Approach are derived from experiences in manufacturing, there has been considerable work on their application to a wide variety of other domains, including Services. It was a small but significant step to popularize Lean concepts derived originally from manufacturing by presenting them in such a way that a general audience could consider the application of Lean to practically any type of process, particularly those that have sequential and repeatable characteristics. This was accomplished in the publication of *Lean Thinking*.[1] For many, this book represented a jumping point to a new way of looking at processes, one in which Lean practices could reasonably be tried and tested in any industry and for a wide variety of purposes. The distillation of Lean concepts resulted in, among other things, a short list of Lean characteristics that we can think of as essential indicators or objectives of Lean applications, and include those identified in the model shown in Figure 4.1 as associated with Lean Thinking.

Some of these essential concepts relate to and, in a sense, provide the Lean response to the question of Business–IT value chain alignment presented in Chapter 2. All work is organized around the objective of deriving customer value and, to that end, all tasks or activities that do not directly and clearly support this objective are candidates for scrutiny and possible elimination.

At its core, Lean is about things that do not necessarily have to be associated with Lean, such as problem-solving. In a sense, there is essential work at the core that comprises *what* we do, and this work is necessary but perhaps not altogether unique to Lean, and then there are those characteristics that represent *how* we do this work; together they comprise the Lean Approach. Lean continually strives to improve value, optimize flow, and eliminate waste. That general statement summarizes core Lean Thinking.

Customer Value

One of the essential indicators of many quality initiatives, and also of Lean, is the importance of customer value. This means that there is a deliberate effort to understand value from the customer's perspective so that products or services that are designed, created, and delivered to customers will truly meet their requirements.

Lean begins by specifying the customer's perception of value for any defined product or service. All operations (processes and activities) are then organized toward the delivery of customer value. Processes and activities typically fall into three categories: (1) those that clearly create value; (2) those that do not create value, but are nevertheless necessary; and (3) those that are neither value-creating nor necessary (the latter constitutes waste). When a customer calls the Help Desk with a service request, for example, perhaps he or she needs a simple password reset. Any time spent directly helping the customer is value adding. Any time spent with the customer to gather information, for example to establish the customer's identity, is certainly necessary, but it does not add value to the customer experience because it doesn't directly help the customer. If you could ascertain this information from their phone number, you would not need to bother the customer with this step. And, of course, as we all know from personal experience, any time spent waiting in the queue is completely nonvalue-adding time, and from the customer's point of view, is waste. It is, after all, not necessary that the customer has to wait.

This focus on customer value is common across all quality management systems. Within Six Sigma, for example, we associate customer value with what is called Voice of the Customer (VOC). With ITIL® (IT Infrastructure Library) there is a similar focus on customer value. The primary delivery component within the ITIL framework is a *service*. Services are designed with reference to business and customer value, and are defined in business terms rather than IT terms. In this way, IT services are positioned strategically within business service operations. All Service Management lifecycle phases contribute to this alignment between IT and the business in order to ensure the delivery of value.

The key point here is that we need to identify customer value *from the customer viewpoint*, so whether this is based on formal or informal sensing is perhaps less important than being able to make the connection and continuing to validate this connection as we design and deliver services. From the Lean perspective, we then need to think of each activity in our work processes as making a contribution toward delivering value.

Value Stream Flow

The concept of flow refers to the unimpeded progression of products or services through a value stream. In other words, products or services are created through the value stream without wasteful activities (e.g., unnecessary delays). A value stream can be viewed as the flow of work where customer value is created. Practically any process can be conceived and represented as a value stream. With Lean, problems with value stream flow (e.g., backlogs, bottlenecks, defects) are subjected to analysis, root cause is determined, and fixes are implemented.

Value Stream Mapping (VSM) is a tool for representing value streams and identifying which activities within the flows add value and which do not. In this respect, a typical VSM exercise will often reveal many examples of waste. In general, VSM is used in the framework of an *as-is/to-be* approach toward improvement (understand the Current, *as-is* State as a precondition for design of the Future, *to-be* State). The Current State is represented so that all essential variables of flow are depicted (e.g., throughput time, waiting time, etc.), and the Future State is designed so that problems are addressed and flow is optimized. A value stream map will show both the flow of materials and the accompanying information flows that support production activities. Within IT, of course, information is often the product that is created (and, thus, is analogous to material flow). The derivation of reports based on data analytics from supporting data streams is analogous to a material flow, whereas the messaging that tells us when the reports should be produced, or the databases mined, would be equivalent to an information flow.

Elimination of Waste

Waste is often identified through value stream analysis, where value-added (VA), nonvalue-added (NVA) but necessary, and unnecessary tasks of no customer value are identified. The latter is what we call waste, and we should properly think of waste as a symptom of some underlying problem. Lean works to eliminate waste by understanding the causes of these problems and addressing them. The concept of waste is typically identified in Lean by types of waste, and include the following:

- Overprocessing: More processing than is necessary to meet customer requirements.
- Transportation: Moving things unnecessarily from place to place.
- Motion: Unnecessary movement in performance of a task.
- Inventory: Too much work-in-progress.
- Waiting: Delays of any sort, waiting for parts, for resources, for decisions.
- Defects: Quality imperfections.
- Overproduction: Producing more of a product or service than is necessary.

There is an often-cited "eighth waste," the waste of human potential that one might associate with the frequent declines in quality that characterize many service delivery operations, and are frequently attributed to poor morale, lack of training, inefficient resource allocation, etc.

When we look at real-world examples of IT operational processes, we often find examples of waste, but sometimes they are not easy to see. This is because it's easy to become habituated to wasteful processes. Indeed, we often become unwitting participants in the very inefficiencies that we casually critique. When individuals talk about waste, they mean it seriously but unscientifically, as in commenting that something is a "waste of time," a "waste of money," or a "waste of talent." In the Lean approach, we apply a more stringent set of criteria to evaluate waste but, in a sense, the bottom line is often the same. We believe that waste in IT operational work is pervasive enough and important enough to deserve some focused attention as a prelude to considering Lean approaches to identifying and eliminating it.

In order to help the reader open his or her eyes to the existence of waste in IT, we have identified a number of examples (see Appendix at the end of this chapter) and we think it's worthwhile to consider these. As a thought activity, the reader might see if any of these seem familiar. Awareness of waste is important because it provides the basis for doing something about it.

The goal of this exercise in waste identification is to help readers see where it exists around them. Not wishing to be dramatic, but the reader should be forewarned that once one's eyes are opened to the existence of waste, it's not uncommon to be aghast at its pervasiveness, and once sensitized, it's hard to go back. However, it's important to remember that seeing waste is just the beginning. We don't stand dumbfounded and retreat in despair. We view these as problems to solve and opportunities for improvement. Viewed this way, rather than seeing only the pervasiveness of waste, we rather see endless opportunities for improvement.

One of the Lean ways of addressing waste is to do things that will make it more transparent and thereby make it easier to remove. In the manufacturing domain, for example, reduction of *inventory* is one means by which operational inefficiencies are identified and then eliminated. Less inventory means fewer products are "on hand" and, thus, they must be delivered "just in time." If they are not at their destination when needed, it exposes operational inefficiencies.

Inventory has a less obvious analogy within IT, but it can be viewed generally as referring to any type of *work-in-progress* (WIP). Within the Help Desk or Service Desk environment of an IT operation, for example, we can view the Service Desk queue, or backlog of incidents (tickets), as WIP. Likewise, we might view incidents in a pending status as another example of WIP. Both of these examples, of course, are commonly accepted within IT operations. They represent, in a sense, business-as-usual activity. Following the Lean approach, we would be encouraged to understand the process dynamics underlying this WIP as a way of addressing systemic problems associated with backlogs, bottlenecks, or defects. Implementing an end-to-end flow of incidents in such a way that we remove the backlog altogether, or reduce all pending incidents to a minimum, might be a rather radical solution for typical Service Desk operations. However, it encourages a line of inquiry that may help to address underlying root causes of these problems.

Continuous Improvement

The quality foundation of Lean is underscored by its emphasis on continuous improvement, aspiring toward perfection. This seemingly unreachable goal underscores the continual aspect of improvement activities and the institutionalization of behaviors that lead to a high quality orientation on the part of all employees (sometimes referred to as *Lean Culture*). We presented a simple model for process improvement in Chapter 3 that can be viewed as the essential core of continuous improvement. The Lean method that directly supports the aim of Continuous Improvement is called *Kaizen* (Japanese for *continuous improvement*). Continuous Improvement is more than just making changes. Continuous Improvement leads an organization into a continuous cycle of learning that aids in adaptation to an environment where change is the norm. It is the difference between saying that it's time to do capacity planning (e.g., once a quarter) and doing capacity planning *all the time*, while at the same time continuously improving the capacity planning process itself.

Lean Learning

In addition to these essential concepts and objectives of Lean Thinking, there are some additional principles that we believe contribute to the overall objectives and goals of adopting a Lean orientation. Some of these principles of the Lean Approach suggest an even more general analogy with *learning*. The notion here is that we will learn how to do things more efficiently by adopting a Lean orientation. We get to a better Future State in an incremental way by applying concepts and practices derived from Lean. Whereas we sometimes feel in IT that gains are made by magic or luck, we rely here more on science and hard work to get to where we want to be.

From this perspective, when we think about what it means to eliminate waste, for instance, and transform processes from their Current State into a more efficient, *leaner* Future State, this is really an example of organizational learning and we can use more personal analogies as a way of understanding the underlying approach to Lean that we are emphasizing here. For example, think about the process of learning to play the piano or learning to swim (please think of your own example). How actually do we learn these activities? First, we apply some methodology or approach to learning. This is often transmitted through an instructor or coach, and the methodology may be very simple (do this exercise on the piano, repeat it 20 minutes a day, and then we'll introduce new exercises). Following a method provides guidance and consistency. In our case, we are using Lean as the method. It's worth pointing out that it is an extremely versatile method that is complementary with any other methods or approaches that are in use, such as Six Sigma, ITIL, CMMI, ISO 9000, ISO/IEC 20000, or COBIT.[*]

With Lean, we have two closely related approaches to learning that contribute to our ability to do effective problem-solving. The idea is that as we solve problems we learn how to do things better. These related approaches are A3 Thinking and Plan–Do–Check–Act (PDCA) and, because of their importance, we want to spend some time discussing each.

A3 Thinking

A3 refers to a size of paper that is used to develop reports, called A3 Reports, which is a Lean tool for identifying and analyzing problems along with proposed solutions. We can think of this as a highly disciplined, scientifically based suggestion box. The template for A3 Reports typically captures

---

[*] We discuss and provide references for Six Sigma and ITIL elsewhere in the book; CMMI refers to the Capability Maturity Model Integration process improvement approach of the Software Engineering Institute at Carnegie Mellon (http://www.sei.cmu.edu/cmmi/); ISO 9000 is a set of Quality Management standards produced by the International Organization for Standardization (http://www.iso.org); ISO/IEC 20000 is a set of IT Service Management standards, which are based on ITIL® (http://www.isoiec20000certification.com/); COBIT is a framework for IT governance and control (http://www.isaca.org/Knowledge-Center/COBIT/Pages/Overview.aspx).

the following information: problem definition and description (with data), problem analysis (with root cause), implementation plan (actions to correct problems), and results.[2] We will be talking more about the various components of A3 Reports as part of our general discussion of problem-solving.

The requirements for content in an A3 report are not only structured, according to the template criteria, but also very detailed. These are not reports that are thrown together casually, but require time and attention in order to derive the right level of detail and validation. Data to support Current State analysis and metrics to measure Future State success are critical. The proposal relative to the Future State (the solution to the problem) is also subject to great scrutiny and serves in some ways as a hypothesis does in a scientific experiment. Indeed, A3 Thinking is very scientific in its approach, which underscores the rigor that must be applied to its use. By the same token, use of A3 is inherently egalitarian, i.e., anyone with an idea on fixing a problem can and should fill out an A3 report, as this then becomes the set of candidate improvement projects.

The rigor of the reports and the intention of empowering any worker to use them suggests the broader and deeper aspects of A3 that suggest its use more as a way of thinking about problems than it does the report format itself. A3 Thinking is about being able to see problems in the first place, and in their apparent absence, to make problems visible, on the general assumption that there are always problems to solve.

At the same time, A3 Thinking is about being able to analyze problems, which means being able to clarify the problem and accurately state its causes and effects. We sometimes say that getting a problem clearly understood and articulated is the largest part of problem-solving. Get the problem understood right and the solutions can be more readily identified. This begins to sound like scientific reasoning and, in fact, the Lean practitioners who exercise A3 will very likely think of it in exactly these terms.[3]

There is also a cultural context that surrounds A3 Thinking. We find in practice that teaching others to exercise A3 is quite difficult, and for this reason, Lean practitioners identify the importance of mentorship as an important aspect of doing A3. Rather than simply teaching workers how to do A3 Thinking, the goal is to help them practice it, and in so doing, help them gain a better understanding by learning on the job.

We can find useful analogies for this in many aspects of daily life. We all know intuitively that even simple tasks can require many years of practice in order to do them at a high level of performance. Many of us can throw a ball, but very few can propel it at 90 mph to a very precise location that is 60 feet away. Many of us can be taught how to do a simple knot or stitch, but it takes years of practice to weave a high-quality rug. In these two cases we can get books on the subject, watch videos, and otherwise take advantage of many tools or methods, but there is probably no substitute for having direct instruction that helps us understand the subtleties of technique and the progression of understanding that leads to higher levels of performance. For this, we would like a teacher or a mentor. It is this same rationale that leads the Lean practitioners to think of A3 problem-solving as the outcome of a relationship between student and teacher. Is this mentorship the role of management? In the Lean community it is, and this underscores some of the significant differences between Lean work environments and those that are not.

A3 Thinking also helps us understand the art of seeing problems. We can begin with the task of identifying waste, but A3 helps us learn to see the root causes behind the waste as well. It also helps us to appreciate how many problems and their causes are hidden from view, and this leads to an understanding of how we can make problems more visible.

A3 involves for many a different way of asking questions because it is extremely analytical. It translates into a different way of talking about things as well. Above all, it is more than just "thinking outside the box" because it requires rigorous and disciplined thinking. In a sense, this approach to problem identification is tantamount to improving our observation skills, which is why the concepts of A3 Thinking are often equated with *learning to see* and embody many of the essential elements of *scientific reasoning*.

A3 also embodies people concepts because, in the effort to increase levels of awareness regarding problems and opportunities, it is important that employees are on board and engaged. They are the ones who are closest to the work, so they are the ones who should actively identify opportunities for improvement. They can see where the pain points are because they live with them daily. There are important enablers that help sustain this approach, including employee training and employee empowerment. Conditions can be created in organizations to make this work well, yet we often see constraints and roadblocks placed in front of employees (indeed, sometimes under stressful circumstances) that make it practically impossible to support employees in this way. We'll talk more about this in Chapter 8.

Plan–Do–Check–Act

We talked briefly about the Plan–Do–Check–Act (PDCA) cycle in Chapter 3. It is the way that the Lean practitioner moves from the Current State to the

Future State, and from a defined solution to an implemented solution. It is also how improvements are made over time, with each small incremental improvement planned and implemented using PDCA. It turns out that PDCA is simple to describe and understand, but often very difficult to do correctly. The reason is mostly because there are so many distractions in our typical IT environments that each step of the cycle can require more rigor and discipline that is conventionally applied to *any* endeavor.

Perhaps overstated somewhat, but we who work in IT are used to doing planning which is less than optimal (in fact, it's often messy), and when we go to implement tasks, we find that rescoping and reprioritizing of these tasks is practically a necessity in order to overcome the roadblocks that often get in the way (changing requirements often introduce delays, a resource planned for is unavailable, a policy intended to support the initiative is stuck in decision making, coordination of resources is complicated by delays in acquisition, etc.). By this time in the PDCA cycle, frankly, we are often spent or otherwise stuck so that there is essentially no attention to the Check and Act phases. We call this variation on PDCA the "Plan–Do–*Stop*" or "Plan–Do–*Drift*" cycle and it is much more common than one might imagine. An example would be planning a survey, then conducting a survey, and then doing nothing with the results except perhaps to generate a report of findings.

It's not diagnostically nuanced but essentially correct to say that many projects fail because they have not done PDCA faithfully and completely. Often this is shrouded in mystery to the practitioners who are part of the failed initiative because it is easy to miss this simple diagnostic amidst all the heat and tension. It is rather like an individual who wants to play the piano, invests in the instrument and in a teacher, and in books or videos as supplemental aids, and then never practices. Despite the investments, not much progress will be made.

We want to pause here to make sure we emphasize this point. PDCA *is* the method for implementing and improving work. Because it is so simple, it is easy to say, "I know that. Tell me something I don't know." And, then it is easy to miss the point by not practicing it. In learning any art, we sometimes say that everything you need to know is taught in your first lesson, and then you spend the rest of your life trying to understand it. The same applies to use of this concept.

In the Lean approach, use of PDCA is not a one-off exercise. It is a means to an end and becomes part of the routine for routine problem-solving, just as daily practice is the routine for learning any new skill.

Identifying solutions is part of planning and this leads us naturally to PDCA as the means by which the solutions are implemented. Some solutions may call for identification of standardized procedures and, for that reason, we can identify a variation on PDCA called SDCA (Standardize–Do–Check–Act).[4] Given our previous discussions about Lean, it will make sense to the reader that a prerequisite to standardization is *simplification*, e.g., we don't want to standardize an inefficient or overly complicated process (and complexity usually introduces inefficiencies).

It might also happen that effective use of PDCA results in changing back to the original way of doing things. That is, our Check activity results in a decision to do this, so our Action is to restore the original state. This might seem like lack of progress, but if it was learned that the planned solution was not going to work, it really represents an appropriate outcome of the PDCA experiment. Similarly, it's possible that an intended sequence of planned solution projects is modified based on changes that result from the implementation of an earlier solution. PDCA may cause appropriate course corrections and is a good example of how PDCA is part of an overall learning process.

Once solutions are implemented, we don't stop there. We do two more things: (1) we implement other solutions related to identified problems (this is done continuously); and (2) we improve the solutions we have implemented. Viewed from either perspective, the bottom line is that once we commit ourselves to the Lean journey, we use PDCA as a fundamental method and tool, and we will continue to go "round and round" the PDCA cycle. In so doing, its practice becomes habitual and ingrained within the culture of the organization until it becomes fundamentally part of the Lean Culture.

One implied corollary of using PDCA is that we need to incorporate metrics as a baseline to measure where we are, as an objective so we have a measurable target, and as observations to show our progress along the way. We will discuss metrics further in Chapter 8, but for now, we want to emphasize that we do not need sophisticated metrics and measurement systems to get going. We need "just enough" to have a simple and meaningful way of understanding where we are, where we want to be, and how we are doing.

We mentioned some of the typical hazards of practicing PDCA, including operating under stress or distraction. Lean enablers will help (again addressed in Chapter 8), but for now we want to introduce some remedies for this common environmental condition. First, PDCA can be done under duress if the work scope is kept relatively small and manageable. Using project parlance, we want tightly scoped, short-term projects where we can reasonably control the variables (maybe not all, but many of them). This emphasis on *small, incremental improvements* is fundamental to doing PDCA under these circumstances. Big projects often fail, so don't do them, especially for Lean projects, because the Lean Approach is designed to see positive results. Hence, we set the work up so it is achievable and we can more likely leverage the success. They may be small projects with small results, but—this is the Lean difference—we don't care because we know we are not just doing PDCA once, but rather we are going to do it again and again.

Working with PDCA over time represents practice in and for itself and this becomes part of the ingrained behavior of a Lean organization. The cumulative effect of small, incremental improvements also begins to change the landscape for problem-solving, since we have begun to change the nature of problems by introducing solutions. This provides feedback that, in turn, influences our approach to problem identification and analysis, represented by A3. Along with A3 thinking, then, we now have the complete recipe for doing IT work in a way that more approximates science than it does magic or luck.

When we think about learning Lean, we also can identify the following notions derived from learning studies, which, we believe, are equally applicable to organizational learning that results from adopting the Lean approach. These include the following observations:

- Visualizing desired results helps, as does seeing signs of progress along the way; Lean is helpful here because it emphasizes transparency, clear objectives, and observable results.
- Learning any new skills or behaviors is easier if manageable "chunks" are rehearsed; it's fine to design an entirely new incident workflow, for example, but Lean would encourage focus on a component (e.g., the priority incident escalation process), and rehearse that until it is repeatable and efficient.[5]
- For this reason, it is good practice to deconstruct processes into components that can be addressed more easily; some may decompose to linear flows and that's exactly what we want to see happen.
- Rehearsal means repetition, so that is the antidote to the common experience of introducing new processes only to have them revert over time to old ones; the usual explanation is that the method or approach didn't work (e.g., "This ITIL stuff doesn't work."), but the real reason is that there was no repetitive practice, so nothing was learned.

- Better to learn by doing than through passive learning; we can't expect to sit in a workshop, agree on a process, and then expect it to work correctly right away; it has to be put in place, practiced, and then improved.
- Making mistakes is okay if it's done in the spirit of long-term improvement; nobody plays the piano perfectly when they are a beginner, and we can't really expect a group of people attempting to do work differently to "get it right" without making some mistakes.

One of the takeaways of these notions is that, for the IT practitioner, it is sufficient to begin the practice of Lean Thinking by simply working with the concepts within one's IT work domain. This is the starting point for the Lean Journey and it is in no way different from becoming a pianist by simply *starting* to play the piano and then *practicing* to gain improvement. There is no right way to get started—modest beginnings are warranted— and there is plenty of room for error, as long as the long-term objective is to get it right. We believe this is one of the attractive aspects of Lean. Concepts and tools are straightforward to learn and adopt, and then it will be in further adaptation and experimentation that improvements will be realized. Above all, it means that the IT practitioner who aspires to be a Lean practitioner can begin the Lean journey at any time (right now, for instance), and all it takes (by analogy) is to sit down in front of the piano and begin to practice.

As simple as this is, note how challenging this can be in typical IT environments, where there are plenty of distractions including lack of focus and attention (limited "bandwidth"), lack of clarity on work scope and objectives (making planning difficult, not to mention the common habit of going off plan), predominance of reactive (versus proactive) behaviors, and so forth. However, the point is that Lean has something to say about all this as well, and Lean Thinking is the starting point for that.

For example, how often has the reader been part of an IT project where the scope of work (what do we do) and the governance mechanisms (who decides what) are so unstructured that, six months into the project, an outside observer might comment that the project team is *still* deciding what to do and how to do it? Here we are talking about contributions that Lean can make where the activities themselves are not even necessarily sequential and repeatable. The essentials of Lean Thinking help to clarify objectives by asking who the customer is, for example, and forcing attention on customer value. For each task in the unstructured project mentioned above, we can ask how that task contributes to customer value. That exercise right there is probably sufficient to modify or eliminate many of the tasks in the plan.

Lean Problem-Solving

The path to waste elimination is characterized by a pervasive orientation toward solving problems. The reason is because, in order to eliminate waste, we need to first identify the root cause of the waste. This is one critical aspect of problem-solving, namely identifying the right problem to solve. The second critical aspect, of course, is actually doing something about the root cause problem. Together, this orientation becomes, in the Lean Approach, a constant guide and methodology that impacts everything that Lean practitioners believe in and apply in their daily work.

This is a very simple script and could actually be associated with many other methodologies, and not just Lean. It is a good example of where we have a core element that represents *what* to do and, with the additional context and narrative provided by Lean Thinking, we gain the perspective of *how* to do it. Each of these simple steps, in turn, then can be understood with some clarity and purpose (Table 4.1).

We think of this script for Lean Problem-Solving as having two perspectives, each of which we associate with a specific method. The first perspective emphasizes identifying and understanding problems and helps with identifying solutions, and we associate this with *A3 Thinking*. The second perspective emphasizes planning, implementing, managing, and improving solutions, and we associate this with *Plan–Do–Check–Act (PDCA)*.

Lean Tools

There are many tools and techniques in the Lean toolbox. Not all of them will be addressed in this book because our primary focus is on *use* of tools, both in the particular context in which they are to be used (*what* tools), and also in the larger context of *how* and *why* these tools are used. We have selected ones that directly support the aims of Lean Thinking and Lean Problem-Solving, and which we will have reason to explore further in the following chapters. We are presenting these tools in this way so that the reader can have enough sense of context and application to begin to use them immediately. We also encourage the

Table 4.1   What and How of Lean Problem-Solving

What	How	Tools
1. Identify the problem	Using A3 thinking, learn to see the problem, make problems visible	***Chapter 5*** Process mapping, Swim Lane diagram, RACI chart, Cause and Effect Diagrams, Value Stream Map, 5 Whys, Go and See, Removal of WIP, 5S, Visual Management, A3 reports
2. Understand the problem	Using A3 thinking, Root Cause Analysis	
3. Identify and plan the solution	Using A3 and PDCA, scope solution so it is doable and small enough to implement rapidly	***Chapter 6*** Brainstorming, PDCA, Checklists, Mistake Proofing, Pull (versus Push), One-Piece Flow, Rapid Changeover SMED, Work Cell Optimization, Workload Leveling, Rapid Improvement Events
4. Implement the solution	Using PDCA, implement quickly so that results can be seen as soon as possible, move on to the next solution, so that rapid incremental improvements are made over time	
5. Manage and improve the solution	Using PDCA, tune the solution until you get it "right enough" then improve it to make it better	

reader to read other books on Lean tools so that his or her own toolbox can be expanded over time.

This is a good time to communicate a philosophy that the authors share and that we believe is consistent with the principles and objectives of Lean Learning. Specifically, while we could provide a detailed description of each Lean tool we will discuss in this book (beginning in Chapter 5), we do not believe that it is either necessary or helpful to do so. To begin with, as stated above, the reader can find these in other books. In addition, we believe that simple, modest starts with basic knowledge are sufficient to "get going." While there are always better ways of using these tools, we believe the Lean practitioner will learn this through practice and experience. Thus, in starting off, there is no single correct way of doing things. Take process mapping, for example. There are certainly process maps that are more useful than others and the goal, of course, is to create good process maps that serve a particular purpose. However, even a rough map can serve that purpose, so any emphasis on detailed conventions or techniques is, we believe, something that the reader can sort out over time.

It is for this reason that many of our models or examples beginning in the next chapter are somewhat rough or even incomplete. We believe that if we show the reader a final product that is the result of a great deal of work, then we will give the impression that this is how one starts. We want to help you get started, so we are using examples that should approximate what you can reasonably expect to accomplish yourself in a relatively short period of time. Consistent with our philosophy, we believe that you will use this as your foundation for continuous improvement.

Lean Enablers

The phrase "lean and mean" usually connotes one of many unfortunate associations that IT practitioners have of life in the modern IT world; one characterized by downsizing, cost cutting, and the challenges of trying to do more work with fewer resources. We introduce this here as a counterpoint to what we mean by Lean. Lean is not about cost cutting per se, although reduced costs may very well be an outcome of adopting Lean practices. Likewise, Lean is not about downsizing, even though it may be possible to do more work with fewer resources due to the efficiencies gained through use of Lean. The typical approach to cost cutting and downsizing, however, typically has nothing to do with Lean. In large part, this is because the entire approach to gaining efficiencies is done essentially backwards. In the typical "lean and mean" approach, you cut costs or reduce resources and do either nothing about waste in the process or else hope that it gets addressed one way or another along the way. In the Lean Approach, by contrast, you focus on reducing waste as a way of gaining efficiencies, and only then identify the cost/resource impacts of doing work in a more efficient way. It is sometimes thought that reducing headcount can force efficiencies, but this is completely alien to Lean Thinking. All this does is add stress to employees, which increases variability. It turns out, in fact, that the Lean Approach would never begin an initiative of identifying and eliminating waste by alienating the very people who are critical to doing this, namely, the workers themselves. For this reason, the Lean Approach places great value on employee empowerment and satisfaction.

Other values that are representative of the Lean Approach include training and mentoring; management support; positive communications; and quality awareness. There are others that we will discuss in Chapter 8. These enablers can also be thought of as critical success factors for implementing sustainable improvements. This underscores the continuous improvement value we identified as part of Lean Thinking.

We do not mean to suggest that all of these enablers need to be in place in order to have successful implementation of Lean improvements, although, of course, if they are in place, the process will be easier. We have mentioned earlier that we believe that Lean improvements can take place even in the absence of management support. However, it is certainly possible to regard the absence of enablers as an issue or problem that needs to be addressed, and to that end, we can use Lean methods to determine root cause of these problems as a prerequisite to addressing them. You just need to get started and use Continuous Improvement to move forward.

In the next chapter, we will begin to look in detail at what it means to take a problem, identify root cause, and provide a solid basis for identifying appropriate solutions.

Summary

In this chapter, we provided a contextual understanding of the Lean Approach by reviewing components of our Lean Improvement Model. This is the model that will guide our discussions for the remainder of the book. Along the way, we also discussed two critical conceptual foundations for the model, namely A3 Thinking and Plan–Do–Check–Act, which together allows us to place the entire endeavor of problem-solving on a rational and even scientific foundation. It is how they build cars and it is how we will build processes to enable and improve IT operational work.

Appendix: Examples of Waste in IT Work

In order to help the reader open his or her eyes to the existence of waste in IT, we have identified a number of examples (derived from multiple sources)[6–13] and we think it is worthwhile to consider these. As a thought activity, the reader might see if any of these seem familiar. Awareness of waste is important because it provides the basis for doing something about it. Remember that the criterion for waste is that it adds no value to the customer experience and is not necessary for any other reason. In some cases, we might argue that these are necessary, even though they have no customer value. However, Lean encourages us to consider them more likely as examples of waste, perhaps by asking first for proof that they are necessary.

- Overprocessing: More processing than is necessary to meet customer requirements
  - System gold-plating (building more than the customer asks for)
  - Unnecessary data processing (with no required or useful output)
  - Spending more time on a customer call than is necessary to address customer needs
  - Churning on issues in a meeting without resolution
  - Unnecessary reports
- Transportation: Moving things unnecessarily from place to place
  - Unnecessary transfer of a service ticket
  - Transferring customer calls from place to place without resolution or updates along the way
  - Phone tree menus that customers must navigate that are time consuming or nonintuitive
  - Too many steps to navigate through applications to accomplish repetitive tasks
- Motion: Unnecessary movement in performance of a task
  - Searching for information that is required to resolve tickets
  - Searching for solutions or assistance from others via email, phone, instant messaging, or blogs
  - Excessive opening and closing of screens as part of normal operations
  - Retrieving anything essential to the task at hand that is not easily accessible (physically or online)
  - Walking around to find files or documentation, or to find out who to talk to about something
- Inventory: Too much work-in-progress
  - Calls or tickets waiting in queue
  - Backlog of pending tickets

- Work sitting in in-boxes (physical or virtual), or partially completed tasks or documents
- Redundant data, files, or documents
- Unutilized or under-utilized hardware
- Teams waiting for work assignments or for decisions that clarify these assignments
■ Waiting: Delays of any sort, waiting for parts, for resources, for decisions
- Consistently slow system response times
- Time spent waiting for reviews, approvals, decisions, or additional information
- Manual escalation procedures
- Slow employee on-boarding, or new employees waiting for phones or equipment
- Delays at handoffs, e.g., between coding and testing, or test and documentation
■ Defects: Quality imperfections
- Abandoned calls
- Reopened tickets
- Bad code
- Inadequate documentation
■ Overproduction: Producing more of a product or service than is necessary
- Overstaffing of agents when the call volume is low, understaffing when the volume is high
- Knowledge-base articles that are on topics out of scope for the purpose of the knowledge base
- Delivery of products or services of unknown customer value
- Redundant or poorly tested troubleshooting procedures
- Reinventing the wheel for commonly performed activities due to lack of standardized processes
■ Human potential: Underutilizing employees or preventing them from fulfilling their potential
- Limited decision authority requiring frequent escalations with associated delays
- Failure to capture good ideas or acknowledge them once identified
- Not including employees in decisions that affect their productivity
- Lack of employee training
- Inability to exchange data or information between systems

- Absence of standards, incompatibility of standards, or noncompliance to standards
- Manual data entry due to lack of automation
- Frequent reassignment of roles and individuals
- Too much work placed on individuals
- Providing no guidance to employees on how to prioritize work
- Not providing employees tools they need to do their jobs
- Unrealistic or impossible timeframes for completion of work

It's also possible to find waste in the information and communication "fabric" of an organization. When you call a Help Desk and you are put on hold, and then the agent provides you with information that contradicts what another agent told you earlier, you are seeing the symptoms of incomplete information, fragmented information, and/or inaccurate information. Whatever you call it, you recognize it intuitively as waste. Likewise, when we see people operating at cross purposes, evidence of misaligned goals, lack of clarity of roles and responsibilities, excessively long decision-making cycles, or conflicting messages that are intended to guide behavior, we are seeing signs of waste in communication. These may be evidence of systemic, cultural attributes, or they may be dysfunctions attributable to abnormal conditions, but the bottom line is the same.

The examples we have just presented might be rare in your organization, but that's not likely. It is important to emphasize that the examples are not about being critical (who is to blame), but rather to underscore how waste is very commonly tolerated. We just don't see it. Lean doesn't approach things this way. If it is waste, we should do something about it or at least call it out for what it is. Learning to see waste thereby becomes the means to making improvements to problems that otherwise trip us up all the time.

References

1. Womack, J. P., and D.T. Jones. 2003. *Lean thinking*. New York: Simon & Schuster.
2. Rother, M. 2010. *Toyota kata*. New York: McGraw-Hill.
3. Shook, J. 2008. *Managing to learn: Using the A3 management process*. Cambridge, MA: Lean Enterprise Institute.
4. Imai, M. 1997. *Gemba kaizen*. New York: McGraw-Hill.
5. Coyle, D. *The talent code*. 2009, New York: Bantam Dell.
6. Hicks, B. J. 2007. Lean information management: Understanding and eliminating waste. *International Journal of Information Management* 27: 233–249.

7. English, L. 2005. IQ and muda: Information quality eliminates waste. *Information Management*. Online at: http://www.information-management. com/issues/20050901/1035293-1.html (accessed July 15, 2012).

8. Escobar, D. and E. Revilla. 2005. The customer service process: The lean thinking perspective. *IT Working Paper* (WP05-13), Instituto de Empresa Business School (Madrid, Spain), November 3.

9. Damelio, R. 2008. Improving knowledge work: Lessons learned. ASQ Lean Six Sigma Conference, February 11. Online at: http://asq.org/le/2008/05/lean/ improving-knowledge-work-lessons-learned-en.html?shl=088852 (accessed July 15, 2012).

10. Lafever, D. 2011. Eight wastes of the support center. *HDI Community Blog*. Online at: http://www.hdiconnect.com/blogs/community/040711/1316/eight-wastes-of-the-support-centerpart-1.aspx (accessed July 15, 2012).

11. Spencer, D. P. and G. Plenert. 2007. Win in the flat world: Apply lean principles across the IT organization. *Manufacturing Business Technology*. November 1.

12. Spencer, D. P. and G. Plenert. 2011. Lean on IT: Applying lean manufacturing principles across the IT organization. *InfoSys View Point*. Online at: http:// www.infosys.com/industries/industrial-manufacturing/white-papers/documents/lean-on-it.pdf (accessed July 15, 2012).

13. Waterhouse, P. 2008. Lean IT: Waste not, want not: Strategies to reduce eight elements of waste in IT. *Enterprise IT Management Strategies White Paper*, Computer Associates, November.

Chapter 5

Lean Problem-Solving: Identifying and Understanding Problems

Beginning with this chapter, we will look closely at the Lean Problem-Solving script as a component of the Lean Improvement Model. Our initial focus will be on identifying and understanding problems using the concepts associated with A3 Thinking. We also will turn our attention more directly at the domain of interest for application of Lean practices, specifically, IT Operations. Using examples and scenarios derived from IT operational work, we will show how Lean tools help in identifying and understanding problems.

The central role that waste elimination plays in Lean Thinking provides an excellent starting point for identifying problems. This is not to suggest that waste is the only type of problem we might encounter, or that problem-solving is the only basis for identifying improvements, but waste is significant and pervasive enough to justify focusing our attention on it. Simply stated, waste is everywhere, and all waste is a problem.

Identifying Waste

In our discussion in Chapter 4 of waste in IT Operations we did not give enough credit to efforts IT practitioners make in their day-to-day work to identify and eliminate it, and we should say something about that here.

We do, in fact, confront pain points indicative of waste frequently enough, and sometimes have no choice but to do something about them. We also make concerted efforts to address problems as we confront them, and this can occupy much of our time (sometimes, unfortunately, in a crisis mode). Sometimes we address these problems in a thorough and conscientious way, and sometimes, due to other priorities, we need to defer on problem-solving until another day. Sometimes known problems get deprioritized and become all but forgotten until the pain we experience from them comes back to haunt us. Typically, despite our best intentions, we approach problem-solving in a rather unsystematic way, addressing what hurts us most and tolerating other problems as part of our business as usual.

One of the benefits of Lean is that it approaches the identification and elimination of waste in a systematic and disciplined way. The waste we identify easily is addressed, but other sources of waste that are perhaps less easy to identify also are rooted out and eliminated. Lean approaches waste elimination as more of a cultural orientation than a one-off exercise. In the Lean orientation, there is no end to benefits that can be gained from addressing problems that underlie waste.

Below we will address three different scenarios where waste is identified. These three scenarios represent variations on the same theme, but they are common enough in real life to warrant our attention. The three scenarios include:

■ Stumbling on waste from pain points
■ Identifying waste in clearly identified workflows
■ Clarifying complex workflows as a prerequisite to identifying waste

In addition, we will discuss a Lean practice whereby problems are purposefully identified by surfacing and exposing them when they might otherwise remain hidden.

In the course of each scenario, we will introduce Lean tools that may apply. It is important to say, however, that we are not mapping tools to scenarios in a prescriptive way. We are beginning with simple tools (ones that you may not even associate with Lean), primarily as an indication of how simple it is to incorporate them into a Lean practice. At the same time, the reader will hopefully appreciate that the tools are intended to be used in practice in a thoughtful and deliberate way, and any of the tools might reasonably be used for any of the scenarios we are exploring.

Stumbling on Waste from Pain Points

A number of technical consultants were deployed on a customer site in order to do the implementation work for an enterprise software application. They were ready to go on the assigned date according to the project plan and the commitments within the statement of work. There was only one problem. There wasn't any hardware on which to work. In fact, as it turned out, the hardware had been received the week before and was waiting to be provisioned, but for a variety of reasons (all of them quite familiar to the customer, as it turned out), there were numerous delays in completing the work associated with server provisioning. There were several different groups involved in all the various activities, each of which had its own process for approval and implementation of work, and there was essentially no coordination between the groups. Each group would finish its tasks, then toss the work order over the wall to the next group. There were delays at practically each handoff, and despite the priority of the work from an enterprise perspective, there was little sense of priority within each of the separate groups. By the way, it took nearly one week for the hardware to be ready, and during that entire time the consultants were being paid to do essentially nothing.

Although it was not clear how commonplace this situation was, one thing was certain—it was perceived as waste ("of time and resources") despite the fact that it was tolerated. This is one fairly common reaction to seeing waste. People complain, issues are raised, individuals are blamed perhaps, but at the end of the day, the cause of waste is never really investigated and nothing is done about it. In this particular case, you could say that the opportunity, such as it was, was practically stumbled upon. It emerged as an obstacle to project progress, so it was, in that sense, pretty hard to miss. However, while it loomed large, it nevertheless escaped more careful investigation, so we could say that we never really looked at it sufficiently to identify the real opportunity for Lean improvement.

The solution to this problem at the time was for the project manager to crack the whip and push the process along until the work got done. This is also fairly common—to have a short-term solution that never gets to the real root cause of the problem.

By the way, our server build case is a good example of sequential, repeatable operational work that is identified as a task within a project plan. As we discussed earlier, project plans are a good place to look for this type of work and, during reviews, it is fairly typical to associate these with sources of project delays. The key takeaway is that this is not a project issue to solve, but it is rather an operational process that needs to be subjected to Lean improvement.

We begin with this example because we believe it represents a rather common occurrence in IT. We can make casual observations and see many examples of waste. We can have good intentions of doing something about it, but there are many competing demands for time and resources, and it is often the case that these opportunities for improvement are simply missed. One could argue that when decisions are deliberately made to *not* address inefficiencies in operation (perhaps due to cost or simply because there are other priorities) that this may be sensible, but when opportunities are neglected because there is no capability of attending to them in any systematic way, this is evidence of a reactive, undisciplined environment. Realistically in these environments, there is no thought whatsoever to attending to them in a systematic way.

Looking for Lean opportunities, then, is on the one hand quite simple. We just look around for signs of waste and inefficiency and there you have it. We could do formal assessments or audits and perhaps identify further opportunities (things we might not see by adopting a more casual approach), but quite likely the things observed casually are as good a starting point for Lean analysis as other things identified more formally. If waste is everywhere, as we argued in Chapter 4, then we should be able to find Lean opportunities practically anywhere we look.

One of the simplest ways of identifying these examples is simply to ask employees. They often are well aware of these problems because they work with them (and *around* them) every day. These problems are experienced as pain points or obstacles to getting work done and very often can be identified simply by asking employees what their challenges are or what prevents them from getting their work done.

In this case, we stumbled on the waste and nothing was really done about it. It was a problem, for sure, and in fact, the causes of the problem were roughly understood (attributable to the siloed nature of the organization, the absence of operational agreements between different IT groups, and the absence of commitments by these groups relative to tasks in the project plan). We are not declaring with certainty that this was the cause of the dysfunction, but the point is that the customer was aware enough of the potential causes not to be surprised by the effects.

How could they have addressed the problem in a different way? As they essentially did nothing, our updated scenario is hypothetical, but it is also quite simple and straightforward. Using the Lean Improvement Model, we would like to find a way of representing the problem in such a way that it can be addressed. One way of doing that is to clearly identify the process, or work-flow, associated with the task objectives for server provisioning. For this, we use a tool that everyone is familiar with and, in our case, in service of our Lean orientation, we include within the Lean Toolbox. The tool is *process mapping*.

Tool: Process Mapping

A process map is an end-to-end workflow of the process of interest, in our case, the server build process. Its primary purpose is to clarify and under-stand the process and, to that end, it is often developed over a period of time, incorporating inputs from various stakeholders (principally those who do the work, but others as well). This suggests a related purpose of the pro-cess map, namely to socialize and foster agreement on the process itself. It is commonplace for stakeholders of a process (even those who work together) to not quite see things the same way as regards to "how the process works"; therefore, one benefit of a process map is to get everyone on the same page.

Recall from our previous discussion on process analysis that there are dif-ferent levels of representation and the one of particular interest to us is the Current *as-is* State representation that shows how the work is really done (versus how we think it is done, how it should be done, or how it may have been designed). Oftentimes it is difficult and time consuming to capture this level of detail all at once and up-front, and this suggests the requirement to scope the process map accordingly. One simple way of doing this is to map it out at a high level, understanding that there is a level-down of detail that remains to be done before real analysis can begin. Figure 5.1 shows an example of how we might begin this mapping exercise.

We derived this model by asking various stakeholders what is required, at a high level, to get the work done. We know that this level of representa-tion is more like the Current *as-designed* State than the Current *as-is* State, and there is lots of "real work" detail that is not represented here. Yet, at the same time, it provides some high-level structure for further drill-down by clustering related tasks and capturing a rough sense of sequence. It is some-thing to work from.

Even at this high level of description, it's possible to do some preliminary analysis. We knew from general awareness (because it was a conspicuous pain point) that the overall process was taking too long. Ideally, we begin to capture data at this point in time to get some idea of duration of time spent on each activity in the process, but even with subjective assessments based

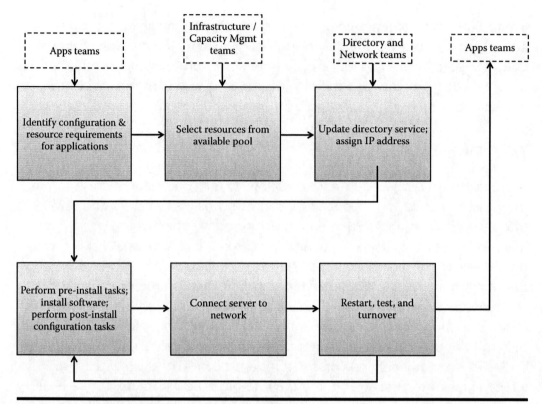

Figure 5.1 High-level, server build process map.

on testimony, it may be possible to hone in on one particular activity as a starting point for further drill-down. In this case, we determined that it was taking too long to identify server configuration requirements. "Too long" is a subjective assessment for sure, but as it was perceived as such by stakeholders, it sounds like waste.

In further analysis of this process, we want to drill down within this activity and get to a representation of real work. But it is important to see how we got to this point, and also to see that we have been guided entirely by good judgment, assessment of stakeholders, and a little bit of subjective data. It is rather like forming a hunch (not quite a hypothesis) that might initiate an informal scientific inquiry. We think this is a problem area, and we believe it's worthy of further analysis.

What else might we want to know about this high-level representation? In building out the model, we might want to identify other pain points as experienced by stakeholders. For example, they might believe that another set of activities (e.g., updating directory services) also takes too long. We can capture that, and then this also gets factored into our decision making about what warrants further analysis. We also might want to know who is responsible for any of these activities, and for this there are two additional tools we can call upon. One is a *swim-lane diagram* and the other is a modified *RACI* (Responsible, Accountable, Consulted, and Informed) chart. Let's do a quick diversion to look at these tools and then return to the process map.

Tool: Swim-Lane Diagram

For our purposes, at this level of analysis, the swim-lane diagram helps to clarify responsible roles (Figure 5.2). As a visual representation, it is the picture that readily conveys roles and responsibilities. In addition, it shows touch points and handoffs very clearly and these are often candidates for investigation in doing Lean analysis because they are often where delays, bottlenecks, and defects can occur. As we clarify and verify the process map, we ultimately want to focus on the process and not the people because it is too easy to have these problem-solving exercises turn into blame sessions where individuals get called out for not performing their

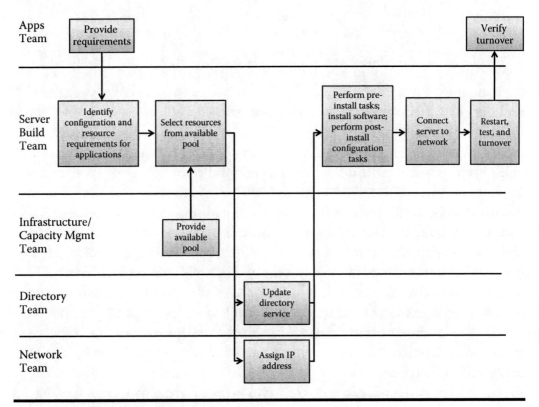

Figure 5.2 Swim-lane diagram.

jobs. This is not the Lean Approach. Here we are interested in identifying individuals so that we can clarify roles and also to identify everyone who can help to clarify and verify the process further. We can take this a step farther by using a RACI Chart.

Tool: RACI Chart

A RACI chart is a matrix that identifies specific tasks and activities and then maps these to roles according to the following scheme:

- Who is **R**esponsible for performing the task/activity?
- Who is **A**ccountable for results?
- Who needs to be **C**ommunicated with prior to the task/activity?
- Who needs to be **I**nformed after the task/activity is performed?

Variations on this RACI scheme exist, but we would like to suggest a very simple way of using the concept. At the level of analysis we are working with here, we believe that the most important element of the RACI is: "Who is Responsible?" Clarification of this question alone will often gain great advantage in understanding a process. We often find that there are delays in IT work simply because people do not know who they should go to for some particular task to be fulfilled or some information to be provided.

Sometimes RACI charts are worked on too soon in an analysis exercise, and they often feel academic or like busy work. At worst, they can be very painful exercises where groups feel disconnected from their purpose. It is almost as if they are a surrogate way of trying to figure out the nature of the work itself. While they can be useful to identify roles and persons who need to be interviewed about a process, they are not a substitute for the process mapping work itself. At the right point in time, however, a full RACI chart can convey quite a bit of information, including gaps ("Nobody is accountable") or overlaps ("I didn't know you did that too"), and can help to identify bottlenecks in resources because it will be apparent that certain individuals are responsible and/or accountable for a lot of work. Our rule-of-thumb is that when this type of inquiry becomes relevant, then a RACI exercise is called for and, until that point in time, just make sure you know who is Responsible. They are the people you are going to talk to further to clarify and verify the process.

Table 5.1 is a simple, generic RACI chart that conveys the ideas we just reviewed. Here we have highlighted in gray areas that probably require

Table 5.1 RACI (Responsible, Accountable, Consulted, and Informed) Chart

Roles Tasks	*Server Team Admin.*	*Server Team Manager*	*Directory Team Admin.*	*Apps Team Manager*	*Network Team Member*
Task 1	R		R		
Task 2		R			
Task 3					
Task 4				R	

some further attention (two roles responsible for the same task, Task 1; nobody responsible for another, Task 3).

More on Process Mapping

Notice that the mapping activity we have done to this point is somewhat informal and we have chosen not to address more formal conventions that might be used. We do this on purpose because we want the reader to understand that even this informal level of representation is sufficient to "get going." Below are a few guidelines on building process maps, but keep in mind that the really important thing is what we do with process maps.

- Avoid too much complexity too soon (take time to understand what's happening as you develop the map).
- It takes time to get to the right level of representation and you will use an iterative approach to get there (work on the model, talk to people, clarify and verify, socialize and improve the model).
- Solicit different points of view (in workshops or interviews).
- Represent it as a picture that you can show people (ask: "Is this what you do?").
- Clarify Roles and Responsibilities with swim-lane diagrams and simplified RACI charts (as discussed above).
- Eventually, everyone should agree that that is how the work is done.
- Include tool steps as embedded work instructions, not as identified tasks in the process map itself, even if you believe there may be inefficiencies in the instructions (in other words, deal with them separately, but visually reference their existence; see Chapter 2, Figure 2.5, for an example).

■ It is okay to identify pain points and even improvement ideas along the way, but put these in a parking lot for further analysis *after* you have agreement on the Current State. It's too easy for people to mix things up and start talking in circles, so make this principally an exercise in developing and verifying the Current State process flow.

Recall from our original scenario that we stumbled on waste, in this case, long delays in getting servers built. We would expect, therefore, to find some evidence of this when we drill down into the process map that corresponds with how the work is really done. In our case here, what we are going to do is to drill down into an activity of interest where there is reason to believe we have evidence of waste. In our scenario, we have discovered in talking to stakeholders that the process of identifying configuration requirements from the Apps team seems to be taking too long. Our data analysis may or may not confirm that, but for now, let's drill down into that activity and derive a Current *as-is* State model that represents how the work for that activity is really done. That model might look something like what is seen in Figure 5.3.

Here, we have begun to identify some problems that may help to explain the original assessment, albeit, subjective, that server builds are taking too long. Still without gathering any data, we have identified in the steps that comprise the real work activities some evidence of delays. Specifically, there are delays between each of the first two steps in the workflow (we don't know why yet), and we have indicated with the star that there is at least anecdotal evidence that this evaluation activity takes too long (again, we don't know why).

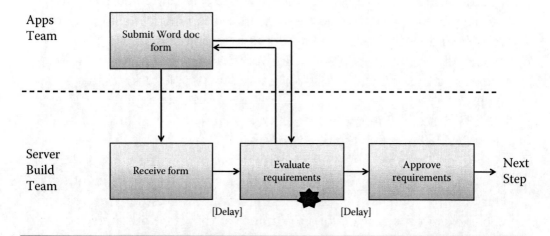

Figure 5.3   Process map for identifying server configuration requirements.

Because we are now talking about real work, it is definitely time to start looking at how we can verify our hunches, and to that end, we need to gather some data. If we were doing analysis using a Six Sigma approach, we would need comprehensive and accurate data in order to proceed. While this is always desirable, we would argue that even a limited set of fairly representative data is sufficient for our purposes. Notice that we are being somewhat subjective about this. What we are saying is that we don't need to be too precise in order to have data that has value for our purpose. Please keep in mind that many "experiments" in IT are based entirely on hunches with no data whatsoever, and we want to avoid that extreme as well. What we want is data that we can start to consider in our continued analysis. In this case, we would like to get data for the following:

- How many forms are received (in some time period)?
- How many forms are processed through each activity (in some time period)?
- How long does it typically take for a form to go through the entire process?
- What is the typical (average) delay between the activities noted?
- How long does the evaluation activity take relative to the total timeline?

We have identified data points here based, in some cases, on averages. A precaution is that averages can be misleading, so it's also important to gather low and high data points as well.

In gathering this data we will talk to stakeholders, but now we want to rely on more than just anecdotal evidence. We might use reports if they contain the desired data, but we probably don't want to rely entirely on these either. We need to verify that we are getting a fairly accurate snapshot of what is going on. We want to apply our observation skills and do something like the following:

- Follow a number of requests through the process from beginning to end, capturing time data along the way.
- Have everyone who touches a request document timestamp it as it passes through their activity.

From this, we can start to build a more accurate representation of what is going on. Because the development of this level of representation includes talking to those individuals who do the work, this is as good a time as any to introduce one of the issues that can arise when doing this level of analysis. Specifically, it is possible that stakeholders don't want to be completely forthcoming about the work they do and the level of performance they exhibit. They, in fact, might be resistant. However, if our goal is to capture the work as it is really done and to include some data collection, then we need to derive this from the people who do the work. There are many ways to motivate stakeholders to be a partner in this level of investigation and some obvious rules of conduct include having good relationships with them in the first place, not to mention tact and persuasion. But, these are really personalized ways of saying that we respect the employee and his or her role, and for this reason, we call out employee-related factors as enablers of success. We will discuss these further in Chapter 8.

With data in hand, we will know whether we are chasing up a tree or not. "Too long" will now have actual duration data associated with it, so it's more than just a subjective hunch. How long does it take? We know that now. How long *should* it take? We can't really address that yet, but it's quite probable that it doesn't need to take as long as it does. We won't know that until we explore the causes behind the delays and, for this, we will need to engage in *Root Cause Analysis (RCA)*.

Before we look at RCA, it's reasonable to ask: "Didn't we leave a bunch of unanalyzed waste in the process?" After all, we just drilled down to one activity among several, and some of the others also might have delays that explain the overall timeline for server provisioning. The answer is "yes," we did leave potential waste unexplored. We were guided principally by pain points, which isn't a bad way of proceeding, but we could very well have other sources of delays elsewhere in the overall process and these will need to wait until some other time to explore them further. Using our Lean perspective, we would expect there to be more waste, suggesting once again that there is a very large opportunity space with which for us to work. In the next scenario, we will talk about identifying waste in a somewhat more systematic way, but for now, let's continue our analysis of delays in identifying server configuration requirements.

Root Cause Analysis (RCA)

Once we have represented the end-to-end process in such a way that we can see how activities interconnect, we also can identify where the pain points are experienced. These are the most likely symptoms of underlying problems, or the *effects* that we will associate with probable *causes*. For our purposes here, let's focus on the primary pain points, which are delays associated with waiting.

Waiting might be completely without purpose, as when something simply waits because it's in somebody's inbox. It is also possible that waiting has a legitimate purpose (well, maybe we should question that), such as when we wait for approvals in order to proceed with work. The bottom line is that waiting as a source of delay is very often a candidate for waste, and we would like to know how much of the time it takes to do something is actually spent in this suspended state. What we will often find is that the great majority of time is spent waiting, and that it's possible to quantify the delay. After some data gathering and analysis, let's assume that of the total time it took to process an individual form with configuration requirements—one day—it turned out that value-added work only took two hours on average and the rest of the time (22 hours) was delay due to waiting.

What are the causes of the delays? For this, we will need to talk to our stakeholders again, in addition to making our own observations, and from these inputs, we may identify a number of possible or probable causes that contribute to the effect that we have observed (that is, the delays).

One of the ways of capturing the underlying causes of these symptoms of delay is use of a *cause-and-effect diagram*.

Tool: Cause and Effect Diagram

The diagram in Figure 5.4, sometimes called a fishbone diagram, represents a template that might conventionally be used to solicit and document probable causes. Our goal ultimately is to identify causes that are both valid (i.e., we have reason to believe that they are the *real* root cause of the problem) and tractable (i.e., we believe we can do something about them). Our goal, after all, is to address the underlying problem, so we would like to know that we have correctly analyzed it and also have set the stage for doing something about it. In order to do this, we need to gain consensus as well from all critical stakeholders that they agree with the analysis.

Please notice that some creativity in thinking is needed in order to identify causes. As a group activity, it is important that various individuals weigh in with their thoughts and ideas. As a brainstorming activity, this also sets the stage for considering solutions to the problems once they are analyzed. We will explore brainstorming as a tool in the next chapter.

The categories in the template are somewhat common and conventional, but do not preclude creating one's own. Used in this way, the categories can

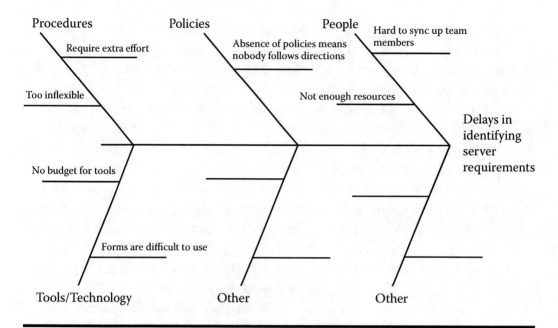

Figure 5.4 Cause and effect diagram.

serve as a checklist of sorts so that each can be considered in turn, asking, for example: "What are some possible *procedural* causes of the delays?"

The causes we identify in this way may or may not qualify for what we call root causes, but they represent the landscape that we work with in order to identify candidates that deserve further attention. Some additional homework may spin off from this level of analysis, perhaps including further data collection. For those issues that require further investigation, the diagram can be used as the basis for assigning individuals to that task.

As a supplemental aid in doing this kind of analysis, it sometimes helps to use *analogies* as they may trigger a line of reasoning that allows us to more readily visualize underlying dynamics. For example, we might view a Help Desk as similar to a fast food restaurant where customers stand in line to be served. Or, perhaps, we can think of work in a queue as similar to traffic flowing through a tunnel. Analogies can be very powerful if properly conceived, and it is one of the benefits of exploring other Lean applications to be able to visualize similarities between work done in these other domains (e.g., a factory) and work in IT.

How do we know if we have identified a *real* root cause (as opposed to an indirect or proximate cause)? This is where the logic and method of A3 Thinking applies. We are conducting what is like a scientific investigation, and our research orientation will help drive us in the right direction.

Even though we do not have to submit our preliminary results to the rigor of scholarly review, our perspective should be both scientific and practical. Our general assumption is that the problems we are investigating are *solvable*, so we want to identify causes that suggest things we can do to address them. Therefore, the *best* root cause is a cause that identifies such a control and also does not appear to have any deeper causes which help to explain it. However, it is sometimes the case that we either cannot identify a root cause or we can identify one, but it does not appear to have any easy solution. It can also happen that we have no time to identify a root cause (due, perhaps, to a crisis situation), so we have to settle for proximate causes and seek solutions to these. The point here is that identifying root cause is not a simple matter, so it requires a style of thinking (A3 Thinking) that is more like scientific investigation. To that end, we should always be thinking how we can derive data to confirm our root cause hypotheses. Finally, application of A3 Thinking suggests that we may not get the root cause identified correctly every time. It means we can get better and better at finding them over time.

While we want to find root causes that suggest opportunities for control (so we can do something about them), sometimes root causes can appear intractable, such as when we identify something like organizational structure as a root cause (e.g., we are a siloed organization and this is causing a lot of the delays we are experiencing as we make handoffs across boundaries). Another common example is when the root cause is determined to be lack of investment or resources. In these cases, we may accept the judgment, but still find that there are opportunities for control when we begin to identify solutions (e.g., let's form a cross-organizational team and clarify the workflow that traverses organizational boundaries, or let's identify low-cost solutions).

Another rule-of-thumb in identifying root cause is derived from the Quality Management school of thought and is summarized as: Human error is never a root cause.

The reason we make this assertion is that we want to focus on the entire system (People, Process, Technology) with special attention to Process, on the assumption that people make mistakes because something in the process is not conducive to minimizing errors. People make mistakes, and this can sometimes lead to critical conditions, such as outages, but we need to understand why the mistakes were made, and when we do, we often find that they are attributable to causes that we have some control over (inadequate training, too few supporting resources, too much overtime, etc.). The real question that helps get us correctly oriented here is to ask what prevents employees from performing according to our quality criteria.[1] This is a Lean line of inquiry because it shifts the attention from people (who is to blame) to the process (what is needed to facilitate the work).

Continuing with our scenario for identifying server configuration requirements, let's assume that the following possible causes were identified for the delays we documented:

- Procedures require teams to evaluate each form according to a set of criteria that may not apply to all types of configuration requirements.
- The form itself is cumbersome and requires time to transfer data from the Word® doc into a spreadsheet where a team tracks requirements through the rest of the workflow.
- The form instructions are not clear so the Apps team often leaves out critical information.
- Evaluation requires lots of back-and-forth between the server build team and the Apps team, and there are multiple delays in getting the right people talking together to resolve issues or collect required information.
- Tools would help, but budgetary constraints have prevented investment in better solutions.
- Not enough people to share the workload so individuals become overloaded (this explains most of the delays between steps).

We actually generated this list quite readily and even if some of them might not yet be at the root cause level, we would like the reader to underscore how relatively simple this is as long as the foundation work has been done in advance in creating the process map and establishing the right communication with stakeholders. Everyone looks at the same visual representation (the process map), identifies pain points, and then begins the root cause investigation, using tools such as cause-and-effect diagrams. We might observe that we often do this in an unsystematic way when grappling with problems, but Lean does this systematically, with a lot of attention on generating valid outcomes.

We will leave this scenario right here for the time being, acknowledging that further root cause analysis is needed. We will explore another tool for root cause analysis in the next scenario, and this will help to dive deeper into root causes. In the next chapter, we will pick up the scenario at this point and talk about how we identify solutions based on our analysis of causes. Basically, what we will do is to review and prioritize the causes and then brainstorm around ways of addressing these. The clarity we have gained in understanding the problems will make generating solutions that much easier.

The reader might feel we have left this particular scenario a bit too soon. It doesn't feel complete yet. But what we would like to suggest is that we have just now provided a couple of simple tools that can be used to practice the approach we have outlined. It's enough to get going. It's not too soon to look around your own IT work environment, identify a candidate for waste (an obvious pain point), and then work through the few steps that lead to a good list of probable causes. You might be surprised how substantive and relatively complete the analysis you achieve will feel compared to the approach we often adopt in day-to-day work.

Identifying Waste in Clearly Identified Workflows

In the previous scenario, we stumbled on waste and then we identified the process workflow in which the waste was evident. In this scenario, we want to begin with a workflow and discuss how we can identify waste and, therefore, opportunities for improvement. The reason to approach the matter from this perspective is because we don't always stumble on waste and yet there is reason to believe that it is there. In fact, it is the likely scenario that waste is there, even if we don't see it right away, because as we suggested earlier, systems (the coordination of People, Process, and Technology) do not naturally evolve to a state of maximum efficiency, but rather to the point where waste is tolerated, and efficiency is only gained through deliberate effort to make it so.

In this scenario we will look at the process of patch management, referring to a set of activities that provide updates to software for various purposes, for example, to enhance security or address known problems.[2]

In our scenario, patch management is performed by different groups for different products and applications, on various schedules, with varying degrees of planning foresight, and with results that require some level of management in order to ensure that correct versions are maintained and properly identified. In this scenario we do not have the benefit of having a configuration management system, so there is some degree of uncertainty at any point in time as to which products and applications are at a particular level of versioning. This introduces complexities, although they are not particularly unusual in many IT environments. The control is to do patching as required and with some level of documentation and monitoring, establish the baseline as, in effect, what we know to be the case. Another control is by having different IT groups assume responsibility for different parts of the infrastructure so that one group does patch management for operating systems (OSs), for example (subdivided perhaps by OS type), while others do patch management for applications. Still, it's quite apparent that there are significant coordination issues that come into play here, and these are often indicators of potential delays or defects, as happens when one team applies a patch without clearing it with other teams that need to know about it.

Let's look at the workflow for patch management for the Windows® OS team. While we don't want to lose sight of the fact that there are touch points and relationships between the work of this team and other teams that also apply patches, we want to begin by focusing on the work of just one group, if only to start the analysis in a somewhat easier way. Applying what we know about process mapping, and going through the exercise we described in the first scenario, we talk to individuals involved in patch management, asking questions as basic as: "How do you do patch management?" We can then identify a first-pass workflow that looks something like what is shown in Figure 5.5.

This process map is quite informal and a little different from the one in the previous example. We have done it this way on purpose, because it

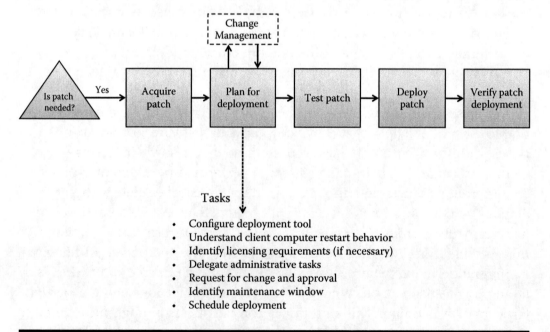

Figure 5.5   Process map for Patch Management.

underscores some of the liberty that can be taken in doing process mapping. There is no "right" way of doing it. We are just trying to figure out the workflow and represent it in such a way that stakeholders (especially those who do the work) can look at it together and agree that it's how things are done.

If we show this workflow to anyone on the Windows OS team, we will likely hear something like: "Yes, that's how we do it," although if we listen carefully, we may discover that there are some variations on the process that are exercised by different individuals on the team, and there may even be some differences that are unknown until we start the conversation. Some of these differences may even be disagreements about the correct way of performing the activities. The point is that we don't know that until we can start to show everyone how the process actually works, based on testimony from those who do the work. This is not a design exercise and it's not about the desired Future State. It's an analysis exercise and it's entirely about the Current State.

As the process takes shape, it is best to listen to how the work is done. But, you need to verify the workflow. Ask the team to track an item through the system, for example, or use past projects as a means to gather a time estimate. In practice, estimates of how work is done often vary greatly from what is actually done, so it is important to verify whatever information we collect.

In order to represent this process in such a way that we can apply further analysis, let's use another tool from the Lean toolbox. This is actually a variation on the process map and is called a *Value Stream Map*.

Tool: Value Stream Map

A Value Stream Map (VSM) is a process map that is designed to encourage a particular line of inquiry that supports Lean objectives. It asks us to identify the value added at each step in the value stream (and if there is no value added, we consider whether the step is necessary). Related to this, it also provides the context for identifying both nonvalue-added (NVA) activities and waste, the latter being the familiar starting point for problem-solving that we described in the first scenario.

In considering value, we have to ask: "Value for whom?" Ultimately it is the customer, but this begs the question: "Who is the customer?" The end user or party that pays for the service or work may be a good starting point to answer that question, although the concept of customer is fluid and might include anyone upstream or downstream from this process. In this sense, then, Change Management might be viewed as a customer of the Patch Management team, and, conversely, Change Management might view Patch Management as one of its customers. This consideration of value all around is necessary in order to clarify whether work is truly necessary.

In considering value, we ask the question about every step in the process. This is the meaning of a value stream; value is added at each step along the chain of activities. If it doesn't, then we need to probe it further to determine if it is NVA or waste. The criteria for waste include an assessment that it is neither necessary nor of value to the customer. Indications that it may be waste are often suggested by comments such as: "We do it this way because that's the way we have always done it," or "It's the required process," or frank admissions, such as: "I have no idea." One common rule-of-thumb is to ask whether anyone would care or notice if the activity were not done at all. It's important to say here that just because an activity at a high level of representation passes the litmus test for value (that is, it is neither waste nor NVA) doesn't mean there isn't waste hidden within it that we will only identify when we drill down in detail. Before we drill down farther, let's look at what else a Value Stream Map provides.

The VSM can be used to identify pain points as well as critical indicators of performance that may suggest waste, most commonly task duration (because long durations probably are attributable to delays). This is simply an extension of the concept we used in the process map in the previous scenario, only here it is somewhat more conventional and formalized within the VSM. Again, we do not want to be prescriptive about how a VSM should look, but encourage focus on the variables we have just described.

The diagram in Figure 5.6 carries this one step farther, showing task duration and also pain points we observed in working the model with stakeholders. We have included information assessments within the diagram, which is not a convention for a value stream map but something that reinforces the spirit behind it.

From this VSM, we will follow observational hunches. Where are the pain points? How deeply are they experienced? What impact do they have on customer value? This is the line of inquiry we follow and we will identify data to validate our hunches (or not) as we go along. Because we always want to quantify and verify information, and because we may be relatively new to the task of building a VSM, we will want to use simple measures and not get too complicated. But, we still want to be diligent about quantification and verification. If someone says, for example, that it takes five days to do planning, we can ask questions, such as: "Okay, when was the last time that

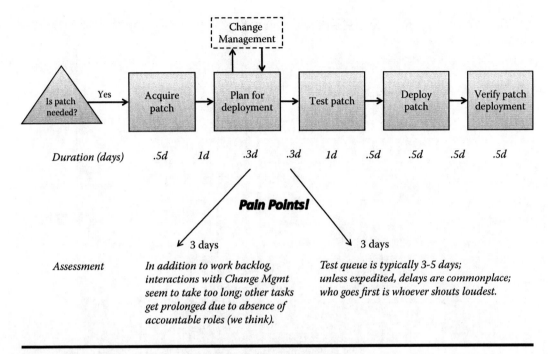

Figure 5.6   Value stream map for Patch Management.

it took five days?" Or, we might ask to look at records that have been kept, in the course of which we might find that the historical data either validates the duration assessment or not. Again, we want to be careful with averages so as not to develop a biased perception of actual conditions.

We might look at a workflow of this sort and see pain points in several different places. This is not uncommon and is one of the reasons why we tolerate these, because it seems difficult and complicated to address them. Lean encourages us to keep going.

Subjected to the value litmus test, we identified in this scenario that Plan for Deployment is necessary, value-added work, but we note that the duration to complete the work is a pain point. Simply stated, it takes too long to get the work done. With this, we can drill down a level, and now we will include some additional data that helps to clarify what exactly is happening as we plan for deployment.

The model in Figure 5.7 is a slight variation in terms of format, but we do this so that we can focus on getting a useful model for our purposes. Here, we have included derived data on duration of value-added work, along with estimates of delays that are associated with each step.

We have again included some assessment in the model, principally to indicate that we have captured it as we built the model in interviews with

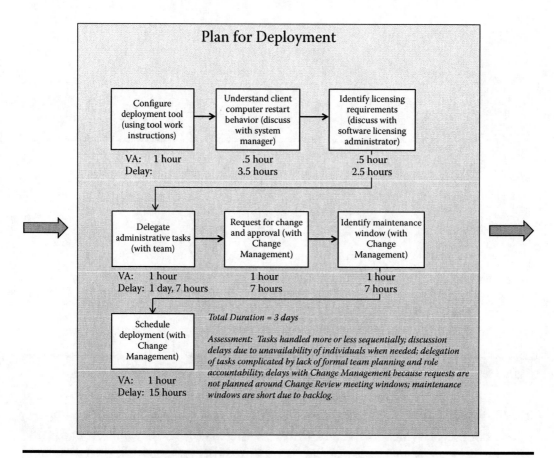

Figure 5.7 VSM for Plan for Deployment.

stakeholders. This assessment provides guidance for data collection and further drill-down as needed. We might identify numerous points where further investigation is warranted and several areas where we can identify candidates for waste. A couple are fairly readily identified here, and these are the ones with long delays, an indication of either NVA or waste. Why, for example, do the activities involving interaction with Change Management have so much delay time? Now we are at the level of detail where our value criteria apply, even though it was not visible at the level of representation above this. From this, we can now look at the work one level down, specifically looking at the interactions with Change Management. The model for that might look like that shown in Figure 5.8.

Hopefully, the reader can see that we are on a hunt. We are hunting for waste. We didn't stumble on it up-front, but found it readily enough simply by looking at the process through the lens of a Value Stream Map.

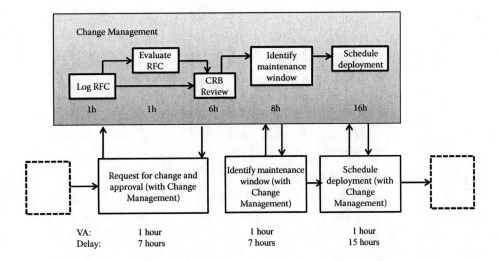

Figure 5.8 VSM for Change Management interaction.

With this level of representation, we have also shifted our focus from the Windows OS team to the Change Management team. For the delays we identified in this activity, we can see where the delays are located. It's in the work that the Change Management team does. We can also see in our assessment where possible sources of defects might be found. With this level of analysis, we can clarify the work further or else pause at this point to begin some root cause analysis. Likely we will do both.

This VSM allows us to engage in focused brainstorming with our stakeholders. What we sometimes discover when people look at a VSM together is that they recognize, perhaps for the first time, how they may be performing the same tasks in different ways, and in so doing, this leads to unnecessary complexity that could be reduced by agreeing on standardized approaches. Because this is still an analysis exercise and not a design activity, we may want to park that particular discussion while we continue to get the Current State represented faithfully and accurately. In the course of doing this, we will identify delays perhaps, just as we did in the first scenario, but may identify other types of problems as well.

Another outcome of this exercise is that we may identify *sequential, repeatable* work even though many may not have thought it was there at the outset. For example, each change in our example is handled within a jumbled flow, but there appears to be an implied linear flow within the mix and we would like to explore that as a candidate for formalized process work. The difference may lie in how we handle changes, as groups (batches) of changes that work through the process or as individual (one-at-a-time) changes that sequentially flow through the process. We will explore this concept more in the next chapter.

We have indicated in our assessment with the VSM some of the possible explanations for the delays we have observed. This is often what happens once we reveal the process through the VSM; namely, we see things in vivid colors and it's hard to miss some of the underlying causes. In this case, too, it's hard to miss some of the communication and informational aspects of the situation. Specifically, several of the connection points (handoffs) are problematic, and there is loss of information or knowledge along the way. For example, the OS team has information about the planned deployment (change) that never gets properly evaluated by the Change Management team.

We have focused on delays as a type of waste in our discussion of the patch management process, but we might just as well have identified defects in the process. That is, we could find through our analysis that there are a number of errors or issues that have resulted from the nature of the work, and we can think of these as defects of the process. These defects might include some of the following: incorrect identification of a patch, incorrect application of a patch, incorrect sequencing of patch installations, lack of proper testing, and so forth. These defects, regardless of their cause, result in consequences that may include rework or remediation, which in turn are sources of delay in completing the original task. It is easy to see how defects and delays are closely intertwined.

Just as we have done for delays, we can do analysis of defects to identify root causes, some of which may be the same as we identified above, although we may find some new ones as well, e.g., lack of standardized procedures within the patch management team, inadequate training, lack of coordination between different teams, etc. We won't know until we do Root Cause Analysis.

In addition to this list of problems, we might identify a few others if we look outside this particular VSM and do a similar exercise with other teams that also do patch management. What we discover is that each team has its own particular set of problems, but they also may have some problems

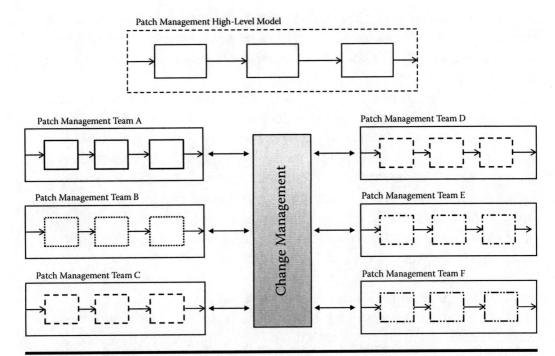

Figure 5.9   VSM for Patch Management teams.

in common. We might discover that each one of them has issues related to coordination with other teams (who does what patch in what sequence may be a lively topic of discussion between various teams). Coordination is a problem because it results in delays. In addition, all the work involved in coordinating activity can lead to defects. Each team may identify these common issues, but it is sometimes very difficult for members of these separate teams to step outside the worlds they work in and address this issue, which spans across several teams.

We may find we can identify the problems more readily when we can represent each individual VSM within the context of a higher-level work-flow that embraces the work of multiple teams, as suggested in the model in Figure 5.9. This model depicts the separate, but related, work of the various teams, each of which performs Patch Management. Not shown here are all the various coordination and communication touch points between each team and other teams. We have shown the central coordinating role that Change Management can (and should, from an ITIL perspective) play in this coordination. However, the reality in many IT environments is that there are parallel, and often confused, interactions between teams. To help align this work, we have identified a generic, high-level model suggesting the commonality of work. We would use this model to help all the teams that apply patches to visualize how they operate in the same general framework. By the way, this is no small accomplishment in many IT environments where disparate teams do work without any coordination with, or even knowledge of, the work performed by other teams.

In the diagram in Figure 4.9, we have depicted each patch management workflow as being *more or less* the same, with variations suggested by the variation in box outlines. These separate VSMs, all depicting the same general work of patch management, although flavored differently by the product or application focus of each team, together comprise a higher-level patch management process. From the bottom up, we have created an organizing framework for addressing a fairly wide range of potential problems (Lean improvement opportunities), and from the top down, we can think of this as a process decomposition activity. In other words, we could have started at the top and drilled down, whereas in our case, we began with one team and built the VSM from the bottom up.

Given the number of different areas where further drill-down might be warranted, doesn't this suggest that we might find waste anywhere? And would we not need to do detailed investigation of each and every area where we either have pain points or observe evidence of waste in order to verify this? The answer is, "yes." Again, this is why we say the landscape is rich with opportunities. In rigorous Lean solutions (such as we find in manufacturing environments), work over time is taken to eliminate any and all sources of waste. We would argue, however, that we don't need to eliminate all waste in order to realize significant benefits. We start with those areas where we are likely going to see the biggest benefits (by whatever criteria we provide for that), and then keep the improvement activity going over time. Using this guidance, we certainly never run out of things to do in the spirit of continual service improvement.

Returning to our set of problems, what do we do next? Using the script from the Lean Improvement Model, we know that we need to analyze the problems to identify root cause. In the first scenario we used cause-and-effect diagrams, and we could use that again if we chose to, but let's use a different tool this time, called *5 Whys*.

Tool: 5 Whys

5 Whys is a tool for identifying root cause and proceeds as a series of questions and answers that selectively lead to factors that explain observed problems. So, in our case, we have evidence of delays attributed to activities

within the Change Management team and we would like to understand what's behind these delays. We might begin our inquiry, for example, by asking why there is a five-day turnaround in processing change requests. The Q&A might go something like this (conventionally, questions may be asked by a facilitator and answered by stakeholders, but we don't want to get too distracted by that, since a team of people can work both sides together in order to establish consensus).

Q: Why is there a five-day turnaround on change requests?
A: Because we need to sync up with the Change Review Board review cycle (they meet weekly) and we often have a high volume of requests that require us to push certain requests into the next review window.
Q: Why does every change get handled in exactly the same way, when all changes are not the same?
A: We need to avoid risk by all means possible and, to do this, we handle each change on its own merit.
Q: Why don't you categorize changes so that some can be handled with maximum review and others with less scrutiny?
A: We assume risk is likely even with seemingly low risk changes, so we handle each separately. Besides, our tool is not set up to categorize changes by level of risk.
Q: Why doesn't the tool allow categorization at this level?
A: Because we are using a homegrown tool that we have never gotten around to replacing.

To underscore the flexibility that underlies use of the 5 Whys tool, it's possible to consider other lines of inquiry that could be pursued after the first question is answered. We might for example, ask the following questions:

■ Why is the volume of requests so high?
■ Why are CRB meetings held weekly (and not more often)?
■ Why do we need to wait for the CRB review?
■ Why do we need approval from the entire CRB team?

The reader should be aware of a couple points about these hypothetical, but not unrealistic, lines of inquiry. First, please notice that the line of inquiry is by discretion and could follow any number of different avenues.

The goal for using 5 Whys is to intelligently reveal root cause by taking away layers of explanation that may obscure the "real" root cause. Of course, this is subjective and not always attainable, which underscores the classic challenge of using 5 Whys as a tool. Sometimes, in the right hands, with the right combination of people, it works as intended; and sometimes, if used in merely a perfunctory way as part of standard procedure for RCA, for instance, it can generate outcomes that are not very helpful. It is, in fact, difficult to identify root cause as a matter of practice, and this is the reason why A3 Thinking is so important, since it drives the method behind the tool.[3]

The reader also will notice that the prescription for asking "Why?" five times is completely arbitrary, and we might find that we can identify an adequate root cause in fewer rounds. In other cases, we may need to ask the question more than five times.

Finally, it is definitely possible to probe the wrong line of inquiry and end up someplace that is neither helpful nor conducive to good problem-solving. We might say that lack of an adequate tool is a root cause, for instance, but otherwise have constraints that make it impossible to do anything about it. This is not where we want to be in Lean inquiry. We want to find things we can do something about, so if we can't fix the tool problem, we should be looking for other causes, which we can do something about.[4]

If in our RCA we have identified multiple root causes, it will make sense to prioritize these in some way as a precondition for identifying and prioritizing potential solutions. For this we can use another tool that helps to focus attention on where we might get the most impact from our Lean problem-solving. This is the *Pareto chart*.

Tool: Pareto Chart

The Pareto chart guides our problem analysis by helping isolate those problems with the most significant impact, suggesting a priority for their resolution. Pareto charts are often used to represent sources of defects with some measure of quantity that will suggest impact. With this information in hand, we can represent various problems in such a way that it focuses attention on relative priority.[5] In Figure 5.10, we have captured information gathered for counts of defects associated with Patch Management within a three-month timeframe.

Using the Pareto chart, the priority of these problems will then drive the priority for what we do in an RCA on, in this case, very likely incorrect identification of patches.

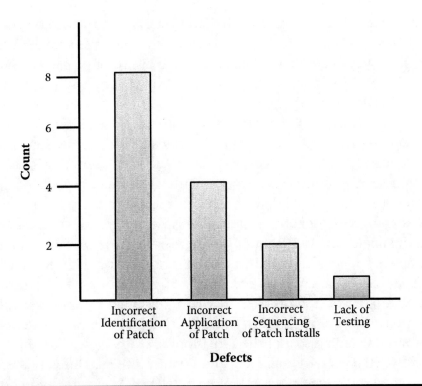

Figure 5.10   Pareto chart for Patch Management problems.

Again, we will leave our scenario here with a good understanding of problems underlying identified waste, and we will pick up at this point in the next chapter when we look more carefully at how we identify and implement solutions. This would be a good time for the reader to practice using these new tools, in refinement of the approach adopted earlier, or as a new exercise involving a source of waste identified through analysis of a Value Stream Map.

Clarifying Difficult-to-Identify Workflows

In this scenario, we have two separate but related challenges. One is to identify waste, but the initial challenge is to identify the process workflow in which it resides. This will often happen when we deal with processes that are fairly complex and involve many different individuals and/or groups, each of which has a different perception of what their work is and how it relates to others, and different objectives for their work, which may be quite different from, or even at cross purposes with, the work objectives of others.

These types of processes often evolve over time in organizations and the steady state is one in which people do their work in large part because that's the way it's always been done. People may be aware of problems (they often are), but the process is sufficiently complex that nobody really knows how to get a start at addressing them. These types of diffuse processes are not only intangible, but they are difficult to clarify without painstaking effort.

Our scenario here involves a set of activities for User Provisioning, basically referring to a set of related processes that allow users to gain access to required services and resources. It includes setting up accounts (e.g., for email), but it is much more than this because it also addresses provision of privileges and access rights to systems, services, and resources in potentially large and complex environments. User Provisioning includes scenarios of adding new users, changing existing users, and dealing with departed users.

We have chosen User Provisioning as our scenario because sometimes we find that the processes associated with it are quite complicated and difficult to penetrate. To begin with, there are different perspectives to take into account, including that of the Provisioning team, as well as Human Resources (HR), Legal, Compliance, and perhaps others. Different systems may have evolved over time to address related requirements throughout the organization. In some cases, these may have been integrated over time, but sometimes these integrations amount to nothing more than data transfer between disparate systems that are otherwise quite different in purpose or maturity. This evolution is sometimes accompanied by absence of clear, overarching objectives for the entire end-to-end workflow. In fact, it is sometimes the case that there is no single individual who has insight into the entire workflow, and this makes it difficult to know where to begin the investigation. Whereas Patch Management had a general set of activities shared by all teams doing that type of work, here we may have quite different work done by different teams using the same name, but meaning quite different things by it.

In this and similar scenarios we find that people can work with (and within) processes that they don't really understand, as if they are employed on one side of a wall, doing their jobs, and then pass along the results of their work to another side of the wall, without really knowing what goes on there (or even who does the work). Sometimes there is awareness over time of who does work directly preceding theirs ("That's John over in HR") or afterwards ("We run a report every month and send it to Compliance"), but again, there is no transparency on how the full workflow operates. It would be very surprising if processes of this sort were to operate efficiently, so it's reasonable to expect that we will find plenty of waste if we just look for it.

So how does the analyst get his or her head around this? We will use the same general approach as in the previous scenario, specifically, interviewing various members of the organization who are involved in one way or another with user provisioning. In this case, however, we need to do more investigative research, and for this we can call upon a Lean tool we refer to as *Go-and-See*.

Tool: Go-and-See (Gemba)

Gemba (Japanese) literally refers to the place where the action is, or to the "real place." Going to Gemba, therefore, means first and foremost being physically present and observant at the scene of activity; the idea being that we go and see for ourselves what's happening.[6,7] It means not only that we see for ourselves, but that we don't necessarily rely entirely on the testimony of others. We also like to see data because this provides tangible evidence of what we may observe. Going to Gemba in our case also means asking others where else we need to go so that we can pull together observations from all the appropriate vantage points in the process. The observations that result from this approach ultimately lead to a better understanding of how things actually work, and this is our desired outcome. Along the way, Going to Gemba necessarily means that we meet people and see work from their perspective. Underlying that is the general assumption that we will build positive relationships with these people as a way of fostering better observation and inquiry.

One implication of adopting this approach is that *we cannot gain a good understanding of a situation without direct observation*. That means we cannot do an adequate job over the phone, working online, or using secondary opinions or observations of others. We need to see it for ourselves. This is much harder to do in practice than it might appear. In factory environments, it's more straightforward. We walk out onto the factory floor and stand around or walk around, as the case may be. It is harder to do in virtual work environments such as we find in IT, but insofar as people are doing work, they are doing it somewhere, and to the degree that it is realistic to do so, we would like to be there watching as they do it. More specifically, we need to drill down into details to identify the data that validates (or not) our observations. If we look at reports, for example, we need to ask questions to ensure we understand what the data are telling us.

Returning to our scenario, with the observations we have made, what we often discover at this point is that the work itself appears as if it is a jumbled flow. (Well, in fact, it probably is a jumbled flow.) When we make our first attempt at a process map or VSM, we may have lines that go every which way, and the characterization of the work is often confused and quite complicated. Very likely at the same time, opportunities to streamline work will practically jump out at us. But, please remember that we want to represent the Current State first and, to facilitate that, we can put all the ideas we might uncover into our Future State parking lot and consider them at a later time. Recall from Chapter 3 that it is not uncommon in discussions that have focus on problem-solving to intermix and sometimes even confuse Current State and Future State. We often find that without some discipline, the conversations go round and round, back and forth between observations on the Current State and speculation on the Future State. The idea in our approach here is to clarify the Current State as a *precondition* for clarifying the Future State. A thorough analysis of the Current State will provide assurance that you are not missing small but important steps.

For this scenario, let's assume that generating a first pass VSM is challenging because we are still trying to figure out just how the process works. We have identified a simple, and still incomplete, process map in the diagram in Figure 5.11, with some honest indicators of what we are not clear about. This is hardly a finished product and is not sufficient to begin RCA, but it is sufficient to show others on our Gemba walk as we seek further clarity.

This diagram is represented somewhat differently than the previous ones in order to emphasize some of the uncertainty that may be encountered in attempting to identify a workflow as a starting point for identifying waste. The idea is that it's complex and confusing and we are not sure exactly where to start.

We don't need to explain all aspects of this model because the point is that we have some areas of relative certainty (the workflow in the center), but the interactions are not well understood. The thick perimeter around the central workflow is a simple contrivance to indicate that we don't understand how information flows across boundaries. When trying to figure out complex workflows, even rough drawings like this can be helpful, and just isolating critical interactions as shown here can be quite constructive.

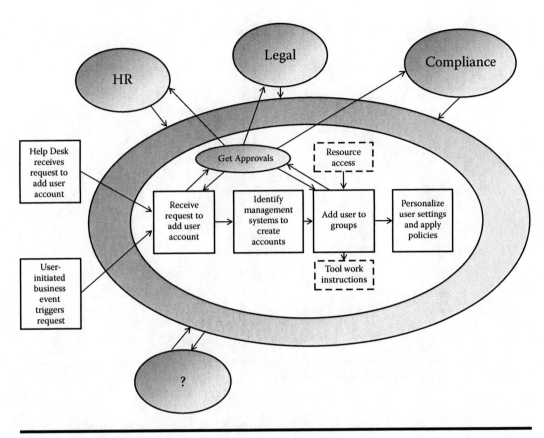

Figure 5.11   Initial process map for User Provisioning.

If the Current State process appears like a complex set of paths through a thick forest that obscures the overall objective, this is not an uncommon observation. Our Lean objective is to create streamlined paths through the forest, but for now, the hard work is to get the Current State representation correct. Rather than becoming completely overwhelmed with complexity, use the simple rules for process mapping identified earlier to give yourself and others the time to absorb the detail, and then, through iteration, derive a map that will look better and better on each pass. Remember that the goal is to get a map or VSM which is *good enough* for the purpose, and this purpose most importantly involves gaining consensus from stakeholders that the Current State is represented truthfully and accurately. There may be quite a bit of work to do in order to accomplish the final objective. We may find that we have to divide the problem at some point and attend to only a portion of the overall process at a time in order to scale it for achieving reasonable objectives. There is no rule of thumb that applies here, but commonsense will usually suffice.

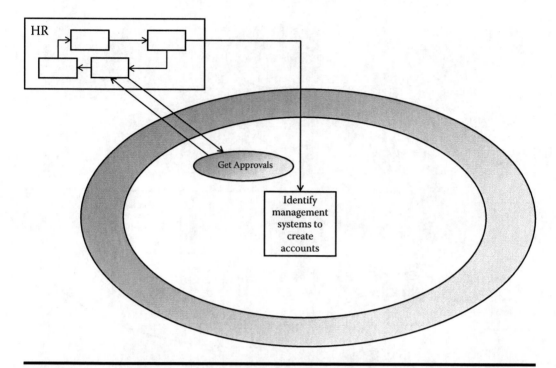

Figure 5.12 Partial process map (clarified for HR interaction).

Scoping and clarifying the process through iteration will eventually result in a process that provides us with a starting point for identification of waste and the problem-solving that follows. What we have done in Figure 5.12 is to just isolate one of the interactions and clarify the process behind the dense wall. Here we find a fairly simple approval workflow within HR, as well as a data flow from an HR application to one of our user provisioning applications. We have left out the specific details because the main point we want to make is that we could generate this level of representation fairly readily by simply isolating the interaction with HR and going to Gemba to understand it better.

What is starting to reveal itself here is the interconnectedness between the Provisioning team's approval activity and the related approval activity within HR. This is how we identify, over time, the full value chain in which these related workflows participate. As a team exercise, we may in fact bring together people from both of these teams to clarify these interactions and discover that this is the first time they have talked with each other, other than one-off point-to-point communications.

Full end-to-end transparency is achieved by looking at these disparate workflows one at a time and clarifying each one in turn. Eventually we get to the level of real work that is required in order to identify problems associated with waste. For that we use the same approach and tools discussed in the previous scenarios. In fact, it may take some time to generate a complete end-to-end value chain and we may choose along the way to concentrate our focus for further drill-down without having completed the full "big picture." That's okay. This could be a several-year endeavor and we will want to achieve some benefits of Lean problem-solving to earn our keep along the way.

One final word on clarifying processes. Sometimes when we talk to stakeholders, we will hear them say: "We have no process." The translation of this should be: "We have no *apparent* process," which is to say, people don't see it and work with it as such. What we discover on clarification of the work is that there is always a process, even if it is characterized by a very confused and unrecognized job shop. The path to finding this process as a starting point for further inquiry is exactly the same as we have described above for user provisioning.

Surfacing Waste and Exposing Problems

In most IT operations, someone, or several people perhaps, are involved in decision making regarding the capacity of infrastructure components such as servers. For any new application, for example, there are capacity decisions that need to be made (how many servers are required, how much memory is needed, etc.). For any operational environment characterized by growth, such as by increased demand by users, there are capacity issues that must be addressed. Some of this work is nonroutine in nature and, therefore, shows characteristics of job shops. Attendance at planning meetings leads to a number of follow-up meetings where functional and performance requirements are identified and discussed, parameters for capacity design must be agreed upon, specific performance information must be obtained, budgetary constraints must be factored in, etc. Beyond this, there are also routine activities that characterize capacity management, such as defining standard build configurations for servers, implementing server clusters in order to optimize performance, and so forth.

Note that the routine activities may or may not be managed as routine work. Defining standard servers to meet capacity specifications may be routine, but the work of defining servers could be done by different individuals using different procedures. Some of these procedures may be efficient and others may not be. Diving farther into the work itself, we might discover, for example, that one employee, let's call him John, who has been doing this type of work for years, has developed a set of procedures and supporting documentation that allows him to define standard server builds quite quickly and, therefore, he can handle a high level of throughput. Another employee, Jim, who just started at the company and who has recently been doing other types of work, may not have received training or may not have had any opportunity to leverage John's experience. Consequently, he does not have the standard procedures in place, nor supporting documentation, and, thus, it takes him considerably longer to define the builds and his throughput is very low.

This type of scenario may sound familiar and, we would argue, is an example of waste. We might be aware of the issue from a management perspective, or we might not. While it may go unnoticed by many, those who are very familiar with the work, and different approaches, of John and Jim, may observe vast differences in the efficiency of their work, and these differences in efficiency suggest the existence of waste. The question is: How might we make this waste visible?

Tool: Removal of Work-in-Progress (WIP)

One of the concepts underlying the principle of waste elimination is that efforts to find it can be facilitated through specific tools that expose problems that may otherwise remain hidden. One of the classic Lean techniques used in manufacturing environments is the removal of inventory, referring specifically to the material WIP that tends to accumulate between steps in production. Inventory is especially common in environments where batch processing is done. The idea behind its removal is that in so doing, inefficiencies in production will be exposed (e.g., where we previously had lots of inventory as a buffer, now we may have no parts where they are needed, and that becomes the problem to solve). In practical applications, removal of WIP will very often increase throughput time.

When we talk about removing inventory, or WIP, we don't mean that we throw it away or simply move it somewhere else (although we may have WIP that has no corresponding value, and this would be a candidate for removal). More likely we are talking about reducing the level of inventory, not only by processing what is there through its workflow, but more importantly, managing the level of inventory so that it maintains only a minimum-level buffer. In other words, we try to find ways to keep WIP at a very low level all the time, which means we have to find ways of keeping the work-flow going so it doesn't accumulate in the first place.

This is fairly straightforward to visualize for material inventory in a manufacturing operation, but less so in IT. While we do not typically think in terms of inventory in IT, we certainly are familiar with the equivalent notion of WIP. When we think of inventory as being work-in-progress (WIP) generally, we will then see that WIP is everywhere we turn, as the following examples illustrate:

- The planning document that is waiting for approvals in order to proceed
- The training matrix that requires some data input from a team member
- Deferred decisions that prevent progress on work that requires them
- Servers that are delayed in the build process (waiting for something)
- Stalled projects while waiting for hardware to arrive
- An application waiting to get time on the test calendar
- An incident that is in an unresolved state

WIP is basically the work underway or in the in-box that everyone has, in addition to the team-based work that is not yet finished for any number of reasons. It is sometimes difficult to visualize the connections between WIP that's waiting for me to do something, and others who need the work from me once I have completed my part. In other words, the work that may exist in a workflow connecting several individuals, each of whom has WIP, is a candidate for delay if each one of us need to clear our current workload in order to get to it. Because each one of us is motivated to clear our backlog at intervals, we often will do our work when we get to it, rather than according to a schedule that takes into account the coordination with other stakeholders. This behavior effectively pushes WIP downstream where it often gets delayed again.

While maintaining WIP always gives us something to work on (whether it's in the ticket queue or the backlog of project tasks), we may not understand the source of delay that we are responsible for or even appreciate how others may be waiting on us to complete our tasks. In many of our day-to-day transactions, lining up resources would be an impossible task; but for work that is sequential and repeatable, the Lean approach encourages us to do so.

Removing WIP means rethinking how we work, and while it may be impractical to simply remove this WIP from our normal IT operations, it is certainly possible to engage in some thought experiments that may help to visualize the consequences of doing so.

What would it mean, for example, to remove the training matrix I currently have in my in-box that requires input from multiple teams before it is ready for approval? I know that the matrix has value, so simply stopping work on it is not an option. In some cases, it might be reasonable to simply stop work if, for example, nobody would notice or care if I did. In this case, removal of WIP means that I clarify the inputs and coordinate these so I can process them quickly and move them on to the next step. In consideration of the full work-flow, this also would suggest that I set the stage for the matrix to be approved by those who need to do so, and to coordinate activities so that approvals can be done quickly. In the course of thinking this through, it might be reasonable as well to ask whether all inputs are needed, or whether all approvals are needed, because each of these discrete tasks will consume time and if they are not necessary or do not have value, then they are candidates for elimination.

Removal of WIP will help a problem surface principally because whatever is needed at certain points in time will need to be where it is supposed to be, or else it will introduce a new source of delay. If I set the expectation that the training matrix will need approval by someone on Wednesday, for example, and the matrix is not ready by then, I have introduced a delay. Everyone is waiting until I finish the matrix and send it out for approval.

Removal of WIP also can expose more systemic problems, as would be the case, for instance, if I remove spare servers that otherwise might be used as a buffer (e.g., when a server is needed on a short timeline). Reducing this buffer means that when servers are needed, all of the coordination work, as well as related workflows that impact availability of servers, must be clarified and made efficient (i.e., Leaned). For example, we might discover by removing the servers as buffer that we identify flaws in our server decommissioning process (because we do not decommission servers in a timely way, we cannot repurpose them). This is how Lean works to surface problems through removal of WIP.

Returning to our capacity management scenario, removal of WIP might correspond to removal of spare servers, as just described, or to the removal of any other work that accumulates in buffers of one sort or another throughout the process. Removal of WIP could include reducing to a minimum the number of workload reports waiting to be analyzed (are they all needed?), shortening decision approval loops for capacity plans (what's the alternative to seeking multiple approvals?), or modifying upgrade schedules to keep queues and waiting times to a minimum. Even if used as a thought experiment, reducing WIP often can expose underlying value stream dynamics that can help in identifying and understanding sources of waste, such as identifying delays for approvals.

Removal of WIP is somewhat like administrative housecleaning. In fact, Lean has a tool that is all about housecleaning called *5S*. The concept behind 5S is that by going through a systematic "cleaning" of an IT operation, it is possible to surface waste and expose problems.

Tool: 5S

5S is a method often used to help create a Lean production environment. It is based on team participation and includes attention to the following activities:

- Sort: Organize and separate what is necessary for work, and what is not.
- Straighten: Arrange work materials for ease of use.
- Shine: Keep everything clean.
- Standardize: Create a systematic way of maintaining and monitoring the environment.
- Sustain: Create mechanisms that provide motivation and discipline.

If you are the type of person with an organized garage, tools hanging neatly on the wall with painted outlines of the tools to show their proper space, 5S will be an easy concept to grasp. 5S is used to place work items in convenient locations, assure that they are returned to their proper place, and to eliminate clutter so work items are always found with little waste of effort.

It is fairly straightforward to see how 5S might be applied in a physical workplace (e.g., a factory floor), but it is just as applicable in an online environment. This method might be applied to file systems, data warehouses, or to data itself. 5S encourages focus on sources of waste and fosters this orientation among all team members who might otherwise optimize only those components of the environment that they "own," without considering other related components.

5S is sometimes used in factory environments as a lead-in to doing more analytic work at a later time. It helps teams of people get familiar with working with each other, an important outcome in itself. We often find IT teams that are split between day and night shifts, and while these teams may have mechanisms to foster communication between them (e.g., shift reports), there may otherwise be very little interaction, even though they are doing essentially the same work. What we find is that they often develop very different ways of doing routine work, and this right away suggests that there are potential causes of delays and defects lurking in the background. 5S as a community exercise helps team members go through their work and clarify how it is best done.[8–10] Below is more information on each of the 5S components.

Sort

Sort is not just about arranging things in a neater way, but is about organizing things according to purpose, which means the nature and purpose of the work at hand needs to be understood and socialized. It also means throwing out things that are not needed. It applies to everything (physical materials, documents, online files, information, WIP). It addresses the common problem of spending time trying to find something, so one test of its success is that it becomes easy (and quick) to find something needed for work.

Straighten

This focuses on having everything in its proper place (both physical and online). The goal is to arrange things needed for work in such a way that they are easy to locate and accessible within the required workflows. Visual aids can help, with maps or labels clearly indicating what is where. This is where we also would ask the question about what is needed for work that we don't currently have easy access to.

Shine

Shine suggests cleanliness, which in a virtual environment also can apply to data and information where the critical criteria are currency and accuracy. This is where we address anything in the work environment that is overly complicated or "messy" (unclear, subject to different interpretations, requires prior knowledge to understand). In addition, a "clean" environment is one where it is easier to identify abnormal conditions.

Standardize

This refers to anything procedural (including the 5S script itself) and the goal is to ensure that work tasks are done the right way, in the right sequence, every time. This suggests use of checklists or other documentation. Standardization is ultimately the means by which we reduce unnecessary variability in work environments, the absence of which is very often an underlying cause of service defects of one sort or another. Part of standardizing work is to assign individuals to tasks (think RACI), and also scheduling (who does what when), and the implication is that scheduling is formal and agreed upon.

Sustain

Sustain refers to the improved work practices that derive from doing 5S, the question being how these improvements can be sustained over the long term. This addresses the very common result of doing improvements, only to see them degrade over time and behaviors return to a steady state characterized by waste. There are some controls that help in sustaining improvements, which we will address in the next chapter, and there is also the important role of enablers in creating conditions for long-term maintenance of improvements (which we will address in Chapter 8).

5S as a tool helps not only to surface and identify problems, but also creates conditions where it is easier to identify problems from that point forward. We think it's a powerful tool, although there is surprisingly little evidence of its use in IT. There are probably several reasons for that, including the cultural resistance in many IT shops to doing team-based work, generally, and doing proactive (versus reactive) work, specifically. Regardless of the reason, we think there are opportunities to realize several benefits that directly impact the outcomes of IT work, including fewer mistakes made (and, therefore, fewer defects in work), higher productivity (easier to get required work done), and better team relationships (improved coordination of work).

Some might say, "Well, we do some of this already." That is quite likely true (and that's good), and it underscores how Lean often appears to systematize what otherwise might be viewed as just good common sense. However, Lean applies focus and discipline to these activities in a way that is not naturally part of typical IT operations, and this is the small difference that makes a *big* difference in the long run.

We have mentioned visual aids as an improvement idea that derives naturally from using 5S. In fact, visual management is a characteristic of Lean solutions, and one of the benefits of managing work visually is that it is easier to spot problems as they arise.

Tool: Visual Management

In many Help Desk environments, it is common to see display boards showing customer wait time, number of customers in queue, etc., and this is a good example of visual management. If we compare this with what we might see in some factories or hospitals, however, we would have to say that many IT shops are not visual at all. For example, it's not uncommon in medical clinics to find diagnostic flows, such as a "Structured Stroke Algorithm," which is basically a flow chart of diagnostic conditions and recommended actions associated with them.

It is not too hard to find examples of diagnostic procedures in IT, and one wonders whether there would not be substantial benefits in making these visually accessible to everyone. In fact, our general observation is that IT shops typically have a great deal of knowledge that is dispersed among team members who may even sit in the same general area. It is very time-consuming sometimes for team members to discover information that might otherwise be very accessible. In addition, we often make the casual assumption that if information is online, it is easily accessible to workers. But we believe there are many missed opportunities to make work and performance against work more visually apparent and, therefore, reap benefits in how the work is done.

The basic idea for visual management is that anything that you want people to know how to do can very likely be displayed in some easy-to-see way, thereby making the activity to perform easier to do. It also is possible to display charts of current activity so that employees are aware of performance or other data that relates to their work. These are very common in Lean factories, and they make it very evident, even to the uneducated observer, what the work is and how it is performed.

These visual displays can have specific purposes as well, such as facilitating access to frequently used resources (e.g., Unix books clearly displayed for ready access) or to indicate that some threshold has been reached, which in turn is intended to prompt certain actions. For example, a color card is flipped to red when cabling or spare parts fall below a certain number, prompting for replenishment of supplies. This is also a good example where something visual surfaces a potential problem; in this case, the problem would be to run out of essential parts.

Tool: A3 Reports

We discussed A3 Reports briefly in Chapter 3 and we mention them here again because they represent another tool for surfacing problems. In this case, they are surfaced by employees who work in the organization and who are closest to the work. They are, in this sense, like "suggestion boxes," only much more powerful, because they are supported by a methodology (A3 Thinking) and are intended to support detailed and rigorous problem-solving.[11]

As we suggested in Chapter 4, use of A3 reports is not a trivial undertaking from the point of view of those who fill out the reports. Nor is it a trivial undertaking for management. If we are serious about identifying waste and its causes, then we have to seriously review and consider all suggestions for change. When an employee submits an A3 Report, we apply rigor in order to ensure that the right homework is done, but in review and evaluation, these should never be treated as just an idea to think about in the future sometime. The back end of the loop, in which the individual who submitted the idea has full and ample opportunity to participate in the evaluation process, is the right focus. For management to say, "We will get back to you on this," is in this context both irresponsible and represents a failed opportunity for improvement. By allowing employees to drive the engine of surfacing and identifying waste, an organization builds into its DNA the ability to sustain positive improvements over the long term.

In this way, A3 Reports as a tool tie back to A3 Thinking as a methodology. Over time, greater sensitivity to problems develops, and this equates to "learning to see." Subjective assessment and intuition can be a guide to identifying problems, but it is also critical that there be data as supporting evidence, and in this way, learning to see equates to scientific reasoning.

Summary

This chapter has walked through various scenarios using a very basic set of Lean tools. The intention is to show how even these quite familiar tools, in the hands of the Lean practitioner, can lead to results that are substantially different than we might often obtain without the accompanying notions of Lean Thinking to guide us. Our intention is also to work through these scenarios in such a way that the reader can see how to do the same in his or her own environment. Further education on these and other tools, of course, is helpful and necessary, but this starter set should be sufficient to get Lean improvement work underway. In the next chapter, we will use well-defined problems as a starting point for identifying solutions to these problems. The connection is quite simple and, in a sense, the hard part is what we have just covered. While our treatment of problem-solving might appear light or even incomplete, we would argue that all the essential concepts and tools needed to do good problem-solving in your organization are now at your fingertips.

References

1. Liker, J. K. and D. Meier. 2006. *The Toyota Way Fieldbook: A Practical Guide for Implementing Toyota's 4Ps*. New York: McGraw-Hill.
2. Nicastro, F. M. 2011. *Security Patch Management*. Boca Raton, FL: CRC Press.
3. Shook, J. 2008. *Managing to lean: Using the A3 management process*. Cambridge, MA: Lean Enterprise Institute.
4. Sayer, N. J. and B. Williams. 2007. *Lean for Dummies*. Hoboken, NJ: Wiley Publishing.
5. George, M. L., D. Rowlands, M. Price and J. Maxey. 2005. *Lean Six Sigma Pocket Toolbook*. New York: McGraw-Hill.
6. Sayer, N. J. and B. Williams. 2007. *Lean for Dummies*. Hoboken, NJ: Wiley Publishing.
7. Imai, M. *Gemba Kaizen*. 1997. New York: McGraw-Hill.
8. George, M.L., D. Rowlands, M. Price and J. Maxey. 2005. *Lean Six Sigma Pocket Toolbook*. New York: McGraw-Hill.
9. Sayer, N.J. and B. Williams. 2007. *Lean for Dummies*. Hoboken, NJ: Wiley Publishing.
10. George, M.L. 2003. *Lean Six Sigma for Services*. New York: McGraw-Hill.
11. Liker, J.K. and D. Meier. 2006. *The Toyota Way Fieldbook: A Practical Guide for Implementing Toyota's 4Ps*. New York: McGraw-Hill.

Chapter 6

Lean Problem-Solving: Identifying and Managing Solutions

If A3 Thinking is the driving methodology behind problem identification and understanding, as discussed in the previous chapter, then PDCA (Plan–Do–Check–Act) plays a similar role in implementing and managing solutions. Fundamental to this is the notion that good problem identification leads readily to good solutions. Well-defined and targeted solutions inherit the analysis done in problem identification and problem understanding because real root causes lead more readily to the solutions that address them.

Starting with Root Causes

With the list of causes we identified during Root Cause Analysis (RCA), we can identify those that, for any number of reasons, seem appropriate to do something about. This suggests that we need to apply some *criteria* to select those causes that seem particularly valid and tractable and, for whatever reason, are of high enough priority to address. Priority for attention may be based on a variety of criteria, including measurable impact, strategic priority, relative ease of addressing ("low hanging fruit"), and so forth. Inputs to this prioritization include data (e.g., from a Pareto chart), as well as subjective assessment and, perhaps, even political considerations.

There are other ways of establishing this priority, some of them systematic (using tools), and others that are less formal, but the bottom line is the same. We want to identify root causes that we have reason to believe will lead to the resolution of problems we identified in the first place. While there is no single best way to prioritize, it is important for stakeholders to agree on the criteria in use. In Chapter 8 we will also discuss the importance of establishing a governance, or decision-making, mechanism, for this purpose, specifically to assist in identifying criteria, selecting improvement projects for solutions, and managing results.

A3 Thinking will guide us to the right set of causes to work from as well, and the experimental nature of this approach means that some trial-and-error to get there is to be expected. Pragmatically, what this means is that we may need practice to derive the optimal set of root causes for any particular problem, but identifying *candidate* root causes along the way can only help us get there. As we mentioned in Chapter 4, it is not uncommon to identify root causes that appear intractable or too big to identify solutions for and, if this is the case, we probably want to look for other causal factors that are more straightforward to address. Above all, we don't want to get stuck in a place where we feel we cannot make forward progress on a problem. It is for this reason that we always want to identify a set of causes from which we can experiment with solutions.

Identifying Solutions

In the server build scenario, we identified several causes and we suggested at the time that good identification of these made identifying solutions relatively easy. For example, several causes related to the forms used by the Apps team to submit their requirements, including the following:

- Procedures require a team to evaluate each form according to a set of criteria that may not apply to all types of configuration requirements.
- The form itself is cumbersome and requires time to transfer data from the Word® doc into a spreadsheet where team tracks requirements through the rest of the workflow.
- The form instructions are not clear so the Apps team often leaves out critical information.

We can argue whether all of these are the best *root* causes of the problems, but they are close enough to start connecting the dots between cause and solution. Given the relative priority of forms as a cause of the problems we observed, it practically goes without saying that we should do something to improve the forms. Improvement of forms then is identified as a solution. In a simple scenario, we clarify the nature of these improvements (features, format, data requirements, access, etc.) and then do the work.

Usually, if root causes are correctly identified—that is to say, RCA is done well and consistent with the principles and objectives of A3—Thinking, solutions are fairly straightforward to identify. In other cases, there may be no clear-cut and obvious connection between the statement of root cause and the likely solution. This may be because solutions are not so obvious, or it may simply indicate that RCA did not go far enough. We mention this because it is not uncommon to have this happen. The remedy is more diligent use of RCA techniques (e.g., 5 Whys) in order to get to the real root cause. For those root causes that do not easily recommend a corresponding solution, we can use some tools to help carry us to the next step. One of the most common tools for doing this is something we use every day, and which we informally introduced in the previous chapter. Here we use it in the service of identifying Lean solutions (so, therefore, it is part of the Lean toolbox). The tool is *brainstorming*.

Tool: Brainstorming

One of the other causes we identified for the server build scenario included not having enough people to share the workload so individuals became overloaded (this explained most of the delays between steps). In the context of a team setting, including stakeholders who may be the same individuals we have worked with in identifying this cause in the first place, but very possibly including others, we will now do some collective thinking about candidate solutions that might address this particular cause. Keeping the conversation focused on the desired outcome will require good facilitation, but there is a lot of room for creative thinking in how the team will work together. While there are many different techniques that might be employed to foster good communication, we think the most important thing is to create an uninhibited atmosphere that encourages contributions from everyone. It is not uncommon for teams to work with a cause that seems to have no good options for candidate solutions. We have picked one of these here on purpose, to address some of the ways that we can work beyond apparent obstacles.

The cause we have identified has to do with resource constraints (not enough people to share the workload). This sounds like a root cause, although we might find that we can take it a bit farther using a tool, for example, 5 Whys ("Why aren't there enough resources?"). Sometimes with this type of issue you can end up walking in circles, so let's look at it from another angle. If the current process is characterized by a certain amount of measurable throughput with a measurable throughput time, at the current level of resource, with certain quantifiable indicators of delays and defects, is it possible to consider other ways of organizing the work so that at least the same throughput and throughput time, with perhaps fewer delays and defects, can be implemented at the current level of resource? Looking at it this way broadens the landscape of solution opportunities. It doesn't mean we have to discard the obvious solution (get more resources), but it allows us to think about the problem with a somewhat wider lens. With this line of inquiry, it may be more straightforward to generate a list of candidate solutions, such as:

■ Get more resources (okay, let's put it up top, but not get stuck there).
■ Specifically, start to measure our current throughput and lead times at current resource levels and make a stronger business case for increasing resources.
■ Do more proactive planning with our user base so we can predict levels of demand well in advance, and otherwise spread the workload over time (in other words, acknowledge that our capacity is limited).
■ Look at other process-level sources of delays and see whether that impacts our ability to do more efficient work with existing resource levels.
■ Purposely limit the amount of work we take on and deal with the customer backlash.

These candidate solutions are not prioritized, and throughout the brainstorming session it is possible that we can identify some that seem "better" than others to focus on further, suggesting again that we have some criteria for evaluating priority. Some solutions are short-term or even stopgap measures, while others may require longer timelines to address. Some may be manual and others may be automated. Some may be addressed through a targeted action, while others warrant attention as projects. In the mix of potential solutions, it is consistent with Lean to identify and do something that starts to change the problem-solution landscape. In other words, we want to do something right away. These are all relevant considerations when identifying and agreeing on criteria for evaluation of priority.

The model in Figure 6.1 summarizes the application of priority criteria for both root cause and solutions.

Here's the script we have followed to get to this point:

- Begin with a prioritized set of root causes for a particular problem.
- Brainstorm on candidate solutions for any of the root causes.
- Prioritize the solutions.

These relatively simple steps represent a starting point for what is essentially a planning activity, a point that we will further describe below. For the moment, however, we want to emphasize how it is that a problem once identified and understood can in a fairly straightforward way lead to identification of appropriate solutions.

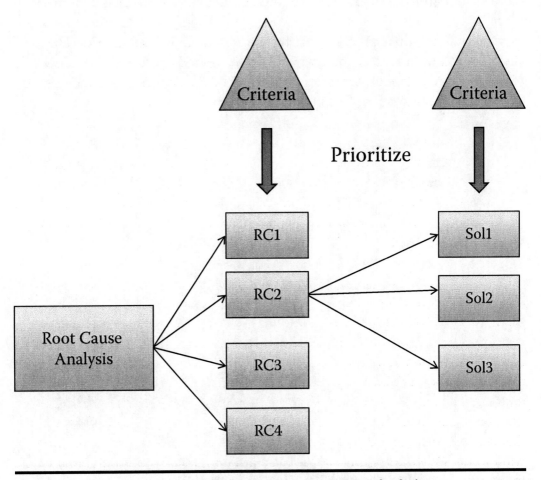

Figure 6.1   Criteria for prioritization of root causes (RCs) and solutions.

Planning, Implementing, and Improving Solutions

Once we have identified the solution, we have begun to engage in what is essentially a planning activity. Our goal here is not to describe "how to plan" in detail, but rather to simply indicate that the planning activity one engages in provides the entry point to the Plan–Do–Check–Act cycle (Figure 6.2).

"How to plan" is no different from any project planning activity except, as we discuss below, we have a bias toward projects that are scoped in such a way that they can be implemented in a relatively short time period.

There is no single best way of scoping work that will be managed through the PDCA cycle. A rule of thumb, especially for beginning improvements as part of a Lean learning process (where repeated practice with PDCA is essential and, therefore, small, incremental improvements prove to be most beneficial) is to scope them small and manageable. It is not unreasonable to identify projects that are implementable rather quickly, perhaps measured in weeks or even days, rather than months. The tendency is often to scale out ambitious projects that have long timelines and considerable complexity. The risk in doing this is that the desired outcomes are either not realized quickly enough to leverage success and see observable benefits, or else, in the worst case, no results are ever seen.

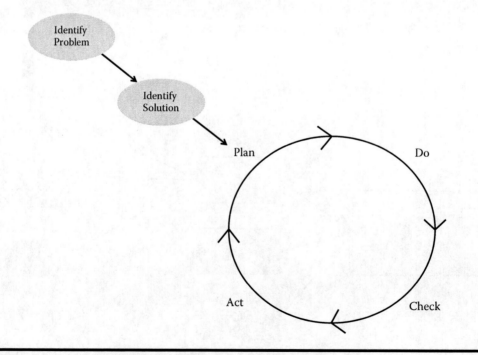

Figure 6.2   Identify solution and Plan–Do–Check–Act (PDCA).

We believe that following the Lean Problem-Solving script will put you often enough in the right ballpark. Good attention to the problem and then, with due diligence and applied criteria in the selection of solutions, should keep the focus on making tangible improvements to real problems. Some solutions often entail desirable benefits that may require investment in either money or time and, therefore, may necessarily have longer timelines. We believe the best approach is to focus on more than one solution, one of which is always something that can be implemented quickly, and preferably without automation, unless this happens to be easily implemented. We want to do something right away, see the results, and then get on to the next improvement.

The hard part in planning is to scope work so that it is doable without getting too large or too long-term because this just postpones the time when something changes. Just as prioritization criteria has a useful function for a governance mechanism, so does scoping. That is, scope and scale should be agreed upon by a decision-making body that can manage projects through their lifecycle.

This may appear too simple or easy, and we certainly do not want to underestimate the potential effort that some solutions may require. However, we believe this part of problem-solving is just about this simple, and appropriately so, if the problem identification work has been done diligently.

Tool: PDCA

We have positioned PDCA front-and-center with respect to implementing, managing, and improving solutions. In this sense, we are using PDCA as a tool, although it also represents an approach and philosophical orientation in the same way that A3 Thinking was an approach and A3 Reports are a tool. As a tool, PDCA is simple yet powerful. It is simple to the point that many may neglect the power of its operation and, while easy to describe, it is actually quite difficult to do consistently in practice, which is why it represents an important tool to practice.

Using PDCA as the means to implementation of the proposed solution also can be tied back to our Value Stream Map (VSM) by thinking of PDCA as the link between the Current State and a new Future State. After all, the solutions we have identified begin to outline certain features of a Future State that, once implemented, will become the Future State. We can think of this as a purposeful design activity. We introduced the model for this in Chapter 3 (Figure 3.9). Using this model allows us to do a couple of things.

For starters, it helps us keep the two states completely separate so that we don't mix up our objectives. Further, when we identify future ideas during brainstorming exercises, a common enough by-product for this type of activity, we have a ready-made "parking lot" to accommodate them.

As PDCA helps in the initial implementation of a solution, it also helps in managing the solution once implemented, as well as in improving the solution over time. Indeed, this is part of the power of PDCA. To begin with, most solutions will not work as planned after the initial implementation. They need to be tuned or improved in order to meet the design requirements. Even when a solution starts to work as designed, it can be improved further, if that seems desirable, and it certainly needs to be managed in order to be sustainable.

There are some additional Lean tools that are helpful to consider when one is actively engaged in implementing, managing, and improving solutions.

Tool: Checklists

A checklist is a surprisingly simple tool that helps to manage solutions once they are implemented. Take, for example, a solution that involves implementation of a new procedure, perhaps to help standardize certain parts of the server build process. These can be captured in a checklist that can be used by the server build team whenever they are working the process.

Checklists serve as a form of mistake proofing because the steps contained in them are rigorously intended to help avoid them. It all seems obvious, and almost too simple to mention, and yet there is some evidence that checklists are woefully underutilized in the service sector. Only recently, for example, do we find testimony of their increased use in hospitals, to considerable advantage,[1] and one can only ask why they were not used more comprehensively earlier. Similarly in IT, we often find many opportunities for use of checklists and there are none in use.

Checklists are sometimes used in conjunction with communication protocols, such as when preparation for surgery includes review of a checklist that includes, up front, introductions of individuals in the surgery room. This establishes structure with familiarity and the combination serves the purpose of these individuals' work in a positive way. One wonders how this same type of protocol might help on many escalation calls we observe where there is sometimes very little protocol and structure, and the objectives of the calls are correspondingly frustrated.

Operational processes and procedures are often developed over time as new information is learned, corrections are made, and the entire end-to-end process becomes stabilized. Sometimes we identify new factors that need to be taken into account. For example, perhaps we are planning migrations that require swapping out hardware and we suddenly become aware of a "green" initiative in the company that requires that discards be handled in a certain way. It may not have been known that this step was needed when the checklist was originally prepared, but it becomes new information to add to it. That type of ongoing improvement to checklists is what helps them become more and more useful over time.

Within the IT Infrastructure Library (ITIL) there is sufficient guidance on how processes should work (and what steps should be taken). This guidance is a very substantial source of checklist content. There are lists of many sorts in ITIL, e.g., requirements for design of Change Management, and any one of these might be used as a starting point. However, it is up to the practitioner to turn this source content into a practical checklist that can be used in daily operations. As with other improvement solutions we have discussed, we don't need to make the checklist perfect up front or completely comprehensive. We just make a start and improve it over time, using—yes, you guessed it—PDCA.

Tool: Mistake Proofing

We mention checklists as a type of mistake proofing. More generally, mistake-proofing techniques are used both to stop mistakes before they occur and to eliminate the possibility of mistakes being passed to the next step of a process.[2-4] This is essentially a diagnostic and design activity, emphasizing root cause analysis of defects and design of controls that will ensure either prevention or detection prior to any impact the defect might have on production activities. Within many IT environments, defects often serve as "reactive agents"; that is, a tremendous amount of effort, time, and cost is expended in a reactive way to address defects (e.g., an outage). The purpose of mistake proofing is to minimize these disturbances and, thereby, maintain smooth operational flow.

Mistake proofing works on the assumption that people do not intentionally make mistakes and, therefore, it is most often the process (and possibly the tools) that needs to be evaluated and designed so that it is physically or procedurally difficult to make a mistake in the first place. Hence, we look at the mistakes that have been made, or that could be made (identified through observation and/or brainstorming), look at each one in turn, do RCA, and identify candidate solutions. In doing analysis of mistakes (or potential mistakes), we want to try to understand everything that is relevant. What conditions do the mistakes occur under? Does everyone make the mistake or just certain individuals?

Examples of mistake-proofing solutions in IT might include use of alerts or warnings below the threshold when a mistake may occur, simple visual presentation of tasks so that it is much harder to vary from the procedural script, use of color coding on devices with indicators of risk (red on devices not to be touched), having two sets of eyes when doing certain tasks as a procedural requirement, or incorporating procedural stop-checks in the procedure itself.

Mistake proofing is a really simple way to ensure better control over work and to reduce variability that may lead to serious defects in IT work. Any procedure where mistakes have serious consequences should deliberately and continuously be mistake proofed. It is risk mitigation at its best.

Creating Flow

In the course of implementing Lean solutions, it may be appropriate to consider how sequential, repeatable tasks can be organized within linear workflows. Further, we can identify actual flow criteria as part of our design. Recall that flow is achieved by relentless elimination of waste, basically anything that impedes the progression of value-added work. The workflow thereby becomes maximally efficient. The server build that may have taken one day or longer now takes a couple hours to complete, because the only work is related to the build and there are few or no sources of delays or defects.

Flow is designed and does not happen naturally. While it is not essential that work flows, it is often desirable to work toward that objective. Many benefits can be gained by elimination of waste even at a minimal level, that is, even without elimination of *all* waste. By understanding where the threshold is for complete waste elimination, we begin to identify the opportunity landscape for ongoing Lean improvements.

One thing that emerges from a clarified process map or Value Stream Map and the problem analysis that follows it, and which is suggestive of the long-term objective of identifying streamlined pathways, is the observation that many activities that are currently managed as jumbled flows could really best be implemented as linear flows. This is a truly desirable observation because it means there are opportunities for significant improvement in overall process efficiency to be achieved simply by reconstructing them as such. It could be, for example, that the initial work in a server build activity needs to be done in a job shop where several individuals are actively engaged in figuring out the best way to do the work. Once this is identified, it is then possible to do this work as a linear flow. The identification of the specific activities that comprise the workflow can be readily derived as part of Future State brainstorming.

The model in Figure 6.3 is somewhat abstract, but it shows the logic behind identifying linear flows from jumbled flows. The translation into our work environments is this: If work is currently done in a job shop, but is in any way sequential and repeatable work, then it is a candidate for a linear flow. It may not be the entire workflow that we recharacterize as a linear flow; it could be only a portion of the entire workflow. By isolating this portion and streamlining it, it is like creating stretches of paved road in a landscape that otherwise has cow paths that have evolved over time. Our long-term goal might be a superhighway from end-to-end, but great improvements can be made through incremental road development.

In the Figure 6.3 diagram, the dotted lines show workflows that are jumbled, as we might find when a new team is working out the sequence of

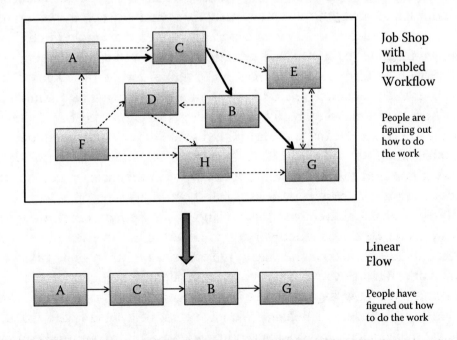

Figure 6.3 Creating linear flow from jumbled flow.

tasks that should take place to achieve some objective. The solid line (A-C-B-G) is based on observation of a frequent (repeated) set of sequential tasks. It indicates that these four activities are habitually repeated in this sequence. This might happen without the people performing these activities even realizing it (hence the importance of observation). This evidence suggests the possibility of segregating these tasks and optimizing a linear workflow from them. There are various things we might do then, in addition to *Leaning* the A-C-B-G workflow itself. We could, for example, move the work location where these tasks are done so they can be further optimized, perhaps around special equipment. More basically, we could allocate the optimized workflow to one team and leave the rest of the work to another team, now a smaller job shop with less complexity. That is, whereas previously many people needed to know how to do work and navigate through the entire process, now we divide the work into groups (one group doing one type of task and the other doing another type). Each person within his or her respective group now needs to know only those tasks that apply to his or her group. It is a way of simplifying work.

By isolating and *Leaning* the workflow (by which we mean organizing it as a linear flow and then removing all sources of waste that may serve as impediments to its efficient operation), we begin to suggest the meaning of *flow* as a principle of Lean Thinking. In fact, we do this type of "peeling off" of standardized work not infrequently, such as when we set up password resets as an automated self-service capability. Another example might be where we initially treat patch update processes as ad hoc and unique, often characterized by team members working to figure out the best way of doing the tasks (which sequence, etc.). In effect, they are working as a jumbled flow. Then, over time, they realize that some types of patches are quite standard in how they can be performed; that is, the work is sequential and repeatable, and they can peel off this work and operate it as a linear flow. Or they might find repeatable subprocesses within the larger patch update process and these can be treated as linear flows. This type of peeling off activity is both natural and systematic using Lean. We may not think of it this way when we do it naturally, but it is nevertheless an example of a Lean practice, and it underscores how readily Lean can be incorporated into day-to-day work. Why? Because you are probably already doing it.

Making work flow means that it is no longer characterized by delays, backlogs, bottlenecks, or defects. We have removed these types of waste by deliberately doing so according to the script from the Lean Improvement Model. It isn't magic. We don't get there overnight.

However, the end result is typically orders of magnitude improvement in overall efficiency.

In a sense, identifying candidates for linear flow implementation is the *sweet spot* for Lean improvements. By isolating the workflow associated with this process (first by seeing it, then by understanding it through closer observation), we can identify specifically where the flow of activities (sequential and repeatable) gets blocked or delayed. We fix those problems and, over time, implement flow.

The fact of the matter, however, is that most work in IT operations does not flow. Indeed, it may be unrealistic in many environments to specifically identify this as an objective. Having said that, we believe that whenever flow is possible, it should be understood how we would get there and what the benefits of doing so might be. If these benefits can be expressed in terms of *twice as much* throughput in a period of time, or *twice the productivity* of employees, for instance, we should probably consider why we do not want to achieve these levels of performance, especially if they can be done with little incremental cost investment. (This may sound outlandish, but these types of benefits are not uncommon in other domains where Lean has been successfully applied.)

We have already discussed the tools and concepts needed to achieve flow, but there are some additional ones that are worth consideration, even if they are not commonplace in IT operations. We would like to explore how these tools might be applied and use this as a thought experiment for further improvement of operational activities.

Tool: Pull (versus Push)

We mentioned earlier that many activities effectively push work to work-in-progress (WIP). We also know intuitively that many activities in IT often feel like we are pushing to get things done. Sometimes this feels like we are pushing against something, but the point is that push is not a bad metaphor for much of the work that we do. (Please see how often the word is used in meetings when discussing work.) Pushing is, in fact, an accurate description of work that is done in operations where products are processed in batches and wait in queues at stages of the production cycle (hence, "batch-and-queue"), so it is really more than a metaphor in practice.

Rather than *pushing* products or services through the value stream, what we desire is for the product to be *pulled*, that is, initiated by a customer signal of demand, with processing occurring only when needed by the next succeeding stage in the production cycle, and only in the required amounts. In some respects, a Help Desk ticket system might be conceived as a pull system, insofar as the customer ticket is a signal to start working on an issue. However, most Help Desks inventory tickets in a queue. An agent selects a new ticket out of the queue as prior tickets are completed, similar to a machine operator taking an item out of a batch of inventory and processing one piece and then selecting another. In this way, Help Desk operations often operate in a push mode because the original customer demand signal is less of a factor in moving the production line of ticket handling than is the backlog of tickets in the queue. Agents often are playing catch-up with ticket volumes, even if the tickets include those with high priority. In extreme cases, even the customer gets involved in "pushing" the ticket to completion, as happens when they are the ones to call the Help Desk to get status or to reconcile different messages from among agents.

The model in Figure 6.4 graphically represents the difference between push and pull.

In fact, it is quite difficult to find practical examples of pull systems applied to IT operational processes. We believe, however, that the explanation for this may be less a matter of it being an inappropriate application of

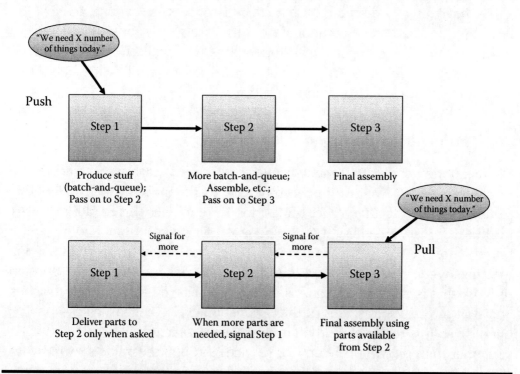

Figure 6.4   Pull versus push.

a manufacturing technique to a service operation than it is a testimony to the degree of difficulty associated with resolving the underlying complexities of these operations. In other words, it is not easy to fix the problems that impede the ability to pull work through the value stream.

In Chapter 7, we will talk about the pull concept as it relates to a Service Desk. We will see that this is an area where application of *pull* is most reasonable, but we will also see why it is so challenging to achieve. For now, we want to just introduce the very simple notion of the streamlined Service Desk, where each ticket pops up in a queue (customer demand signal) and it is taken care of in a just-in-time fashion. The ticket is resolved, and then the next ticket is taken care of. In this simple (and admittedly unrealistic) scenario, the product/service delivered by the Service Desk is initiated by customer demand and then pulled through the Service Desk value stream.

The service-based implementation of pull, which could be adapted to the Service Desk example, begins by looking at the amount of WIP in the system (e.g., tickets in process), and then determining the maximum amount of WIP that the process can handle. Next, we create an input buffer (think of it as a queue in front of the queue) and impose a categorization scheme that allows some differentiation of priority, so that high-priority tickets don't get in the buffer behind low-priority tickets. We then only let the ticket queues handle as many tickets as their WIP capacity permits. Now we can have the agent look at a limited number of tickets in his or her queue and effectively process each one in turn, to full resolution, before pulling another ticket.[5]

Let's consider another example of where pull may work better than push. Take the case where someone does a report habitually, sends it to a distribution list, and that is about the last he or she hears of it. This can happen when practices evolve over time, and while there may have been ample evidence of need earlier, none exists currently. And yet, the work continues. And, let us say, it is going to continue because the message this individual gets from management is that the report is needed. (This should probably be questioned more deeply, but for the time being, let's assume it is of limited value, but nevertheless necessary.) Because nothing actionable results from the report, we can say it is being pushed to WIP (someone else's, presumably). But, what happens if we create conditions where the work is suddenly asked for? We effectively "sell" the report to our potential customers and help them understand its value to their work. We perhaps draw out the connection between the data represented in the report and data they need to do their work. We might call this marketing, in a sense, but the result is that there is now a customer demand signal for it (Where's that report I'm supposed to get?). Now the report is being pulled.

Tool: One-Piece Flow (versus Batch)

Related to this concept of pull is the simple notion of processing one piece of work at a time rather than trying to do components in batches and then pushing them through the workflow. We call this one-piece flow. An excellent example, again using server builds, is to do one server at a time, from beginning to end. It often seems counterintuitive that this could be more efficient than producing in batches and the proof of it must be seen in practice, but we know that in the Lean manufacturing world this is not an uncommon mode of production.[6]

Review boards or weekly status meetings all could benefit from one-piece flow. In practice, issues needing approval before moving forward are batched and held in queue awaiting the weekly Review Board for approval. The weekly meeting creates seven days of nonvalue adding time. If the requests were handled in smaller batches (meeting twice a week), you could reduce the nonvalue adding time by 50%. Just imagine the streamlined process if requests could be immediately (same day) reviewed.

We can experiment with one-piece flow in a lot of our administrative work, and this actually helps in considering its application to team-based work as well. For example, I may have numerous reports that I assemble and the work may often be done in bits and pieces, batching tasks in various places, and then doing assembly as a one-person job shop. It is worth taking an end-to-end view and doing a single report in its entirety, timing steps along the way, and then doing the next report. It is not uncommon to discover new sequences of tasks this way, and the end result may even be surprising in terms of time savings. However, you don't know until you try it out.

Tool: Rapid Changeover

SMED refers to Single Minute Exchange of Die, a tool whereby machine die are changed very rapidly, the time duration of a single minute expressing the emphasis on speed. It is a term used in Lean manufacturing, and while it has little use as such for IT, the concept of rapid changeover does. The idea is that environments that may have multiple uses, such as test environments, may have reason to be set up and configured under conditions of high demand, and as such, would benefit from doing so rapidly.

Changing the configuration of a test environment is obviously not a completely manual activity, and there are automated tools that facilitate the work, but we do find some environments where much of the work is still quite manual and, for these, some thought of how rapid changeover might apply could be beneficial. Basically, we need to identify those changeover tasks that must be done at the moment of change, and others that can be done either before or after. We then create standardized procedures for each type of work and leverage the efficiencies accordingly.[7]

Again, this is the type of tool that requires experimentation, perhaps using a small, manageable environment. Once the variables are understood, it is possible to consider its application in a larger, perhaps more dynamic environment.

Tool: Work Cell Optimization

It sometimes happens that teams of people benefit from being co-located to accomplish a certain task. If you are operating a jumbled flow job shop and "peel off" some linear flow tasks, as depicted in Figure 5.3, you are creating a linear work cell. Of course, in IT, we more often find virtual environments and the argument is that good connectivity and communication between team members is sufficient to accomplish whatever work is needed. However, there is probably an equally strong argument why people benefit from working physically in proximity. What we sometimes find in doing operational work is that even when attempts are made to bring people together, somebody is not there who needs to be there. For example, in doing complex configuration of operational environments, having people there who can grant rights and privileges to others as needed can be of great advantage. Otherwise, what happens is that there are delays in finding the right people and delays in getting the work done.

This concept of bringing people together and co-locating them is called work cell optimization, and it doesn't stop there.[8] Co-located workers can be cross-trained so that resources can be deployed toward higher priority work. Special equipment can be placed so that it is easy for workers to access it within the work cell. Sequential work can be physically arranged to promote flow (admittedly less applicable in a virtual environment). Co-location may be something that can be employed on a temporary basis when a new team of workers is figuring out tasks assignments together.

Then, the same work (in the same sequence) can be done later on in a virtual configuration.

Automation of IT Operations

Automation is frequently part of an implementation solution, and can be viewed as improvement to manual processes with the precaution that the process first be simplified.

The Lean axiom is this: Simplify first; then automate. This applies to Lean solutions that impact the business processes that IT supports (e.g., sales processing), and it also applies to IT itself (e.g., simplify the process of handling change requests before automating). Sometimes we do automation as a matter of routine (e.g., password resets), but may still have opportunities for simplification. For example, if the customer only finds out after they attempt a password reset what the criteria for passwords are, this is not yet a simplified process because a truly simple one would reduce decision making and complexity (and extra steps or rework) on the part of the customer. Therefore, the Leaned process would give the password criteria up front in the process. As an aside, password resets are a great example of nonvalue adding waste. Passwords may be value adding as they increase security for the customer, but password resets are a process built for failure of passwords. If passwords were easier to remember, or if there was another means of identifying a user without a complex code, password resets would not exist. This is a great example of how Lean Thinking pursues lines of inquiry that focus on very small details in the way we work, and even question accepted practices.

Of course, in practice, we use third party tools for certain solutions and this is a known requirement from the outset. However, the precaution is still valid, and lack of attention to process simplification, if coupled with automation, is often a prescription for disaster. In addition, simplification can help avoid some of the common sources of complexity in any IT solution. For example, many solutions involve multiple third party tools, and their interactions can be quite complex. So, there is reason for thinking about these interactions from a process perspective first, and clarifying and simplifying these as a precondition for automation.

Simplified automation also can correspond with simplified IT systems environments (infrastructure and applications), such as when excessive data transfer is identified as waste, and then eliminated, or removing components that are potential points of failure, thereby reducing overall complexity. In other words, we can apply Lean principles to the systems environment itself and, in that context, we will discover that many of our automated solutions (e.g., for monitoring) actually fit quite nicely within the Lean scheme of doing work (in this case, the monitor is an alert that prevents a defect, so it is an example of mistake proofing).[9]

Improving Nonlinear Processes

It is worth reinforcing the point that not all work processes are candidates for flow. Some work is best not handled in this way, and the model for this is a jumbled flow, such as we find in job shop operations. Much of the work in IT can be looked at in this way. Much of this work has variability in demand, variation in process, or frequent exception handling, and often has high customer interface.

Just because it is not organized as a linear flow, or even automated, does not mean that Lean practices do not apply. They do, and often to great advantage. We can still represent the work as a value stream, for instance, and identify sources of waste. We also can ask where value is provided. We can consider as well where resources are best used, as when we shift resources from the back office to the front office in order to have more effective customer engagement. We can provide workers with the right tools to do their jobs, located in the right place, to facilitate work and reduce waste.

The conclusion we draw from this is that there is no aspect of IT operational work that cannot benefit from Lean.

Continuous Improvement

We have indicated that PDCA is the means by which Lean solutions are implemented. We have also suggested that use of PDCA is something that, when used over time, can become systemic and habitual. As a common orientation, it can be embedded in practices, but more importantly, it can be woven into the fabric of the culture of the organization itself. Once ingrained and imprinted, PDCA provides its own answer to the common problem whereby a solution is implemented, but then over time the organization slips back to its old behaviors and the positive effects of the solution become diluted.

PDCA would suggest that any solution needs further improvement. It is this continuous attention to improvement that facilitates the outcomes we desire in the long term, namely tangible and sustainable improvements. The fact is that the more a routine is practiced, the more ingrained it becomes, and this applies as much to Lean improvements using PDCA (where PDCA is the routine) as it does to practicing the piano.

If practicing the piano is the analogy, what then can we "practice" in IT? Well, when we think about it this way, we are actually practicing IT one way or another whenever we do any task. Individuals are learning how to do specific tasks or activities, or how to use tools, and they are also practicing to work with processes and procedures, even if they don't do it very well—rather like playing the piano without much attention to what one is doing.

Consider an escalation procedure for a priority incident: There is an outage. There is a procedure for handling it, which often includes some form of escalation (who gets called, in what sequence; what do people do to coordinate resources; what are the contingencies). All of this is either made up on the fly (not good) or else it is proceduralized so that it can be done quickly (much better), and, in that context, it would make sense to practice the escalation so that there is confidence that it can be done right when there is a real outage. That suggests value in practicing even in the absence of an outage. Why wait for the recital to start practicing the piano?

Another obvious example is disaster planning and contingencies for handling various scenarios. They need to be practiced and mistake proofed. As such, this is an example of organizational learning inasmuch as desired behaviors are imprinted.

Kaizen

Kaizen is a term that refers to continual improvement, so it generally captures the notions we have been discussing. Kaizen is a method for accelerating process improvement by diving deep into identified problem areas and implementing desired improvements. It is conducted by a team (Kaizen team) and may be implemented as a resource-intensive, time-bounded activity (Kaizen event). Within IT, so-called "tiger teams" offer an analogy, but these sometimes become operationalized as longer-term team projects lose focus over time. Consistent with the Lean approach, Kaizen events are well-structured, short-duration activities (e.g., three to five days) with expected outcomes that include immediate implementation of results.

Kaizen events can be scaled according to purpose, but the scale (or scope) we want to emphasize corresponds to what we call "mini-Kaizen" or *Rapid Improvement Events*.[10-12]

There is a philosophy that is associated with Kaizen, and it includes enablers that we will discuss further in Chapter 8, but which include clear goal direction from management and employee empowerment. Kaizen teams are empowered to identify and eliminate waste, and their work is managed to that end. Once the team makes a decision on an improvement, they also are empowered to implement it. Kaizen events, then, put the philosophy of Kaizen into action.

Tool: Rapid Improvement Events

We like the term Rapid Improvement Event because it captures both the spirit of Kaizen, continual improvement, and emphasizes the value of making small, incremental improvements over time as the means to the end. In fact, in this case, the means *is* the end.

Rapid Improvement Events require preparation and we have already identified the critical work that needs to happen. It typically involves Current State process mapping or VSM, and may also include some attention to identifying solutions to problems we have identified. But, actually the preparation is all about problem identification and we often find that the work of validating the problems (and root cause), identifying solutions, and then designing the Future State is done within a team setting (this is the *event*).

Preparation is done so that the events themselves can be short-term and highly productive. They might, for example, be just one to two days in duration, and a "big" event perhaps as long as a week.

Let's consider how use of Rapid Improvement Events differs from a traditional IT project. In a traditional project, there is usually a significant amount of up-front planning before any work is done. The work is conceptualized over the long term, with many hidden assumptions about resources, work scope, and customer requirements. All of these commonly change over time, sometimes dramatically, so that the original assumptions are essentially useless after a period of time. For large projects, there often reaches a point where the best analogy to work is something like a traffic jam—lots of dependencies, lots of delays (much of it related to waste in the operational workflows that the project depends on), and lots of places where things can go wrong. It is like having too many cars of different variety (big, small, some fast, some slow, some performing well, others not) trying to squeeze through a tunnel. All it takes is a breakdown or two (a statistical likelihood) and the traffic comes to a stop. It then squeezes through the other end of the tunnel one car at a time until eventually the bottleneck is relieved. We won't work the analogy out, but we think it is not a bad one for some projects we have seen.

In contrast, the Lean practitioner will look at the landscape of improvement opportunities and select those that will have high impact on known problems. Using our analogy, he or she will try to identify the root cause of waste in the traffic flow using all the tools we have discussed to this point in the book. Short-term projects are identified, then managed to successful outcomes using PDCA, after which other projects will follow.

We would argue that this is a completely different way of looking at how we work, and yet we also observe that the approach and tools are all quite simple to employ. We will talk more about Rapid Improvement Events in Chapter 8.

Summary

This chapter began with good root cause identification as a starting point and we indicated that this is the most important element in good problem-solving. We begin with a prioritized list of root causes for some particular problem, then brainstorm candidate solutions, which then are prioritized as well, and then implemented using PDCA. We also talked about PDCA in managing, improving, and sustaining these improvements over time, using a number of different tools to help in these activities, including several that facilitate flow. Finally, we talked about Continuous Improvement, Kaizen, and the relatively simple approach captured within a project tool for Rapid Improvement Events.

References

1. Gawande, A. 2011. *The checklist manifesto: How to get things right*. New York: Picador.
2. Sayer, N. J. and B. Williams. 2007. *Lean for dummies*. Hoboken, NJ: John Wiley & Sons Publishing.
3. Liker, J. K., and D. Meier. 2006. *The Toyota way fieldbook: A practical guide for implementing Toyota's 4Ps*. New York: McGraw-Hill.

4. Chase, R. B., and D. M. Stewart. 1994. Mistake proofing: Make your service fail-safe. *Sloan Management Review*, Spring 1994: 35–44.
5. George, M. L. 2003. *Lean Six Sigma for services*. New York: McGraw-Hill.
6. Sekine, K. 2005. *One-piece flow: Cell design for transforming the production process*. New York: Productivity Press.
7. Sayer, N. J. and B. Williams. 2007. *Lean for dummies*. Hoboken, NJ: John Wiley & Sons Publishing.
8. George, M. L., D. Rowlands, M. Price, and J. Maxey. 2005. *Lean Six Sigma pocket toolbook*. New York: McGraw-Hill.
9. Liker, J. K., and D. Meier. 2006. *The Toyota way fieldbook: A Practical guide for implementing Toyota's 4Ps*. New York: McGraw-Hill.
10. Bodek, N., and B. Tozawa. 2001. *The idea generator: Quick and easy kaizen*. Vancouver, WA: PCS Press.
11. Martin, K., and M. Osterling. 2007. *The kaizen event planner: Achieving rapid improvement in office, service, and technical environments*. New York: Productivity Press.
12. Tapping, D. 2007. *The lean pocket handbook for kaizen events*. Chelsea, MI: MCS Media.

Chapter 7

Lean IT Service Management

In this chapter, we take a somewhat different view of IT operational work. We are going to look at the domain of IT Service Management, which includes IT operations, but from the perspective of the IT Infrastructure Library (ITIL). The term IT Service Management identifies both a set of capabilities (people, process, and technology) as well as an end-state in which these capabilities support the delivery of IT services. With reference to the IT domain model for identifying applications for Lean (Chapter 2, Figure 2.4), we are looking at the lower right-hand corner of the diagram.

IT Infrastructure Library (ITIL)

ITIL is a framework of best practices that focuses on the provision of quality IT services.[1] ITIL is widely used among IT practitioners and has become an increasingly popular reference model for implementation of both process and technical solutions within IT. In support of that, ITIL identifies core processes to support IT service operations, as well as the recommended workflows for many of these processes.

From the ITIL perspective, IT is viewed as a service operation. All concepts within ITIL are positioned within the Service Management lifecycle, which consists of five phases: Service Strategy, Service Design, Service Transition, Service Operation, and Continual Service Improvement. A set of defined functions and processes provide the specialization and coordination required to implement the full service lifecycle. For example, the phase of the lifecycle for Service Operation consists of a set of processes that are collectively described as "business-as-usual" activities, also sometimes referred to as the "factory" of IT. In fact, other processes supporting other lifecycle phases also have operational elements, and our interest here is with this wider domain of operational activity across all phases.

In ITIL, IT process and quality improvement is achieved through implementation of best practices across *all* lifecycle phases, and not just from within a single phase. Most importantly, the entire phase called Continual Service Improvement (CSI) provides foundation guidance for sustainable improvement. Within ITIL, specific quality systems are identified in the context of CSI. One of these quality systems is Lean.

The process-centric view of IT work provides a useful orientation for implementing improvements in IT work, because it provides an abstraction of work activities that can be isolated and subjected to ITIL best practices. For example, those activities that together enable the IT organization to control changes in the IT environment are addressed within the process called Change Management.

In ITIL Version 2, several processes and one function (Service Desk) together comprised the ITIL framework. We mention Version 2 because it is in the context established in this version where the notion of IT Service Management applies. We call it a traditional view because it is IT-centric and essentially addresses how IT can support the business through the effective and efficient implementation of process-based work.

There is a subtle but significant shift in perspective from ITIL Version 2 to ITIL Version 3. The emphasis in Version 3 is still on IT Service Management, but with a stronger focus on what *service management* means. The notion is that services are defined in business terms, then mapped to service capabilities within IT that directly meet business requirements. This shift in orientation is represented in a service-centric lifecycle view within Version 3.

This should sound somewhat familiar, because it is very closely aligned to the notion of the Business–IT Value Chain, which was discussed in Chapter 2 (see section Business–IT Alignment), and also aligns rather well with the Lean perspective on addressing business process efficiencies as a precondition to identifying supporting IT requirements. From our earlier discussion, we have an understanding of what it means to Lean a process, but the notion here suggests the requirement to Lean processes that underlie the delivery of services. It is a small difference, and from our perspective the approach and activities we engage in are exactly the same as those we have been discussing.

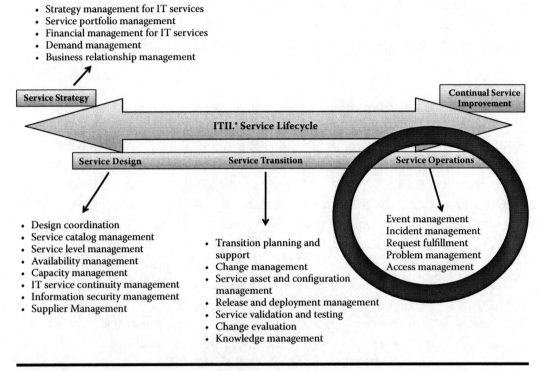

- Strategy management for IT services
- Service portfolio management
- Financial management for IT services
- Demand management
- Business relationship management

Service Strategy

Continual Service Improvement

ITIL® Service Lifecycle

Service Design   Service Transition   Service Operations

- Design coordination
- Service catalog management
- Service level management
- Availability management
- Capacity management
- IT service continuity management
- Information security management
- Supplier Management

- Transition planning and support
- Change management
- Service asset and configuration management
- Release and deployment management
- Service validation and testing
- Change evaluation
- Knowledge management

Event management
Incident management
Request fulfillment
Problem management
Access management

Figure 7.1   IT Infrastructure Library (ITIL) processes.

In ITIL Version 3, then, we still have a strong process orientation, but processes are placed within the context of lifecycle phases. In order to provide a complete view of this framework, we identify in Figure 7.1 all ITIL processes within their respective lifecycle phases.

The processes that align with the Service Operation lifecycle phase will be of particular interest to us here, in part because they lend themselves rather well to a discussion of Service Desk activities (a topic of focus in this chapter), but in addition, Service Operation encompasses all aspects of day-to-day IT operational work, so there is a close correspondence with the domain of work we have been addressing throughout the book. Here we will have the additional orientation toward definition and implementation of formal process activities (Incident Management, Problem Management, etc.) that will provide a top-down perspective on operational capabilities. As we will see, these processes are not unlike the generic, high-level processes we discussed in Chapter 3.

Because it is natural and reasonable to apply Lean concepts to any process, the processes that comprise the ITIL framework are likely going to be good candidates for application of Lean. Applying Lean concepts to Service Operation processes means we will try to identify workflows that represent sequential, repeatable work. In addition, we will look for evidence of waste, and then engage in the Lean Problem-Solving script in order to understand root cause, identify solutions, and manage and improve these solutions over time.

Incident Management

Incident Management is the process of restoring normal operations when an "incident," defined as an interruption to normal operation or a reduction in service quality, occurs.[2] As a process, Incident Management can be represented as a workflow with a set of recommended activities (process steps). For Incident Management, these steps include those represented in the diagram in Figure 7.2. From the ITIL perspective, these steps need to be implemented in order to ensure proper operation of the Incident Management process.

The first thing we notice is that this is a generic, high-level workflow and probably does not represent the process at the level of "real work." For example, there are no indications of where delays, backlogs, or defects might occur, and we know that it is not uncommon to find these in the process of resolving incidents. By the same token, this serves the same function as the generic models did in our earlier discussion. Specifically, it provides the top-down orientation for defining more detailed workflows as part of process mapping or Value Stream Mapping (VSM).

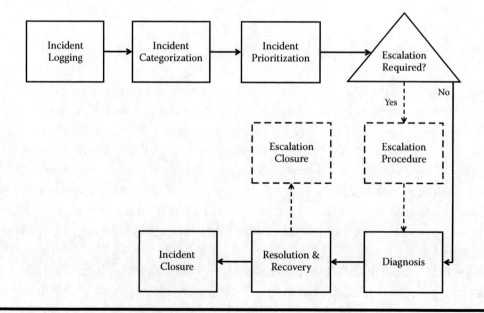

Figure 7.2 Incident Management workflow (derived from ITIL).

In the Incident Management workflow, incidents represent the artifact (product) associated with the service of restoring normal service operation to the customer. We don't want to trip over the two meanings of "service" here, but it's important to distinguish between the service provided by IT (normal operation) and the service provided by Incident Management (restoration of normal operation). Indeed, the service of restoration is best viewed as a service failure recovery process, a point which underscores the critical importance of this service as a factor in maintaining good customer relations. In addition, we should view the incidents themselves as evidence of defects in products or services, and this helps shift our focus from the Incident Management process to the processes that support creation and delivery of the products or services that are defective. We will follow this point further when we discuss the Lean Service Desk.

Inside the Incident Management operation, incidents are opened and flow through the process in conjunction with service delivery. Each step in the process has a defined purpose that contributes to the overall service objective. Several of these support the objective of utilizing standardized procedures. For example, incident models represent predefined "standard" incidents, and when categorized as such, incidents can then be handled through standardized procedures for resolution. While standardization is the desired aim for handling all incidents, exception handling is commonplace due to the variety of incidents and the low volume of each type. Many of these incidents require a high degree of labor associated with their resolution, often with handoffs to more advanced levels of subject expertise (e.g., Service Desk Agents to Level 2 Subject Matter Experts to Level 3 Engineering).

When Incident Management is run like a linear flow, these exceptions run counter to standardized practice and, for that reason, can be a source of great expense and frustration. These nonstandard exceptions are better handled with a jumbled flow, or job shop process, because if they are handled as a linear flow, the process will sometimes fail under duress of high incident variety. Another reason a line will often fail is due to unexpected spikes in incident volume, or unpredictable variation in demand that overwhelms the capacity of the line. This failure is inevitable because service capacity is typically defined by relatively simple heuristics (e.g., 1 support agent per 1000 users) or by cost constraints (this often translates into low-cost outsourcing options), rather than by variables associated with the product within the workflow. Therefore, it's not uncommon to see backlogs, bottlenecks, delays, and defects.

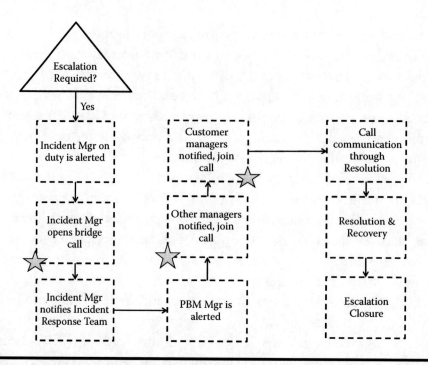

Figure 7.3   Incident Management escalation process.

To Lean the Incident Management workflow, we, of course, need to drill down to a level where we can represent real work, just as we did for processes in Chapter 5. Let us look at the detailed process activity that is associated with escalations, represented in the diagram in Figure 7.2 at a high level, and in the diagram in Figure 7.3 at a lower level that maps to the realm of real work.

Here we have a process map for escalations and we have highlighted those points where we have identified trouble spots, which is to say, signs of waste. The pain points correspond with delays (takes too long for the bridge call to be initiated, takes too long for customer managers to dial in, takes too long for other managers to dial in). In addition, we also identified a problem related to delays, whereby each person added to the call requires his or her own orientation as to the nature of the incident, so the Incident Manager spends a lot of time repeating the incident report, current state, and so forth. Through observations and data gathering, we may ascertain that perhaps 20–30 minutes on an average 80-minute bridge call is spent in this way. In other words, time is arguably wasted.

The reader knows from our review of problems in Chapter 5 how to work with this type of process map, identify the underlying root causes of the problems, and then identify appropriate solutions. It is done exactly the same way we described in the previous chapters. What is interesting, however, is that in many IT environments problems of this sort are tolerated as being part of the course of doing business, and/or signs of these as waste go completely unnoticed, despite the fact that a significant amount of time is spent in doing unnecessary work, which is of questionable value to the customer. While we could argue that the customer benefits from having the nature of the incident explained to him or her (and, therefore, it has value), we should temper this by remembering that the incident itself represents waste for the customer (nothing should have broken in the first place). In addition, if the customer's time has value, then it's incumbent on the service recovery system to use it wisely.

In addition to this, we want to emphasize that a pure ITIL orientation on improving Incident Management as a process by and large means implementing the workflow that is identified as best practice (Figure 7.2), and does not specifically address the requirements for improving lower-level component workflows (Figure 7.3). This is where Lean comes in, and this is why Lean and ITIL are very compatible. ITIL provides top-down structure and guidance on process capabilities and high-level activities, and Lean addresses the process-level improvements that necessarily follow from implementing the ITIL processes.

We think this is an important relationship because we often find that organizations will implement (or try to implement) ITIL processes as if they are out-of-the-box solutions for addressing process dysfunctions in their current operations. Once implemented (usually in an incomplete way because they have not had adequate scope definition and/or disciplined use of Plan–Do–Check–Act as the means toward implementation), they will exhibit their own evidence of dysfunction (basically signs of waste), which are often attributed to the observation that "ITIL doesn't work."

Once we identify a solution to our problem associated with escalations, another Lean takeaway is that we cannot expect the improved process solution to operate smoothly unless we implement it, manage it, and improve it over time. Some of the tools we discussed in Chapter 6 could be brought into play, and we might then realistically expect to see a bridge call that used to take 80 minutes on average now take only 60 minutes. This is the kind of chopping away at waste that characterizes Lean.

We could apply this discussion of ITIL process implementation to any of the other ITIL processes. We would follow exactly the same script, using the same tools derived from the Lean Improvement Model. Rather than review this same approach with other ITIL processes, we want instead to look at how other characteristics of these processes relate to various notions we derive from Lean Thinking.

Problem Management

In the ITIL framework, problems represent the underlying, unknown root cause of incidents, and Problem Management is the process that identifies root cause, resolves problems, and thereby helps resolve their associated incidents.[3] This should sound familiar. It's exactly like Root Cause Analysis described in Chapter 5. It's not surprising, then, to know that Problem Managers often use tools, such as cause-and-effect diagrams or 5 Whys, as ways of identifying root cause in the course of their work. In this context, Problem Management also can be viewed as a component in a higher-level quality management process that pertains to the product or service that exhibits the incident and problem. In other words, it serves a function in providing feedback regarding the defect of the product or service.

At the same time, Problem Management can be viewed as the process for managing problems. For this there is a corresponding workflow defined by ITIL as best practice guidance, and this provides the top-down framework for implementing Problem Management as a process, in exactly the same way the Incident Management workflow did for that process. We therefore would expect to find evidence of waste in Problem Management workflows (at the level of real work). One of the "problems" with Problem Management, as it turns out, has to do with waste in the form of defective outcomes of the process itself. That is, we sometimes find that Problem Management is not very good at identifying and resolving the problems they are investigating.

One of the common reasons for Problem Management not effecting good problem resolution is because good Root Cause Analysis (RCA) is hard to do. We discussed this earlier, and all the guidance around A3 Thinking and use of tools, such as 5 Whys, applies to the Problem Management process itself. For example, we sometimes find that 5 Whys is used in a rather perfunctory way, and the consequence is often that a root cause is not identified. Use of 5 Whys alone is not an indicator of a more mature Problem Management process. We also find that the Problem Manager may not have good A3 Thinking skills to guide him or her, so his or her understanding of problem-solving is limited. We think that complementary guidance for Problem Managers should include A3 Thinking because it has everything to do with Problem Management as a process.

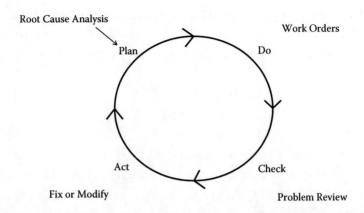

Figure 7.4 Problem Management and Plan–Do–Check–Act (PDCA).

At the same time, we can relate Problem Management activities to PDCA, as represented in the diagram in Figure 7.4. In this model, we view the outcome of good RCA as the input to an implementation of a solution, and we can map activities that should be part of the overall Problem Management workflow as corresponding to steps in the PDCA cycle. However, we sometimes find the same issues in management of this as we find with other dysfunctions in use of PDCA, most commonly signs of Plan–Do–Drift or Plan–Do–Stop.

Finally, we can draw attention to the ITIL distinction between *reactive* Problem Management (responding to incidents and problems after they occur) and *proactive* Problem Management (where we try to identify potential sources of incidents and problems before they occur). This maps quite closely to the Lean notion of surfacing problems, so the approach and tools we discussed for this in Chapter 5 could all be applied in supporting this particular objective.

Service Request Fulfillment

In the ITIL framework, a Service Request is a trigger for a Request Fulfillment process that delivers services, such as password resets, granting of privileges, procurement, office moves, and so forth.[4] There really is no limit to the type of services that IT might provide, and ITIL is not prescriptive about this, except to indicate that the Service Desk should be the request point *except* when self-service options are available. Because Request Fulfillment processes are often quite customized within an organization's environment, ITIL does not provide top-down workflow guidance as it does for Incident Management and Problem Management. Nevertheless, these processes once implemented in any environment can be subjected to the same level of analysis as any other process; in other words, they can be Leaned.

We like to think of Service Request Fulfillment as a supply chain that delivers products and information to customers in various types of packages. This is consistent with the ITIL point of view and, of course, is completely consistent with the Lean way of thinking as well. However, a supply chain is nothing more than a value chain and, consequently, we can map the supply/value chain and consider the contributing value of each activity, as suggested in the diagram in Figure 7.5.

With this model, we have identified the Service Desk as having both a customer-facing front office and a back-end operation that could be conceived of as a job shop for packaging of components that are derived from linear flows. We will work with this idea further below, but for now let's focus mostly on the back-end linear flows that comprise the supply chain. When a request is made for a new computer, this triggers a procurement process that corresponds to a supply chain of material flow. When a request

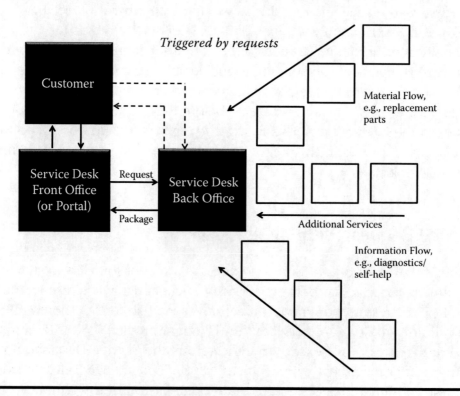

Figure 7.5 Service Request Fulfillment supply chain.

is made for information, this might similarly trigger a process for generating content that can be managed through a value chain. Finally, we may have requests that require the Service Desk to request supporting services from other service providers, such as when the Service Desk is a broker for access to diagnostic support services from third-party vendors. From a Lean perspective, all of these requests are a "pull" signal for initiating a service fulfillment process.

By thinking of this as a supply chain, we encourage analysis of the associated workflows from a Lean perspective, looking at sources of waste as a precondition for eliminating them, in exactly the same manner we described earlier using tools such as VSM. One outcome of adopting this line of reasoning could be the simple observation that the Service Desk role is itself a potential source of delay. Focus would then be drawn to the sources of delay and appropriate solutions can be identified to address them, for example, by implementing more self-service options. Or, we might decide that some of the back-end flows can be completely outsourced in exactly the same way that outsourcing of supply chain components is done in the service of greater efficiency.

Service Desk

Service Desk is a function in the ITIL framework. Process capabilities enabled within the Service Desk include Incident Management, Problem Management, and Service Request Fulfillment, the process areas we discussed in the previous sections. This is somewhat simplified, as other processes also may be supported, but it will be sufficient in this section to address requirements and considerations of interest to us. Most importantly for our purposes, we view objectives of each separate process as determinants of Service Desk functional objectives.

The Current State of many service desks can be characterized as a jumbled flow. There are lots of front-end, customer-facing interactions, as well as many back-end activities that support requirements of the customer interface. If we spend some time within a service desk environment, we also will see many activities that we might otherwise associate with waste. Some of these include many alternative paths (physical and virtual) to accomplish same or similar tasks, lots of exception handling, many handoffs (routed and linear, but also ad hoc and sometimes misdirected), requirements for data collection with follow-up clarification, and complicated information flows that often exhibit signs of incomplete, fragmented, and incorrect information. In addition, service desks require specialized skills that need to be deployed at different, sometimes unpredictable, points in the workflow. Finally, we often see evidence of backlogs, bottlenecks, defects, and delays, all of which are the result of handling volume with variety, process variation, and overall variability.

We have represented the Service Desk in this somewhat extreme way, despite the fact that many service desks do a good job of keeping up with the demands made upon them. However, as many practitioners who work in these environments know and understand, there are points in time in which even relatively stable processes become stressed to the point of breaking.

The following description of Service Desk activities will lead us naturally to a hypothetical design of a *Lean* Service Desk. The idea is to build on Lean concepts and practices and develop some practical notions of how a Lean Service Desk can be designed and implemented. Ideas for this section are derived from multiple sources.[5–8]

External View of the Service Desk

From a Lean perspective, it is important to adopt the perspective of customers not only in order to understand the customer experience and provide better customer service, but also in order to define the work we do in providing that service. If the work we do does not add value to the customer, why are we doing it? In the case of incident resolution, Lean encourages us to initially adopt an *external* view of the Service Desk and its role in managing incidents.

From the customer perspective, the work they do is what is most important, whether this be working on a factory floor or working in an office. In the course of doing their work, they may use a variety of products, tools, or services. For the moment, let's consider their use of a product, say, a computer. Anything that may interrupt the normal operation of the computer is from their perspective a "defect" or a "break" that requires remediation. In their search for resolution, they may interact with a service recovery system that may include a Service Desk. From the point of view of the Service Desk, service recovery is synonymous with incident resolution, but it is important to note that for the customer, they probably don't care what it's called. They simply want remediation, and anything that delays this outcome is, from their point of view, *waste* (i.e., a waste of time).

There are multiple sources of frustration to users when they experience
a break requiring a fix. For starters, they can no longer do their work. Then
they need to reach out and engage the service recovery system, an activity
that can include searching for it in the first place (whom do I call?), trying to make a connection (navigating phone trees, finding the right person,
often with delays in response), and then any number of issues with getting
satisfaction for the problem at hand. Of course, within organizations where
attention to these sources of frustration has been made, the customer experience is better, but most customers would still regard all of this activity as a
waste of their time.

Actually (and ironically), anything that takes place from the point in time
when the break occurs to when successful resolution takes place is, from a
Lean perspective, waste, even if it is value-added activity from the perspective of the Service Desk. Services should not break, and any breaks represent defects in the process. This notion corresponds to ITIL's notion of the
Expanded Incident Lifecycle,[9] and is in contrast to the much more common
practice of only capturing measurements within the ticketing system (i.e.,
from when the ticket is open), instead of when the defect actually occurs.
In fact in many operational environments, we often find that measurements
are not representative of the complete end-to-end workflow, which compro-
mises the value of the data for capturing the true state of affairs.

In viewing the complete end-to-end customer experience, we can, of
course, isolate component processes and identify waste, especially with
the aim of streamlining activities that may introduce unnecessary delays. In
addition to streamlining the process and presenting positive results to the
customer as quickly as possible (resumption of normal operations, so the
customer can get back to work), it is also important, from a Lean perspective, to remove all defects that led to the incident in the first place. That is,
without remediation of product defects and the improvement of product
quality, service recovery is nothing more than a band-aid. Simply stated, if
product defects are the cause of incidents, then the way to reduce incidents
is to improve product quality. We can combine these notions in the diagram
seen in Figure 7.6.

Lean emphasizes these aspects in such a way that it allows analysis
of the Current State and also design of the Future State. That is, we can
use this model to see how our current operations align with it, and also
as the basis for design of operational improvements. We may very well
find examples of current practices that address these Lean requirements,
but more often than not, we find diluted expressions of these, or even

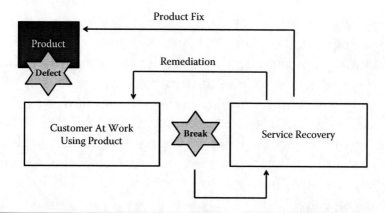

Figure 7.6   External view of Service Desk.

inadequate, disconnected, or dysfunctional renditions. We may have good service recovery, for example, but no effective links between the incident resolution process and the product quality processes. Or, there may be long time delays that effectively mute the effectiveness of the process, as when, for instance, product developers have a huge backlog of fixes, so anything introduced by the service recovery operation is likely to have a long delay before being addressed. We may accept this as the "way things work" or "business as usual," but from the point of view of customer value, this is waste.

Note that by drawing attention to these external perspectives, we have not specifically addressed the role of the Service Desk itself. While the Service Desk may have no direct responsibility for other components in the product quality workflow, the Lean perspective compels the Service Desk to understand its contributing role.

Internal View of the Service Desk

Just as we can apply Lean notions in the depiction of an external perspective, we also can apply Lean to the work of the Service Desk itself and thereby adopt an *internal* view of its activities. The conventional internal view would have us look at levels of support (e.g., Level 1, Level 2, Level 3), resource and skill allocation, functional subdivisions, etc. In addition, adopting ITIL as our frame of reference and looking once again at Incident Management, we can isolate the Incident Management workflow with inputs and outputs that together fulfill the objectives of the process, in this case, service recovery or incident resolution. From our discussion earlier, we can

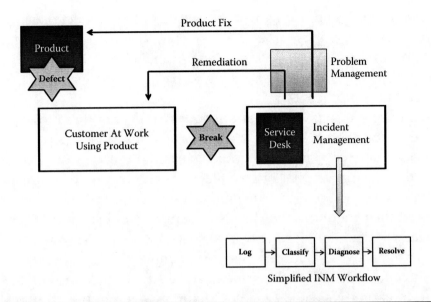

Simplified INM Workflow

Figure 7.7 Service Desk activities.

view this workflow as a value stream and focus our attention on what adds value throughout the workflow (ideally, each activity) and what does not add value (this is a candidate for waste). In addition, we can position the related work of Problem Management in this same context, because it provides the essential activities supporting Root Cause Analysis for incidents.

We can position this internal perspective within the larger set of objectives driven by external factors (Figure 7.7). From this diagram, we can start to identify specific objectives and requirements that represent a mapping of sorts between internal activities and external performance criteria. For example, if product and service quality is a paramount consideration and Problem Management is the critical activity in support of that, then every incident should have a corresponding problem, or else how do we know if we have really resolved the underlying root cause of the incident? Looking at the customer interface, given that all time expended by the customer waiting is waste, we need to ask how we abbreviate the interaction while also adding value. One outcome from this line of reasoning might be that higher levels of specialized support, which we conventionally think of as back-end support, e.g., Level 3 Engineering, should be deployed at the front-end interface where needed. We also might conclude that Problem Management activities should likewise be deployed in this fashion because it is where the most information can be derived about the nature of the problem itself.

We also can ask questions about the nature of the product or service that the Service Desk is delivering. In the case of service requests, as suggested earlier, we can think of this almost as an assembly operation, and we should consider efficiencies in the supply chain as part of the management of the request fulfillment process.

As we think through these various ideas and apply them to our current models for Service Desk operation, we begin to see gaps. Lean suggests one way of viewing the objectives, and our typical Current State operations that suggest that other objectives are at play (e.g., operate at lowest unit cost, respond to incidents or requests within established time limits, and then route to other levels of support, and so forth). These objectives are commonplace and "realistic," but they have nothing to do with Lean objectives. Consider this, for example. Typical Service Desk queues tolerate backlogs, which mean the customer has to wait, which is waste. It is pretty simple. One could almost say that the waste is designed into the process because we know that if we deployed enough capacity, we could keep up with the demand. However, we don't do this on purpose because it would cost too much. Thus, while we might not like to admit this to our customers, the fact is that we have intentionally imposed wait times.

Lean would adopt a different design perspective by suggesting, for example, that a ticket opened is resolved as quickly as possible, and then the next ticket is opened. Capacity is deployed to handle the volume and variety of tickets deployed. The only way to realize this objective is to adopt Lean practices from the very beginning of the interaction to the very end. Stated otherwise, we should think Lean at both the front-end and at the back-end. If we realize maximum efficiencies at the back-end, we can deploy our resources at the front-end where they add the most value (because they are customer-facing). This is exactly the same consideration that a library makes, for example, when it maximizes efficiencies in processing returned books in the back room so it can deploy its staff out on the circulation or reference desk.[10] Or it's also seen when customers are able to select services from a catalog (at the front-end), triggering self-service or automated options (back-end), rather than their having to wait in line only to get routed elsewhere (which often enough is what happens).

What we have begun to do here is to tease apart the front-end of the Service Desk from the back-end, and we will use this model to consider how Lean drives different considerations at each end. The model in Figure 7.8 shows one rendition of this, whereby an agent either operates

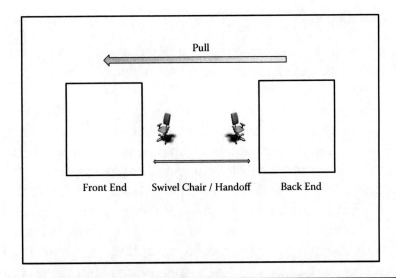

Pull

Front End

Swivel Chair / Handoff

Back End

Figure 7.8   Service Desk front end and back end.

in a swivel seat capacity between front-end and back-end, or else effects a handoff. We have also shown how this model begins to look like a pull system.

In order to implement this high-level model, every activity in every component workflow needs to be subjected to Lean analysis. That sounds like a lot of work and perhaps even unrealistic, but this is exactly what Lean practitioners do on the factory floor, and it is exactly how efficiencies have been gained in other service environments, e.g., in hospitals.

We need to ask what work gets done in the front-end and what work is best done in the back-end. For work on either side of the Service Desk, we need to ask whether the work is best done as a job shop with a jumbled flow or as a linear flow. Both jumbled flows and linear flows can be optimized using tools we have covered earlier in the book. Above all, we can look for signs of waste in how work is currently done and use the Lean Problem-Solving script to identify and eliminate it. An example might be to look at the information exchanges and handoffs that occur between levels of the Service Desk (Level 1 to Level 2 to Level 3) and as end-to-end workflows, surface and identify evidence of waste within them. Even well-managed Service Desk operations will show some evidence of waste, so there are very likely many opportunities for efficiency gains.

Lean Service Desk

The various notions communicated above begin to define what we mean by a *Lean* Service Desk. Let's present one more model to help draw out all the relevant concepts (Figure 7.9).

The first thing one might ask when looking at this model is: "Where's the Service Desk?" The answer is that it's everywhere, from customer interface to front-end to back-end. Each separate component of this model can now be viewed from the perspective of its functional role, from which specific objectives can be identified, along with Lean solutions for addressing these objectives. For example, all access options at the customer interface serve the purpose of facilitating easy incident reporting or service requests. The objectives are to have intuitive interaction, with the fewest number of steps, and the least amount of customer time expended in interaction. Lean solutions require us to identify the workflows for each mode of access, optimizing value and eliminating waste in each. For phone access, for example, we might start with the ideal of one-ring pickup (no phone trees), but if phone trees are a "reality" in the current environment, then we need to systematically match user requirements against phone tree options so the user can

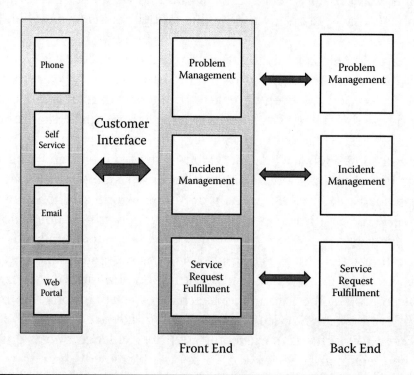

Figure 7.9 Lean Service Desk.

easily get to the option in the least period of time. Most of us know from personal experience that many phone tree options are nonintuitive, frustrating, and often a complete waste of time. This is the opposite of a Lean solution.

Turning attention to the front-end of the Service Desk, we can look at the value-adding activities that should be part of the engagement between customer and Service Desk agent. We need to address rapid information capture, accurate and detailed categorization of needs (to facilitate back-end handoffs), along with as much custom interaction as possible (addressing *my* needs, respectful of *my* time, and providing as much constructive guidance as possible, as soon as possible). As suggested above, that may mean pulling in more specialized resources at that point in time, rather than as a handoff where someone picks up the work after an unspecified delay.

Finally, we can turn attention to the back-end activities where the objective is rapid resolution or fulfillment, enabled very likely by linear flows. Again, we isolate the workflows, optimize the work, and eliminate waste.

By splitting each of the core processes into front-end and back-end components, we also help differentiate values that are important for each component. For the front-end, it is customer interaction, while for the back-end, it is efficiency of operation. Some of this is counterintuitive from a conventional ITIL perspective, for example, by suggesting that Problem Management has a role in the customer interaction, but it follows rather naturally from a Lean perspective.

In this model, the Lean Service Desk is a set of separate but interrelated functional and process areas, each defined in such a way that the separate components can be optimized around Lean objectives. It is a decomposition of typical Service Desk operations and their recomposition as Lean workflows, all contributing to customer value.

We believe that this model helps liberate us from constructs of Service Desk operations that are perhaps, in some respects, archaic. If we think of the Service Desk as a reactive function that gets bombarded by incidents and requests, we very quickly end up with an operation where everybody is pushing things around. This means things are pushed to work-in-progress (WIP), which means we can't get work to flow. Soon enough (it's just a matter of having volume that is too high and/or variety), we will see delays, backlogs, bottlenecks, and defects. We can tolerate this, and even operationally fulfill the requirements imposed by management with respect to cost constraints, response time targets, and so forth, but quite likely the customer isn't happy and quite likely the Service Desk agents aren't happy either.

Lean wants us to turn the whole matter around, starting with the customer experience and then identifying ways that products and services are pulled through the workflow. The purpose of this model is to help encourage ways of thinking about Service Desk activities from this perspective.

Applying Lean to Other ITSM Processes

There are other processes that are derived from ITIL and that comprise the domain of IT Service Management, and we could walk through any of them and consider the Lean implications principally by looking at workflows and considering opportunities for Lean problem-solving. In some cases, ITIL defines high-level workflows and, in other cases, not. In all cases, we know how to find the workflows embedded in real work within the organizations and this, of course, is where the action is for real Lean improvements. Let's consider a couple ITIL processes where there are some additional Lean perspectives or applications of particular interest.

Availability Management

Availability Management is about ensuring high levels of availability of services to customers. A simple example is providing 99.99% availability (uptime) for email services. Achieving high levels of availability is neither simple nor cheap, and there are several tools and approaches to support the objective, including some that map very closely to those familiar to Lean practitioners. Simplification of the overall infrastructure and architecture reduces potential points of failure, for example, as do applications of mistake proofing, use of monitoring, and statistical tools that derive from Six Sigma, with focus on zero defects.[11] Doing Availability Management well is practically synonymous with doing Lean, because all waste needs to be eliminated in order to achieve high levels of availability.

Event Management

In the ITIL framework, events represent the continuous flux of computational activity that underlies delivery of IT services. It includes the ebb and flow in network traffic, the volume of data handled through batch routines, or the fluctuating changes in customer requests. These events are ever-present and changing, and not all are observable, but the ones that are important are monitored so that observations can be made, and many of these are actionable. That is, we monitor an activity so we can do something if thresholds are reached; we monitor so we can identify trends over time; or we simply monitor because something happened in the past and we want to make sure it doesn't happen again.

For this, we use monitoring tools and, as we saw in Chapter 3, the processes that accompany monitoring are subject to Lean inquiry. The interplay between process and tool also is important as the following examples illustrate. Alerts set at the wrong thresholds will trigger actions that represent waste, not only because actions may be taken unnecessarily, but it also impacts the ability to react appropriately to the *right* conditions. Over time, unless the implementation of alerts is reviewed, they can become unneeded overhead (inventory) that complicates the environment. Even when managed correctly, it's possible to see other evidence of waste, as when an alert triggers widespread communication to various team members, not all of whom understand the meaning of the alerts or the actions to take. This can result in unnecessary work, misdirected efforts, or confused communication, all evidence of waste.

Change Management

Change Management is a core process within the ITIL framework, representing a control point for changes that are made within an environment. The process itself is represented as a high-level, generic workflow, and therefore, in its implementation could be subject to Lean analysis. In fact, it is not uncommon to see a number of issues associated with Change Management, all of which can be viewed as signs of waste. Examples include the occurrence of unsuccessful changes (defects), imposition of complicated administrative requirements on users who submit requests for changes (causing delays and dissatisfied customers), ineffective or time-consuming risk review processes, or procedural workarounds where users bypass or misuse the process in order to avoid the administrative requirements or to expedite a change. In addition, Change Management can be subject to high volumes, high variety, and lots of process variation, so from an Operations Management (OM) perspective, we can practically view as inevitable the occasional break in the process where, for example, a change results in an outage. When this happens with frequency, it is not uncommon to impose additional administrative controls, or even a moratorium, and this translates into unhappy customers and delays in moving work forward.

We have described a scenario that will sound familiar to many Change Managers and have also represented the issues in such a way that they can be viewed as candidates for Lean applications.

Implementing Lean ITSM

As consultants, we are often asked how to implement ITIL, which also can be translated as how to implement IT Service Management. Perhaps the question is somewhat more specific, such as how to implement Change Management. One approach is to educate stakeholders in ITIL best practice guidance, and then generate high-level models and processes that implement this guidance. Knowing what we know about Lean, we can see just from saying it this way that that is probably not going to work too well. How will the stakeholders get from the high level *as-designed* state to the Current State of real work? Unsystematically (and not uncommonly), they do something that amounts to a combination of "figuring it out," while wrestling with the legacy of these processes that are already in place in the organization.

For example, even if stakeholders claim that they have no process in place for Change Management, they most certainly do; although it may be hidden from view and is probably dysfunctional and/or highly inefficient. When they want to implement ITIL's best practice guidance for Change Management, they somehow have to bridge the gap between what they want to do and how things are currently done. Merely designing the desired Future State won't get them there because they still need to fix the issues in the Current State. We can imagine a scenario where it's possible to "begin again," essentially replacing altogether the current process and starting over with a new one, but this is really quite difficult to do because the old processes (however obscure or dysfunctional they might be) have a way of sticking around even when new direction is established. For this reason, we believe the task at hand is the familiar one whereby Current State is analyzed, Future State is designed, and deliberate and incremental transition work (using PDCA) bridges the gap.

Lean, of course, can help with this, so we can view the Lean Approach as one way to implement ITSM (IT Service Management). The reader may observe, however, that Lean is so comfortably suitable for process implementation that improvements to Change Management, for example, might take place even without the use of ITIL best practice guidance. That is exactly correct. Insofar as ITIL has guidance to offer, however, we can very easily use it along with Lean to implement the desired Future State.

Using Change Management again as an example, we can develop process capabilities by both fixing problems in the Current State, and introducing new capabilities as a design activity for the Future State. When we think of the development activity, we can think in terms of small, focused projects that accomplish specific objectives in a short period of time. When we say that these process capabilities are derived from ITIL, we mean that we have identified and selected best practice guidance contained in ITIL and used this as the basis for our design and development activity. For example, we might identify creation of Change Management policies, controls for unauthorized changes, procedures for submitting Requests for Change, or formation of a Change Review Board, as the kind of discrete activities that together comprise the Change Management process.[12]

By working with ITIL in this way, we are using best practice guidance as a checklist of sorts, and over a period of time, we will thereby develop capabilities that align with ITIL recommended capabilities. People sometimes ask how they should work with ITIL content, and this is one very important way. By starting with small projects and working on new ones in succession, we can eventually develop fully robust process capabilities. This approach is what we mean when we say that we are "building out" process capabilities. Each successive improvement to Change Management builds on what has already been developed, and improvements to existing implementations effectively represent practice at doing things better and better. Practical demonstration of this might be seen in rehearsal (simulation) of new Request for Change procedures, for example, followed by implementation of the procedures and remediation of issues that were observed upon their introduction. This is all simple PDCA and represents how we integrate and over time imprint desired behaviors within an organization.

Building on a model we introduced in Chapter 3 (Figure 3.9), we can represent the overall reference model for implementation of ITIL using Lean as seen in Figure 7.10.

Please think of this model as a "wiring" diagram of sorts. That is, to the degree to which each component and flow activity is considered and implemented *well*, it strengthens the integrity of the overall approach. A weak governance mechanism will compromise the ability of the transition from Current State to Future State to take place. Conversely, attention to enablers and critical success factors makes the transition go better. In this model,

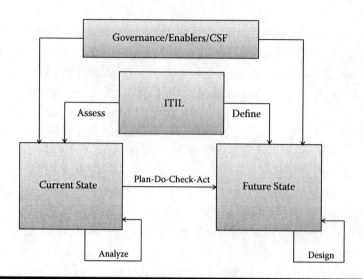

Figure 7.10 Implementing Lean Service Management (ITSM).

ITIL serves as a reference model for both assessment of the Current State (which must be analyzed) and as definition of the Future State (which must be designed). Getting from Current State to Future State should look pretty familiar (PDCA).

This Lean way of implementing ITIL begs an important question. When do we introduce specific Lean improvements using the Lean Problem-Solving script? The rule-of-thumb is that you *first* implement ITIL (in some well-scoped, properly implemented project), and *then* use Lean tools to gain efficiencies. Specifically, you implement ITIL processes, let the process stabilize a bit, and then Lean it. The reason for this sequence is fundamentally that Lean works more effectively on real processes not on processes that only exist in design, so you need to have something in place to work with.

This approach also addresses the very common experience whereby organizations implement ITIL (but not very well) and then decide after a period of time that it doesn't work. Please don't fall into this trap. Assume that the initial implementation will have flaws. It has to be figured out over time, and you are going to use Lean as the way to do that. In fact, there is something to be said for the casual philosophy that these flaws (and even mistakes) don't even really matter much. The important thing is what you are going to do about them, and that is where Lean comes in. You are going to fix the defects and other sources of waste, one by one, over a period of time that both implements real improvements and also teaches you and the organization how to instill a Lean orientation and culture.

One more reminder of our simple analogy to playing the piano. Will the beginning student make mistakes? Of course. What is important is what they do about it, and fundamentally what they have to do is practice playing better and better over time.

In the next chapter, we will address something that is probably on the reader's mind. This is all well and good, you might think, but we have to operate around real constraints and realities. If we don't show evidence of progress for major efforts, we will never get another chance. We can't go in front of our management and tell them that mistakes were made, and that's okay. So, how do we deal with that? As we will see, these questions are pragmatic and also pertinent to the realm of activity we call Continuous Improvement, or in ITIL, Continual Service Improvement.

Summary

In this chapter, we have applied the Lean concepts and practices to the realm of activity we associate with IT Service Management. In one respect, this is exactly the same work that we described in earlier chapters for problem-solving, only here we have adopted an ITIL orientation to see how the same notions apply. We also discussed how Lean and ITIL are entirely complementary and, in fact, their use together is both desirable and recommended.

References

1. U.K. Office of Government Commerce. 2007. *The introduction to the ITIL service lifecycle book*. ITIL Version 3. Norwich, UK: TSO.
2. U.K. Office of Government Commerce. 2007. *Service operation*. ITIL Version 3. Norwich, UK: TSO.
3. Ibid.
4. Ibid.
5. Womack, J. P., and D. T. Jones. 2005. *Lean solutions*. New York: Free Press;.
6. Kannan, N. 2006. Applying Lean Six Sigma to help desks. *Support World*, Sept/ Oct 2006, Online at: www.thinkhdi.com/topics/library/supportworld.aspx (accessed July 15, 2012).
7. Lafever, D. 2011. Personal communication, November 16.

8. Wicks, R. V. 2011. Improving customer service from the inside out: An IT service desk utilizes Lean principles to lower its abandoned call rate. *Support World*, Sept/Oct 2011, Online at: www.thinkhdi.com/ topics/library/support-world.aspx (accessed July 15, 2012).

9. U.K. Office of Government Commerce. 2007. Service operation. ITIL Version 3. Norwich, UK: TSO.

10. Huber, J. J. 2011. *Lean library management*. New York: Neal-Schuman.

11. Gygi, C., N. DeCarlo, and B. Williams. 2005. *Six Sigma for dummies*. Hoboken, NJ: John Wiley & Sons Publishing.

12. U.K. Office of Government Commerce. 2007. Service operation. ITIL Version 3. Norwich, UK: TSO.

Chapter 8

Implementing and Sustaining Lean IT Improvements

We ended the last chapter with a dose of reality that characterizes many IT environments. Specifically, it is hard to implement improvements when there is so much work to do just to keep up with demands. Let's put aside for the moment the fact that the problem we just represented is an example of waste (backlog of work), and focus instead on the real dilemma of how an IT organization can start to work on Lean improvements with all the competing demands on time. The analogy that is sometimes used is that it's like changing tires on a car when the car is in motion. While that is a graphic analogy, we don't think it is the right one, or rather we would prefer to look at it this way: Race cars need to change tires all the time in the middle of a race, and they don't change them while the car is in motion. What they do is streamline the process of changing tires so they can do it very quickly.

There is another set of problems that we suggested in the last chapter as well, and it has to do with how we can justify the initial investment in improvement solutions and then demonstrate the progress of these efforts along the way (specifically, to management). We said that many of the allowances that the Lean Approach presents, for example, that it is okay to make mistakes, may not be the sort of message that you want to take to management when reporting on progress of improvement efforts. What we will suggest below is that we can do things to scope the work so results are seen sooner rather than later, and increase the probability of success in our efforts. Both of these will help in communication with management and it will allow you to focus on your successes in these communications rather than on mistakes that may appear to jeopardize your credibility.

Finally, there is the problem of how we can make sure that when we make improvements in process, they will endure over time and the organization will not slip back to old ways of doing things. We call this *sustainability*, and it is a very real problem underlying any improvement effort, regardless of the methodology employed. We actually already have laid the foundation for how we can achieve sustainability, but we will clarify that in more detail below, specifically by addressing the role of various Critical Success Factors, or Lean Enablers. We have identified the contribution these make in the Lean Improvement Model, and, in this chapter, we want to spend some time discussing specifically what they are and how they help.

All of these issues can be addressed in the context of what we refer to as Continuous Improvement in the Quality Management (QM) domain, and what ITIL (IT Infrastructure Library) calls Continual Service Improvement. We will adopt the QM terminology here, but the meaning is exactly the same.

Continuous Improvement

As we have suggested at several points throughout the book, our philosophy of Continuous Improvement relates to two different avenues for improvement. One pertains to the continual attention we give to identifying and understanding problem opportunities, which we have suggested is essentially limitless in scope because of the pervasiveness of waste. The second has to do with the necessary attention we give to the ongoing improvement of solutions we have implemented, in order to tune them, make them work, and make them work better. This philosophy suggests the continuous use and refinement of various practices that reflect A3 Thinking and disciplined use of PDCA (Plan–Do–Check–Act). This philosophy also corresponds to that of *Kaizen* as practiced by Lean practitioners.[1]

In conducting the work of IT in the spirit of Kaizen, or Continuous Improvement, we have suggested several practical recommendations throughout the book, including the following:

- Use the Lean Problem-Solving script (from the Lean Improvement Model)
- Ongoing solicitation of problems from those closest to them, namely employees

- Selection, scope, and prioritization of projects that address solutions so they can be implemented in relatively short time periods
- Leverage of successes so that subsequent projects can be supported and managed through their own improvement lifecycles, suggesting a lineup of projects where new ones commence as old ones complete

In a sense, it is the implied *again-and-again* aspect of this that underlies Continuous Improvement. This is the practice that leads to perfection over time. Because this orientation is inherently strategic, that is, it is about where we want the organization to be in the long term, it therefore is permissible to tolerate mistakes along the way. We mentioned this earlier as something that you may not want to confess to management, but it is a reality in the implementation of work of this type and complexity, and it means first and foremost that we don't just do a project, walk away, and assess it later. In fact, our understanding of the integrity of PDCA as a lifecycle makes that sound funny just saying it that way. We do the project work, check it immediately, and act on those things that are necessary in order to correct the mistakes and get it right. And then we plan how we proceed from there. Therefore, the continuous loop of PDCA is the engine underlying all Continuous Improvement.

The use of Kaizen Events as a practical mechanism for doing Continuous Improvement projects is fairly conventional in the sphere of Lean applications. There are guidelines and approaches that characterize Kaizen Events,[2] and we want to explore the use of some of these as they pertain to smaller events, referred to as mini-Kaizen Events or Rapid Improvement Events.[3]

Rapid Improvement Events

We like the notion of doing Rapid Improvement Events precisely because they are short-term in scope, and, therefore, we can see the results more quickly than we can for big projects. This is not to suggest that large-scale projects don't have their place or that they cannot be managed under a Lean Approach. We just think it's an easier way to begin work and forces the practitioner to think about concrete objectives and practical solutions to problems rather than in terms of grand schemes and inherently long-term efforts. It is the difference between declaring we are going to "implement ITIL throughout the organization" and "we are going to fix the problem of backlogs in our change queue." If you do the latter as a one-off project and leave it at that, it will, of course, be of limited long-term value to the organization. However, if this is one of many projects conducted over time, what you are really doing then is implementing ITIL one step at a time.

Rapid Improvement Events are conducted as mini-projects, suggesting there is a related project lifecycle that is adapted for their purpose. Project deliverables and milestones incorporate activities that are derived from Lean. For example, we may have requirements for a clear statement of business justification, a statement of customer value, Process or Value Stream Maps, problem statements with supporting root cause analysis, and so forth. By turning these into project activities and deliverables, we begin to institutionalize Lean practices as part of *any* project. That sounds like a good idea and one that is likely to impact how the organization as a whole thinks about projects over the long term.

We don't need to make this mapping of Lean activities to project activities all at once, or even comprehensively, in order to get things going. Indeed, we could do a mini-Kaizen, which is itself focused on generating the project template we will use for subsequent events, and then we can improve it over time. That is consistent with this approach, in general, and will start to get the right thinking instilled in participants.

In conducting the Rapid Improvement Events, we can think of some of the work as prework, accomplished through interviews and including required outputs, such as a Current State Value Stream Map. This is input to the event itself, which is designed as a group workshop activity (therefore, requiring facilitation). The primary characteristic of the Rapid Improvement Event is just that, it's rapid; so the workshop itself is planned as a two- to three-day event (sometimes shorter, sometimes longer, but always in this general timeframe). It also is planned to have tangible outcomes, represented very likely in a Future State Value Stream Map with specific solutions that are scoped as small miniprojects for implementation after the workshop event.

We have represented the script for these events so it all sounds pretty simple. Keeping it simple is important, because projects typically have a way of getting overly complicated. However, there is hard work and some complexity involved as well. Some of the additional nuances of this approach are captured in the following guidelines.

■ Suggesting that these events are projects, with prework, workshop activity, and post-workshop implementation, suggests that we have an implied role for a project manager, who obviously needs to have a good understanding of the Lean Approach in order to be effective.

- Proper scoping up-front means we have some sort of governance mechanism in place to identify these projects, scope and prioritize them well, and manage them through their project lifecycle.
- All of the prework is grounded in use of Lean tools and practices (e.g., derivation of a Current State Value Stream Map), so comfort with use of these tools is important.
- Successful workshop outcomes depend on good facilitation skills, and this may or may not be part of the skill set that makes for good project managers, so distinct roles for Project Manager (PM) and Facilitator are needed (and these may or may not be filled by the same individual).
- Events are used as well to facilitate Lean Thinking among participants, and this suggests the need for prior training, and also means that the workshops are inherently about *active* participation, particularly since these events are sometimes the first opportunity many stakeholders have had to work together toward a common objective.
- The short time duration of these events means that prework needs to include detailed workshop planning, down to the hour, so that time is used wisely.
- Ultimate success critically depends on acting on results from the workshop, which is all the more reason at the outset to define this work so its doable and tangible results can be seen.
- The focus on having tangible results suggests we have established baseline measures (before the improvement) that we track as evidence of progress and success after implementation of the improvements.

There is an implication in several of these guidelines that we have an infrastructure in place to facilitate desired outcomes, rather like the support structure we might view as critical for the hypothetical beginning piano player we have referred to throughout the book. The young pianist needs a piano, an instructor, some method for practice, but also a variety of intangibles, such as the time to practice, parental support, a way of getting to lessons, guidance when practice becomes frustrating, etc. All of these elements together comprise a support structure that enables success and over time becomes what is really a *culture* in which practice makes perfect.

Lean Enablers

The Lean Improvement Model says that we should "enable everything," the point being that the degree to which we can facilitate the work of the Lean Problem-Solving script, the easier it is to identify and implement improvement projects. This means we are trying to remove obstacles. Surprisingly, we find in many IT (and other) operational environments that obstacles seem to be the norm and not the exception. When we identify Management Support as an enabler, for example, what we mean is that management helps remove obstacles, but again, surprisingly, we often find that management puts as many obstacles in the way as they may attempt to remove.

We have seen this happen. Operational work is characterized by bottlenecks, delays, and defects (indicators of problems, which we now know defines the opportunity space for Lean improvements). Management incorrectly concludes that individuals are to blame, so they replace people (perhaps even fire them), and instead of things getting better, they get worse. From a Lean perspective, the outcome seems rather predictable. Nothing was done to improve the underlying process or the *system* of People–Process–Technology that constrains or facilitates, as the case may be, the behavior of individuals. Replacing people did nothing except, perhaps, instill fear in everyone remaining, and that does nothing but lower morale and inhibit individuals from surfacing problems.

We have started with a description of what does *not* enable success as a counterpoint to our more positive description of enablers in the previous section, mostly because we can think of these enablers, or critical success factors, from both perspectives. We can identify what we need or want to have in place to enable success, and we also can think about what needs to be removed. Thus, enablement is one orientation and dealing with obstacles is another. We will address both in this section.

We can identify Lean Enablers from several sources. Some are directly derived from the guidance we have provided for components of the Lean Approach, e.g., effective problem-solving (employees need to be empowered to identify problems) or proper scoping for rapid improvement events (effective project management governance). In other cases, we can derive enablers from the study of Quality Management as proven success factors identified through research.[4,5] In some cases, however, you will identify enablers directly from within your own organization, by considering how improvement efforts may have been effectively implemented in the past, through lessons learned within projects, or through testimony from champions of previously successful efforts.

Regardless of the source, we can identify these enablers and position them as critically important in order to achieve desired outcomes. By the same token, however, we do not want to suggest that all these enablers need to be in place. In a sense, more is better, and some are better than none. But the fact is that many of these enablers are difficult to put in place, and this does not mean that effective Lean improvements cannot be realized without them. In one respect, we can think of these enablers as cultural artifacts that we can encourage or even create over time, and their implementation is not unlike any other type of improvement effort, except that in some cases, they are more systemic. Management support or sponsorship is the classic example. We can help management in one way or another to become better supporters of our efforts, but it's very challenging to transform management into a true enabler if it isn't already. That is a management fix, if you will, and not something that Lean practitioners will accomplish by initiating a project.

Below is a list of Lean Enablers, with short descriptions of each. As suggested, the reader will want to consider how each one is present (or not) in your own organization, and supplement this list with enablers of your own.

- *Management Support*: Management needs to be in the game, providing value-based leadership. They need to be visibly present, for example, by attending kickoff or progress meetings. They need to be able to communicate how the work being done supports their own strategic objectives (of course, it is incumbent on the practitioner to work this touch point from his or her perspective as well, leveraging notions derived from the Business–IT Value Chain). Management also needs to provide tangible evidence of support through investment in required resources. Finally, they need to listen and help to remove obstacles. One demonstration of support is in active sponsorship of change initiatives.

- *Employee Empowerment*: Lean relies a lot on employees to help identify and solve problems and this can only happen if they are empowered to do so. This means more than tacit permission, but it means they are actively supported and their efforts are reinforced. This means management needs to think about incentives that encourage employees to act in a constructive way, and it means employees need to think about how they can help the organization. While some direct attention to resistance may be needed at points in time, the goal is to move beyond this so that employees identify with their work, are proud of their work, and have motivation to improve how their work is done.

■ *Quality Awareness*: Everyone needs to be aware of the importance of quality and the impediments to ensuring its priority in all aspects of work. From the perspective of Lean problem-solving, this means attention to defects and to their elimination. But quality is also a value point that needs to be considered in any type of design activity, and practical ways of translating that into development or implementation work need to be institutionalized. Quality awareness also suggests the required role of quality oversight to address the need to ensure compliance with quality objectives.

■ *Training and Education*: Implicit in creating quality awareness is the need to provide training and educational opportunities for employees. Specifically for Lean practice, this may include formal training as well as various on-the-job opportunities for learning. One other advisable form of training is for Six Sigma, and, while we cannot quantify the correlation, we believe that presence of Six Sigma belt practitioners and the opportunity for formal Six Sigma training are most certainly Lean Enablers in their own right.

■ *Flexibly-Deployed Skills*: An assumption in some Lean solutions is that employees may need to go to where the work is, e.g., where there may be increased demands for resources. The notion is that by having multiskilled employees, it's possible to deploy these skills as needed. This also creates more opportunities and a higher interest level among employees who might otherwise feel they are stagnating in their roles. Most importantly, however, it effectively increases the capacity of an organization without increasing headcount.

■ *Decentralized Decision-Making*: We have suggested earlier that waiting for decisions is a delay point and, therefore, it represents waste. By allowing decisions to be made close to the point of activity, it minimizes the need to escalate the decision, and thus reduces the waiting time. Pushing decision-making authority down in the organization is also an indicator of trust and empowerment. We see the reverse side of this notion not infrequently, as when ideas are brought forth to individuals who say, in effect, "We will get back to you on that."

■ *Positive Communication*: Communication issues are pervasive in many organizations, as we suggested in our earlier discussion of waste. By positive communication, we mean that there is an emphasis on clear, concise, and complete communication, and also that there is closure on communication, i.e., when the communication of information results in some action or decision, everyone understands what the outcome of that action or decision is and/or is aware of any relevant feedback. If someone solicits input, for example, and some people don't provide any, but rather relate their concerns at a later date, they have not only imposed a delay on the work of others, but have given no indication to the solicitor that they had even received the message. Sometimes positive communication is practiced in very simple ways, as when someone replies to the soliciting message by saying: "Got your message and I'll get back to you tomorrow," because this closes the loop on the communication.

▪ *Project Governance*: We have suggested earlier that having a strong project or portfolio management structure in place can assist in Lean projects because there is a framework of capabilities that can be leveraged. In addition, governance also suggests that there is a mechanism in place that can evaluate Lean project opportunities, establishing criteria for this evaluation and managing Lean projects through their lifecycle. This might also include skills training and resource allocation (finding facilitators for Lean events, or ensuring that employees are properly trained in advance).

▪ *Industry Experience with Lean*: We know that some companies have a head start on Lean because it has been in use in their organizations for some time, the classic example being a Lean manufacturer. It is an enabler because it very often means that other organizations, such as IT, have an institutional if not a cultural framework in which to position their own Lean efforts. They may be required to do so, in fact, and this certainly facilitates its introduction and use.

▪ *Product and Service Design*: The degree to which products and services are designed with Lean concepts in mind will enable other supporting services, such as IT, in finding their appropriate role, and perhaps, also will influence their ability to make strategic contributions. An example might be if a bank designs an online banking service using Lean to design the business process itself and IT is able to offer ideas on how the reach or scope of these services can be increased by use of mobile technology.

▪ *Process Management*: Overall, any organization's degree of experience and expertise in process management, broadly defined, will assist in adopting Lean solutions because of the central role that process improvement plays in Lean. This might be as basic as having employees who are skilled with process mapping techniques and approaches, and also would be evident in how frequently process identification and management is incorporated into the work (e.g., in project management or business process design).

■ *Quality Data and Reporting*: In addition to quality awareness, the ability of an organization to do data capture, analysis, and reporting in support of quality initiatives will most certainly enable its ability to deliver Lean solutions because of the importance of quantitatively measuring progress against quality objectives. By extension, the ability to do this for quality purposes supports the ability to do it for any purpose, such as performance measurement.

As you find evidence of these within your organization, you may find some enablers in place and functioning well, and these can be called out as something to leverage. In other cases, rather than enablers, you may find obstacles, some of which can be addressed using the conventional problem-solving script (i.e., they also are problems to solve). Let's talk more about obstacles, because seeing these is another way of identifying what enablers need to be in place.

Dealing with Obstacles

We have made some passing recognition along the way to the common constraints that characterize IT operational work environments, and to the often unrealistic demands that are placed on IT, where more must be done with less. Simplistically, we might say that obstacles are problems so the Lean Problem-Solving script applies to these as well, and this is true. However, the reality of IT work is that some of these obstacles are challenging to overcome, and even with enablers in place, they can significantly constrain the ability to implement Lean solutions. Let's look at some of the not so uncommon obstacles we find in real life and see how the Lean approach might apply to them. Here is a list of these, many of which may seem familiar.[6]

■ Highly reactive culture
■ Highly distracted workforce (constantly keeping up with events, high degree of multitasking)
■ Organizational silos (with walls or boundaries that have to be worked through, over, or around)
■ Operational complexity, with end-to-end workflows that are hard to identify (lots of cow paths)

- Project complexity, with frequent evidence of backlogs and bottlenecks (low project success rate)
- Insufficient resources and budget
- Employee job insecurity (threats of firing for poor quality work or performance, workforce reductions)
- Low employee morale (for many reasons)
- Lack of management support or sponsorship
- Lack of overall organization objectives, strategy, or direction
- Poor communications
- Lack of supporting Knowledge Management (information is fragmented, incomplete, inaccurate, out of date)
- Lots of legacy effects, with disparate, incompatible systems, forcing lots of manual work
- Lack of metrics and measurement infrastructure
- Resistance to change
- Poor relationship between IT and the Business
- Absence of standards

We could go on, but the point is that we run across these not infrequently, and they are obstacles to progress. Some of these will look familiar because we have talked about them before. Of these, some of the most persistent obstacles are perhaps the ones easiest to tolerate, that is, unseen waste and tolerated waste, as well as the common tendency for people to be so busy doing things the way they have always done them (with all the associated rework) that they feel they have no time to do things differently.

Some of the other obstacles on this list are more systemic, however, and do not lend themselves readily to remedy using Lean Problem-Solving. However, Lean Thinking can still help. For example, the obstacles presented by a poor IT–Business relationship were addressed in earlier chapters as part of Business–IT alignment supported by Lean's focus on customer value. The Lean prerequisite of focusing first on the business process is a way of directly addressing this obstacle.

For the obstacle associated with being a highly reactive culture, we know that the Lean focus on Continuous Improvement is an inherently proactive and deliberate orientation, so we would argue that the way to address this obstacle is by demonstrating the success of approaches that are not just about chasing crises, but focus on solving underlying problems. It necessarily takes time for an organization to move from a reactive to a proactive orientation, and it happens in tandem with the overall process environment becoming more stable. Doing Lean is all about achieving stability in process over time.

What about insufficient resources? This is a very real obstacle and prevents many improvement efforts from getting off the ground. We would argue that the disconnect between required and obtainable resources is often a reflection of the disconnect between Business and IT generally. It signifies that the Business does not see value in the investment. If everyone is tightening their belt, then clearly there is pain experienced everywhere, but everyone also should be thinking constantly of how their work contributes to the larger organizational objectives. How does IT provide value to the Business? The degree to which we can make the connection between IT and business objectives, the stronger the argument for investments that contribute to these objectives. Our takeaway from this is not that it's an easy obstacle to overcome, but that Lean Thinking encourages us to look at the broader context in which the obstacle is found.

It is not uncommon, in the face of budget constraints, to reduce workforce and compel those remaining to take on more work, to do more with less. Now here we can demonstrate that Lean has a lot to say. We know from our understanding of process inefficiency and waste that this approach will not eliminate waste and may add no additional value for our customers. Whether or not a workforce is reduced, we need to seek efficiencies on an ongoing basis, streamline the work, and realize the corresponding productivity benefits, such as same work with fewer people, or more work with the same people.

Because Lean is not "mean," however, we know that we cannot and should not use Lean as the basis for mere workforce reductions. In this sense, Lean is resource agnostic and does not discriminate between People, Process, and Technology. Focus on reducing headcount is contrary to Lean Enablers and values, and certainly won't help to get employees on board for improvement efforts. If corporate directives compel us to reduce workforce, then we should get that out of the way and only then begin our Lean improvements. If management wants guidance on who to eliminate (based on skills, perhaps, or target ratios) we have a conundrum, because Lean doesn't work that way. Our belief is that this is all symptomatic of management instability (they don't know what they want, they don't know how to get there), and as Lean practitioners, we should focus on very tightly managed projects that fix real problems, asking employees to assist in these efforts, but understanding that everyone is operating under a shroud of uncertainty. And, we can help management in this cause as well.

Management as an obstacle or management as the problem also is not uncommon in many organizations. From one perspective, they ultimately own responsibility for establishing the conditions that enable success in the organization. Therefore, they are a Lean enabler. On the other hand, they are themselves under so many competing pressures and incentives that they typically operate under very complex conditions that challenge even the most capable of individuals. It is sometimes easy to be critical of management when there is absence of support or the appearance of imposing unnecessary obstacles, but let's not be too critical and rather think of this in another way, using Lean Thinking.

If IT is a service, management can be viewed as the service owner and, as an owner, has a vested stake in our success. We as practitioners need their sponsorship as we look to improve service and provide benefits and value to the customer—our business partners. One of their objectives is to ensure that their services are successful and the business does not look outside for better, cheaper services.

Another outcome of looking at our management problem this way is to look at our work as that of a service provider. We can provide services to our customers and, in so doing, we are developing a portfolio of service capabilities that our management can support as well. What better expression of the value of our work than to have our management serve in a marketing role. We can consider other supportive structures and roles, such as that of Business Relationship Managers, and this really amounts to building out management capabilities that support our line of work. If our line of work is based on Lean Thinking, then management inherits the benefits of this as well.

From our perspective in IT, management provides governance over our work, but also it can be viewed as a customer of our work. As a customer, management has customer values, and it is our job to identify these and have our work align accordingly. If we are lucky, management values will align somewhat with business values, but they may have their own distinct set of value points as well. Hence, we need to figure out what these are and include delivery to these values in our work. This may be as simple as creating good reports on our work so that the underlying data are comprehensible and it gets easier and easier to show success over time. Our successes should be their successes as well. In other cases, we may need to work on how we present our work to management so it can be consumed by them for the reporting that they are obligated to do. We work on this like we would any other improvement effort.

Lean Thinking also encourages us to think about waste elimination, of course, and this should be of immediate interest to management, because it provides the best way of addressing inefficiencies that otherwise are often dealt with indirectly (e.g., by reducing headcount). With some education on the Lean Approach, we believe this can become a frequent topic for discussion between IT and management and, in the process, management will become more familiar with our work and we will become more familiar with their objectives.

We want to address one other obstacle that may arise during information gathering, for example, in support of developing a Value Stream Map (VSM). It can happen that employees are resistant to the efforts being made to improve the work at hand. They may feel threatened, legitimately or not, or they simply may be resistant to change. They may like things the way they are. This certainly qualifies as an obstacle. As we suggested earlier, having good working relations with these employees helps immensely, and some people are probably better than others in developing the types of relationships that facilitate information gathering. Management support also helps, of course, since they can assuage anxieties and set expectations. We also find that many people respond quite well to simply being asked about their work, what is going well and what isn't, and for the latter, specifically asking them what prevents them from doing their job well. If employees are on board early in the process and can see benefits that can accrue from active participation, they will more readily accept the prospects of change. In general, then, our approach suggests that employee empowerment (an enabler) is the best way of addressing the obstacle. We don't overcome resistance, but rather empower employees to be the change agents that they are capable of becoming.

Tool: 5 Questions

We want to end this section with another Lean tool that addresses several of the elements we have been discussing. True to the Lean approach generally, it is spare in rendition, but deep in implications. It is called the *5 Questions* and is a technique to facilitate implementation of improvements, including elements of both A3 Thinking and PDCA.[7] It also encompasses many of the activities that are typically associated with Kaizen. Here are the 5 questions:

1. What is the target condition?
2. What is the actual condition now?
3. What obstacles are now preventing you from reaching the target condition?

4. What is your next step?

5. When can you go and see what you have learned from taking that step?

Actual and target conditions represent Current State and Future State (here, we begin with the Future State, rather than the Current State as we recommended earlier in the book; this difference suggests that the technique was designed more for implementing new improvements rather than directly for problem-solving). Question 3 is all about obstacles and it's important that obstacles are identified in the context of reaching a target. Question 4 is, by implication, about the use of PDCA, and Question 5 is about Gemba (Go and See). We like this tool as an easy way to foster communication around objectives in a guided path scenario.

Lean Culture

What does it mean to have a Lean culture? We don't believe this should be the goal of an organization. It is perhaps an ideal end-state, but organizations that have what we call Lean culture are constantly engaged in Lean improvement activities and in enablement of these, so one might say that the journey itself is the point rather than reaching some destination.

We believe that the practices expressed in this and many other books on Lean are what will provide the pathways for the Lean journey. There are many routes that might be taken, and sincerity of intent and willingness to work and learn are the most reliable partners. Once undertaken, Lean practitioners learn from practitioners across many other disciplines and industries and constantly work to bring new insights or practices into their own organizations. As Lean IT practitioners, this means we have a lot that can be learned from Lean practices in manufacturing, hospitals, services, administration, and many other areas of application.

At the end of the day, culture is a complex expression of ingrained behaviors that characterize how people work with each other, through process, and supported by tools and technology. These behaviors are the result of practice (good or bad). When employees come to management with ideas for improvement, and management views its role as that of removal of obstacles so that improvements can be made, this is an indicator of a Lean culture. It is also expressed in the language, so that when Kaizen, PDCA, A3, and other concepts and practices are commonly referenced in meetings and conversations, this is another indicator.

While we can insert the right language into our discussions, and perhaps also into the fabric of the organization, by having Lean activities as part of project templates, for example, we know that it is in practice where cultural outcomes are best realized. It is in this way that practice of the philosophy of Kaizen, or Continuous Improvement, becomes imprinted as a cultural footprint. As we build out Lean capabilities over time, they become the routine for how work is done and this is the best expression of embedding practice in culture.

Metrics and Measurement

We haven't talked a lot about metrics throughout the book, except to suggest that data collection to validate observations is important, and that any project should establish a measureable baseline by which to track improvement gains. We also indicated that having quality data and reporting is an enabler, and this also suggests the importance of addressing requirements for metrics and measurement.

From the ITIL perspective of Continual Service Improvement (CSI), metrics are defined by beginning with Critical Success Factors (CSF), deriving Key Performance Indicators (KPI), and then identifying metrics and their underlying measurements.[8] For example, if we identify a CSF for Incident Management as "efficiency of operation," we might identify a corresponding KPI as "size of queue backlog," with the implied trend logic that efficiency is gained as the size of the queue goes down. We can then identify an underlying metric for number of tickets in queue exceeding a certain threshold, for example, longer than five minutes. (We might also identify other metrics that apply.) Finally, we can decompose the metric into actual measurements that will be made, presumably, within the ticketing system. These will map to specific data fields or attributes, and the actual measurement data (e.g., data in queue by time period) are then calculated to derive the metric, which in turn supports the KPI, which supports the CSF. (By the way, ITIL provides examples of CSF and KPI associated with processes within the Library, so this is a good additional source of these for consideration.)

The logic we have just followed is top-down, although the reality is that most organizations already have metrics in place. It is possible to reverse engineer KPI and CSF from the metrics in use, a somewhat strange, but doable, way of answering the question: "Why are we measuring this particular thing?" Often times the real answer is: "We don't know" or "We have

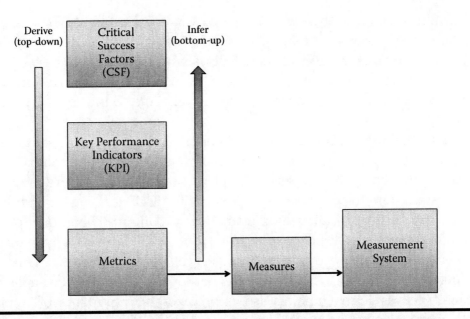

Figure 8.1 Critical Success Factors (CSFs), Key Performance Indicators (KPIs), and metrics.

always measured this," which is not really a good basis for continuing the effort. Many times we see where reporting is done and there are indicators that metrics are not understood or leveraged adequately, as happens when people ask about the meaning of a metric or a trend of data when the report has been used for a long period of time. We also see many examples where metrics are not actionable (nobody knows what to do when trends go up or down). From a Lean perspective, this is all evidence of waste, and so we want to treat it that way.

We can capture this top-down and bottom-up approach in the diagram in Figure 8.1. Sometimes we derive metrics from both of these perspectives until we settle on the right ones. Because supporting measurement systems often introduce their own challenges, it's sometimes very difficult to measure what we want to measure using the tools for data capture and reporting that we may have at our disposal. We probably will have quite enough to work on if we just generate an initial set of 3–5 metrics and work out all the issues associated with their measurement. Implementing a measurement system can be, as we say, challenging, and while we will not get into the nuances of this here, suffice it to say that the nature of the challenges need to be assessed early on, because the timeline for addressing these can sometimes be quite long. The best approach is to understand the current state of the measurement process, treat it like any other workflow where we need to identify waste, and then problem-solve to address underlying root causes. Because measurement systems suggest automation, we need to clarify the process, then automate the solution. This is where timelines can enter in, because these may require customization of existing tools or investment in new ones. Please do not underestimate the degree of difficulty you can find here.

Lean Thinking encourages clarified understanding of metrics (what are we measuring, why are we measuring it, how do we interpret trends, what are our contingencies for trends?). Coupled with this is an understanding of statistical thinking, so there is a good understanding of what trend data means (e.g., is it really a trend or just natural variation?). This is one touch point between Lean and Six Sigma and is one of the reasons why many practitioners wear both hats. Our approach here is that while Six Sigma can definitely help in the Lean journey, it is not a prerequisite for accomplishing Lean objectives. Lean Thinking also emphasizes the importance of quantifiable observation and, from this, we encourage the identification of baseline data for measurement of Lean improvements. This is really where we want the reader to have some takeaways for doing Lean improvements.

We need to understand the Current State of a target process using verifiable data, and while this does not need to be statistically comprehensive, it should be accurate and representative. We don't need precision so much as relevance, and we need to know that we have looked beyond casual observation and personal anecdote to get to some facts from which we can work. We might have three months of trend data, and while this may not represent the best or correct data set from which we will derive statistical results, we know that it is much better than nothing. The litmus test is whether all stakeholders comprehend the nature of the data and agree on their implication. We can improve our statistical approach over time (using Six Sigma), but for our beginning steps, we just need to make sure we are operating in the field of facts and data.

If we have a baseline, we can then identify what changes in data we would expect to see as a result of the improvements we put in place. Where we don't have the baseline data to begin with, we need to identify the metrics we will use to track progress and begin data measurement right away. This is planned activity and not an afterthought.

With before-and-after data, we can track progress of our improvement activities. We can report on this progress, which carries with it both a pure reporting perspective (What data do we report on? To whom?), but there also is a presentation factor that we can take into account. We can look at the requirements of our various audiences and consider how the packaging of the data facilitates the right line of inquiry, for example, or sets the stage for actionable decision making based on observed data. The point here is that an end-to-end perspective on metrics and measurement means that data serve the Check phase function in the PDCA loop, meaning that we need to be attentive to all other phases.

As with any activity that is process-enabled, we will improve our data capture and reporting practices over time. We do so by deliberately attending to it as an improvement solution in its own right. We have all the tools we need at our disposal, and the hard part is really just focusing attention on this as part of our customary way of doing work.

Lean IT at Work

In the remainder of this chapter, we want to show how Lean practitioners do their work in IT. The purpose is to show use of concepts and practices in real-life contexts. In some cases, this is an expression of what works, even best practice, and in other cases, it represents an acknowledgment of what hasn't worked so well. That is reality and it underscores how Lean practitioners take conditions on the ground and use Lean to create new opportunities. In all of these cases, we find evidence of many of the attributes of Continuous Improvement and Lean Enablers that we have discussed throughout this chapter.

Our case examples reflect experiences in IT in three related industries: healthcare, health insurance, and hospitals. These industries have a long history of experience in use of Lean, and it is certainly not a coincidence that we find indicators of use of Lean IT within them. That is to say, Lean IT practices are enabled by the organization's own history and legacy in use of Lean. This is important, although, as we suggested earlier, we don't believe it represents a constraint on use of Lean IT in other industries where this history does not exist. We think that it is more a matter of exposure, education, and practice.

Lean IT in a Healthcare Company

Our first case study is derived from interviews with a senior IT analyst at a large healthcare company where Lean applications in IT have been underway over a period of several years. This is a reflection of the use of Lean within the healthcare industry generally, as well as this individual's own background in manufacturing. Within the company, there is an enterprise-wide programmatic structure for use of Lean within subordinate businesses and functions, including IT. In their case, this is a hybrid approach that combines Lean with Six Sigma (L6S), with flexible use of practices and tools derived from each methodology depending on the needs of the improvement projects.

The experience at this company reflects the common pattern where Lean practices begin in the manufacturing environment and then over time are rolled out to other business areas and functions. Also common within the healthcare industry are issues of integration (e.g., from mergers) and scalability. They have found that having an underlying L6S framework for work helps to implement integration and support requirements for scalability.

Within this company's IT organization, there is also a strong foundation in ITIL best practice. The intersection of ITIL's notion of Continual Service Improvement (CSI) with L6S as a supporting quality system is well understood and has been institutionalized in many ways. The entirety of IT, for instance, has fully vested L6S components, including extensive training for all employees and recruitment of certified Six Sigma black and green belts, with a supporting level of other belts. The purpose of this is to promulgate the "culture" of what it means to approach projects and operational work from an L6S point of view.

While recruitment was a focus in the recent past, an indicator of the degree to which L6S has become institutionalized is evident in the current focus on using L6S resources on projects. Project managers have learned to look at projects from an L6S perspective and, in so doing, they incorporate deliverables that reflect Lean and Six Sigma and also leverage the skilled resources available to them to support their projects. At this point in time, the integral use of L6S tools and approaches within projects has become routine. In support of this, there is an L6S group that has this as its sole function and its scope is enterprise-wide.

Fundamental to the widespread use of the L6S approach is to help project managers, and all employees for that matter, speak a common language about work, processes, and improvement. The core question that everyone is asked to consider is this: What is the problem we are trying to solve and how does the resolution of this problem add value to our customers? Problem-solving and value creation provide the primary orientation that is required for all projects. With regards to projects, the corresponding challenge is to "define the problem" versus "define the project."

For problem-solving, they use the 5 Whys as a common tool and encourage analysts to seek root cause in such a way that the most important factors can be identified ("big whys" versus "little whys") and that quantifiable measures of the Current State can be obtained, in order to provide the baseline for verifiable improvements. For problem resolution, small incremental improvements (versus large projects with long timelines) are not only okay, but, in fact, fuel the underlying engine for long-term cultural transformation. Their philosophy is to not let the search for a comprehensive, ideal solution become an obstacle to seeking immediate, sustainable improvements. The philosophy is simple: "Don't let the perfect get in the way of the better."

In addition to its cumulative effect over time, small improvements also have the advantage of providing additional perspective on the problem at hand. That is, with some ground gained in resolving a problem, it is then possible to look at that problem from a new and better perspective.

An example brings some of these notions together. There was the case where a manager looked at a certain problem in such a way that its resolution would likely take six months to implement. In fact, this manager's idea of problem and solution was not based on root cause, but on motivations that pertained to his role (e.g., he wanted to keep his scorecard green). As a consequence, he was looking at the project and not at the problem. In this case, the lack of a good Root Cause Analysis (RCA), along with lack of transparency on actual metrics to characterize the work of his organization (the "honest scorecard"), served as obstacles to real problem-solving. You cannot get to continual improvement, after all, without accepting that something needs improvement.

Overcoming these obstacles required several different approaches, including getting everyone on the same page, asking tough but important questions (e.g., if the manager can ask the question in the first place, can he also accept the answers he gets?), and encouraging transparency (through quantitative, metric-based scorecards). These themes underscore another philosophical underpinning of their approach, summarized again simply as "Show me the science."

Quantification and good analysis of data are critical to science and critical to the L6S approach as employed by this IT organization. In another case, a group defined and encouraged operational work that showed absolutely no evidence of defects. In the commonplace environment of IT operational work, where there is typically a high level of variation in performance, this stuck out like a sore thumb and encouraged a new look at how the metrics were defined and what value they should provide over time to improve the process rather than accepting performance as perfect based on current metrics.

In addition to incorporating L6S deliverables within projects (e.g., requiring that business cases be developed up front to focus attention on customer value), they also use mini-Kaizen events as a mechanism for facilitating short-term projects. These events are facilitated by skilled individuals who are deployed from the L6S group that governs training and use of the methodology. They are involved in the early stages of the projects in order to do planning and ensure that deliverable requirements are met, and then are used during the Kaizen events to facilitate to the desired outcomes.

Kaizen events involve getting the right people together for the duration of the workshop, typically one to two days in length, perhaps three days, and no longer than five days for larger projects. The goal is to get from problem definition to root cause to problem solution as quickly as possible. Projects are scoped to fit these aggressive timelines, reinforcing the notion of focusing on incremental improvements. In one case, for instance, an implemented change control process was Leaned out, then brought back to a new implemented state using a Kaizen event. The use of Kaizen is about getting to an incremental improvement goal, standardizing the improvement, and then looking for the next incremental improvement.

Even when Kaizen events are not used, L6S concepts are still employed on projects throughout planning, execution, and control, in order to eliminate waste and focus on customer value. An example of a larger project where this applied was for technology/resource consolidation efforts. On these large-scale projects, it is quite common to specifically employ Six Sigma's DMAIC (Define–Measure–Analyze–Improve–Control) methodology.

Other than this distinction, where Lean tools and practices are used on projects with end-to-end requirements for waste elimination, and DMAIC is used on larger projects, differences between the approaches are not emphasized. The focus is more on using tools intelligently to meet objectives; i.e., it is on how the tools are used rather than which ones are used.

Because many of the L6S practices have become institutionalized, there is not much resistance to their use, and this serves as another indicator of the relative maturity of the organization. Everyone working on projects has learned to adopt a business case perspective with focus on the problem they are trying to solve. If it's determined that there is limited customer value in the project, they don't do it. There also is sensitivity to the cost benefit of specifically adopting a Lean orientation, with focus on elimination of waste. Cost savings from removal of waste is understood to result in the benefit of applying these saved monies to higher-value initiatives. Their philosophy is to do more with less and this means continuously "Leaning" the organization.

Encouraging employees to look for opportunities for improvement is supported by general L6S training referred to above. In this way, it helps employees "learn to see" problems and, most importantly, what to do about them. In this way, it's possible to have problem identification driven from the bottom up.

Because L6S has been institutionalized within the project framework, there is a relatively simple path from problem identification to formal review. First, the employee would review the problem with his or her manager. If it seems reasonable to move this forward as a project, it will be reviewed within the project portfolio governance process, which would impose L6S-based deliverable requirements (e.g., business case) as well as rationalize and prioritize the project upon review. Because it enables project work in alignment with L6S objectives, it's possible to view Project Portfolio Management itself as a critical success factor for sustainable improvements.

Also supportive of these objectives are a variety of tools and resources that employees and Project Managers can take advantage of, including online forms and templates, FAQs, etc. There also are award programs and other incentives for employees to follow the prescribed approaches. While these supporting elements contribute to cultural acceptance, they do not eliminate the need for enforcement and reward mechanisms to drive desired behaviors.

Some Lean practices also can be applied to Project Management processes themselves. Whereas it is common to have multiple projects underway, often with conflicting priorities and resource demands, the Lean Approach encourages management of fewer projects at one time as one way of having fewer failed projects. They have observed that, while pressures to meet project deadlines may be unavoidable, it is important as well to do real Root Cause Analysis on project failures. Very often Lessons Learned, in fact, are not incorporated within a learning feedback loop, so that nothing is actually learned about project failure. The aligned L6S and Project Portfolio Management governance capabilities discussed above, therefore, are viewed as mechanisms to avoid this cycle of failure. Continual improvement requires measurement and documentation of failures as well as successes. The focus is on moving past implementation to realization of desired outcomes.

With regards to using this approach in IT generally, their observation is that because many other organizations have used Lean for significant gain over the years, the question for IT is: Why is it any different? Looking ahead to new computing paradigms such as cloud computing, the fundamental questions still remain the same; that is, what is the business case, where is the customer value, and what is the problem we are trying to solve? Because customer value means alignment with business objectives (we need a "line of sight to business values"), Lean is viewed as entirely synchronous with the ITIL orientation toward viewing IT like a service provider. This orientation mandates a service perspective for the sake of survival itself, because if IT doesn't provide customer value at competitive cost (achieved through Leaning), customers will seek other options (e.g., through outsourcing).

Lean IT at a Health Insurance Company

Bob Grinsell is Enterprise Business Relationship Manager at a large health insurer where there is a history of applying Lean practices within both the business and IT. Bob's background in IT Service Management, customer service, process improvement, and project management, along with the strong influence of Lean practices developed within the company, have contributed to his ability to identify and implement Lean IT process improvements in support of the business units he serves.

Bob received his Lean training and had his initial experiences in applying Lean practices in support of Request Management and Service Catalog processes. Early on, they had outdated software in support of ITSM (IT Service Management) capabilities and, in conjunction with a software migration to a new application environment, they addressed a variety of process efficiency needs.

This company began to develop competencies in Lean around 2004, when it initiated widespread training of employees in order to instill Lean thinking within process operations throughout the company. Waves of training over a several-year period and the development of a Center of Excellence for Lean resulted in a locus of specialized knowledge with over 40 Lean practitioners and 100 trained champions and process owners. An internal belt certification (similar to Six Sigma) was initiated to provide consistent competencies and experience among practitioners. By 2007/2008 there had been over 100 Lean events in the company.

The structure of Lean events was relatively consistent. These were initiated at first as four-day events, but eventually were streamlined to fit in three days. The agenda on Day 1 included introduction of Lean concepts, including role playing simulations to help participants start to "think Lean."

By Day 2, it was usually possible to address Current State to Future State activities. There were several enabling controls that were characteristic of every Lean event, including the required involvement of executive champions and sponsors, midevent report outs, and summary reports that emphasized business benefits. In addition, of course, there was typically a good deal of work that went into preparation for events, including proper scoping. One outcome of an event was a Development Plan, which served as the Implementation roadmap, with 30-, 60-, and 90-day milestones. This ensured accountability and helped drive implementation results going forward.

An example of a Lean event involved firewall IDs. In order to access and modify data in production environments, there were a variety of security requirements that had to be met and several processes in place to support them, including a code checkout process and various approval processes. In addition, there were three supporting systems in place, with no data integration between them. In short, this was a great example of an operational process that had evolved over time to accommodate a growing set of needs with a severe trade-off in efficiency of operation. The focus of the Lean event was on identifying a streamlined process.

In streamlining processes, with stakeholders in the room, the question is often asked: Why do you need this information? It is not uncommon to find out upon questioning the reason something is done a certain way that, in fact, nobody needs the information. As supporting tools, it has helped to begin with decision trees and process flows, from which it is then easier to generate a Value Stream Map.

Another example involved the process of reviewing and approving requests for modifications to software, otherwise referred to as the application development intake project. For this Lean event, Bob looked at activities for engaging IT, including estimation of project time. Because development work was moving to an outsourced model, they were careful about how they specified their work requirements because they were paying for it. Improvement efforts were also driven by the company's desire to incorporate ITIL best practices for Release Management, including intake, evaluation, and governance. Full tracking of work was required, because in the pre-event state, there was no consistency in how work was requested.

In preparation, Bob held interviews with business and IT groups, addressing the question: How do you take work in? Additional questions addressed what developers needed to know as the result of the process, and what business requestors needed to know. Various processes and tools were in use and procedures were viewed as cumbersome and complex. Adhering to the controls that characterized all Lean events, there was a high-level executive champion who helped ensure managers saw the value of committing their people's time to the effort. Also as part of preparation, they identified and prepared process flowcharts of the existing processes using Value Stream Maps. Semantics also were addressed by agreeing on shared definitions for business risks or functional specifications. There was an activity-by-activity review from which they identified a Future State VSM as well as a new request template. These efforts, which helped to compensate for the fact that many event workshop participants had never even spoken to each other before, resulted in a unified process and an improved level of idea sharing and understanding. After the workshop, the project team prototyped a new unified intake form plus associated workflow, all of which took several months to complete. The new process was piloted with specific user and support groups, and rolled out to additional participants as word spread about the improvements. Finally, they leveraged the success they had achieved in order to apply benefits elsewhere in the company, and also to assure compliance with the new process. This also led to the development of a Governance Board that resulted in greater participation from the business groups in the prioritization of IT work.

Another project involved requests for funding approval, which included decision-making activities for software acquisition and procurement of consulting resources. This project addressed both process and tools, with a request intake tool being of central focus. While it took one year to go fully live and was characterized by considerable complexity, this was still based on a single Lean event. With greater scope and complexity, more work is needed up-front, including lots of documentation. In addition, work on this project reinforced the general Lean guidance to first simplify a process and only then automate.

Employee on-boarding was another area of focus, involving, among others, Human Resources (HR), IT, Information Security, and Physical Security. The complexity and scope of the process was more than could be addressed in a single Lean event and work in this area is still ongoing. To get a full picture of the interdependent factors, it was necessary to start by addressing the question: Who starts the process? It turns out that this was a surprisingly difficult question to answer. One component of the overall flow began by looking at request processes (e.g., physical access to a building) that led to consideration of the process for new employees requesting access to data centers. In a case such as this, it becomes necessary to control "scope creep" and establish what are reasonable expectations for success. This becomes a challenge in defining a project scope that is both doable and addresses the real underlying efficiency problems.

They streamlined components of the overall flow, addressing questions such as: How long does it take to fill out a form? and How many different forms are required? The new process is more efficient, although Bob acknowledges that it's difficult to quantify results in projects of this sort. (In other projects, it has been easier to identify metrics, e.g., a project focused on inaccurate mailings.) While the measures were intangible, it generated customer goodwill, resulting in better IT–Business alignment, which in this case, was more important than having metrics that showed tangible benefits.

The Center of Excellence provided governance for process improvement and also served as the decision-making forum for prioritizing improvement opportunities. It provided a conduit to submit candidate projects. At quarterly Lean practitioner meetings, work that had been done and work on the candidate list would be reviewed. This was a common vehicle for identifying new opportunities. Further, in order to become a Lean practitioner, one had to be actively submitting event candidates, and also assisting or leading new events. To make all of this work, it was necessary to have a mix of Subject Matter Experts who could be called upon in support of Lean projects (time management requirements mean that you can't call on the same people all of the time). Champions across the organization provided balanced consideration of opportunities.

Champions also were critical because it is not uncommon for employees to be uneasy when asked to participate in Lean events. There is the concern that there will be job impact, such as managing an employee's existing workload while they are participating, or that the Lean event could result in their jobs being eliminated. It is the role of the champion to provide assurance to employees and overall support for the work.

Following these several productive years of Lean activity and promotion, when Lean was viewed as a critical success factor for process simplification and standardization, in 2009, the company stopped practitioner training and the resources of the Center of Excellence were distributed into business support services organizations. This was intended to help socialize Lean practices and otherwise weave Lean Thinking into the fabric of the company by incorporating these practices as business-as-usual for process improvement. While there has been strong routinization of Lean practices, it is also probably the case that these changes have diluted somewhat the focus on Lean, and overall awareness among employees has tapered off.

Despite the somewhat diluted form that Lean practices have in the company now, they are no less important for the work that Bob does, which is reinforcing the notion that effective Lean practices can be applied even in the absence of supporting management structures. In his years of experience, he has also gained a greater understanding of how tools support Lean Thinking. For example, when asked about his experience with mistake proofing, it is clear that in his mind this is strongly aligned with Continual Service Improvement objectives, and can be found in specific practices that reinforce desired behaviors, such as when defects in software are identified during QA testing and especially User Acceptance Testing, where someone asks of the customer, in effect: "Is this what you said you wanted?"

Checklists are another Lean tool, and these can be found in run books, workflow diagrams, and procedure manuals (e.g., with steps identified for accessing a database). The message here that Bob conveys, again aligning the use of the tool with Lean Thinking, is that it is important to make sure that any checklist or guidance of any sort that might be contained in procedure, process, or policy manuals, is kept *simple*. At the end of the day, you don't want thick manuals, but rather guidance that is both useful and accessible. You can publish the greatest procedures document in the world, but if it isn't accepted and used, it isn't actually very useful.

Lean IT in a Hospital

Dan Lafever is the IT Service Quality Manager for the IS organization at a regional hospital system in the Midwest. This is a relatively new position for Dan. Previously when he served as Help Desk Manager, he asked to be mentored by one of the hospital's Six Sigma black belts and attended several meetings on Continuous Improvement at a local Lean network association. He was able to successfully apply Lean and Six Sigma principles and improve Help Desk performance with a number of projects. In his new role, he has a broader mandate to implement Lean throughout the organization. As we will see, Dan has had great success in identifying opportunities for improvement and then implementing improvements using principles and practices associated with both incremental improvement and Rapid Improvement Events. When asked by management how he intended to begin work in his new role, Dan referred to these principles and practices and replied that he would "go where the pain is" and look for opportunities where he could show results.

Dan's experience was that this orientation was neither natural nor accepted practice within IT (not in the "DNA" of IT), so the initial challenge was how to help people understand the mindset of Continual Service Improvement; the idea being that you start here (focusing on attitude and thinking), rather than with tools, on the assumption that as the mind adopts concepts, it becomes easier to adopt tools. In fact, there are many tools that may be used, and very often, simple tools suffice as long as they are used to best advantage.

In order to promulgate this approach to the entire company, Dan used an ideas database (originally developed for hospital employees) to have staff submit IT improvement ideas, looking for opportunities to do small incremental improvements. In addition, he does active marketing of concepts related to their approach toward improvement, with a focus on small incremental improvement as key to his overall strategy. This approach is sometimes referred to as "quick and easy Kaizen."[9]

Fundamental to Dan's approach is the notion of Rapid Improvement Events where the focus is on seeing results quickly. Rapid Improvement Events, based on the "Kaizen blitz" model, are typically a few days in length with lots of prep work. He is now working on an event for a security request provisioning process. There was pain, with too much work-in-progress (WIP), too much delay, and customer feedback that the process took too long (not good turnaround in a timely fashion). First they discussed their motivations. Was it to get quick results or was this perceived as an "incentive project" (where bonus points can be earned)? As a Rapid Improvement Event, pre-analysis is critical and this includes mapping the process, deciding what data can be collected, and gaining inputs from the customer, introducing the issue of how in general to get customers to participate in such an event. They then discuss next steps and meet with the team, with the goal of doing enough prep work so they can do the event in a couple of days and then implement fixes immediately.

This approach encourages focus on small projects, whereas big projects may be more suitable for tools like L6S. With Lean, minimal training is needed in order to introduce concepts and the focus can often be on what's "good enough," with the notion of then perfecting results over time (versus getting it perfect up-front). This approach often lends itself to grassroots efforts (without the overhead of big projects) and it is Dan's experience that successes at this level can naturally lead to leverage of results for other small projects and increased awareness leading to broader interest in use of Lean.

His belief is that people need to have hands-on experience with this approach in order to "get it." Generating concrete examples of how Lean can be used provides testimony of how it works, and also helps to shape people's thinking, so that they can gain confidence in the approach—"Yes, we can do this." In this respect, sharing stories also helps.

Dan cites his own personal story where he managed to win a Help Desk haiku contest by engaging in Lean thinking, including implementing the following steps: First, identify the rules (constraints), one of which was to adhere to the correct number of syllables for a valid haiku (5/7/5). Then, he looked at how he could improve quality, and, for this, he used a syllable checker. Then he added some process checks in generating samples and, in this context, he strived to be creative. He wanted to be able to come up with some way of predicting his success (prediction analytics), and, for this, he searched through tweets of his samples and determined who had retweeted what he had written (this also provides input on VOC). The end result was that he had personalized Lean concepts, reinforcing the approach, and as a result of doing this, he also won the contest. Here is the winning haiku:

> Help Desk horror flick:
> Rogue tech kills main router in
> "Silence of the LANS"

Similarly, there is value in use of analogies to help people understand Lean concepts. This notion could be applied to the use of Root Cause Analysis, for example, by simply asking what other things have the same sort of problems. Dan cited an example of an analogy that worked well for him at a conference he attended. He talked about the badge that was provided to conference attendees, which included the schedule, plus tickets for food and drink. It was a jumble of parts, but Dan worked to improve the packaging (through continuous improvement) and was able to actually measure the positive results by reducing the amount of time it took him to locate the schedule of events he wanted to attend. He shared this experience with the audience and it resonated as a great example of applying Lean concepts in order to realize tangible improvements in a short period of time.

Applying Lean notions to IT has sometimes meant taking ideas from other applications observed elsewhere and then thinking through the process of how it relates to IT. For example, Dan visited a bakery where he observed that employees were looking at quality measures every few minutes. In IT, in contrast, it seemed much less common to look at quality indicators on a frequent, even daily basis, and, in fact, more common to not look at them at all unless there is a crisis. There are many reports (e.g., monthly reports), but Dan works on the philosophy that if you wait until the report comes out, it's already too late. He believes that IT needs to understand how it's doing *right now*, and in that context, the question then is: What are the key quality measures for IT and the business?

The general theme is that it's possible to adapt lessons from other Lean environments and apply them to IT. In a sense, Dan finds Lean learning experiences practically everywhere (Lean Thinking) and tries to tie it back to the work at hand. This characterizes his Lean journey. He also notes that if you adopt the philosophy of Continuous Improvement, you are always learning and this can compensate for simple and common things, such as "missing something" or "making mistakes," because by always focusing on improvement, you will eventually figure it out.

These approaches to use and communication of Lean concepts can help to promote Lean Thinking throughout the organization. When employees believe there is a way to solve problems they experience ("pain points") and management can provide the means by which these opportunities can be identified and worked on, every individual then becomes an agent of change. As Dan says, the best Continual Service Improvement experts already work for you. This suggests that the role of management is more about mentorship and this, in the long run, is more important than training or book learning. In addition, this approach lends itself to a grassroots effort approach to improvements. While this bottom-up approach seems unlike a "big strategy" for Continual Service Improvement, this really represents a strategic orientation that can lead, over time, to a real culture of quality and improvement.

The use of specific Lean tools can now be understood within this larger strategic framework. For example, they have historically struggled with Problem Management at this company. Root Cause Analysis was primarily reactive and ITIL guidance did not seem to help much to get improvements. Dan incorporated *5 Whys* into the RCA process and this is now used to generate results. Importantly, he publishes these results to the entire company, on the principle that it's good to make problems visible. He is now starting to train other employees to use this approach to RCA.

They also have incorporated use of checklists in their IT operations. For example, to support use of their electronic medical records system (EPIC), checklists were prepared for each person in the EPIC call center as follow-up to quick training. Every agent had a checklist for use before a shift began: one when they were working and one as a postshift checklist. A team of individuals created the checklists by identifying possible problems agents were going to face, about which they could do something. For example, they discovered that headset batteries would run down after 9 to 10 hours, so for a 12-hour shift, staff needed to cradle them frequently. This was then incorporated into the checklist.

Improvements were made to these checklists over time, making modifications as needed. For example, some checklists were either not understood or not used (e.g., for go-live certification), so for this, they made observations and did RCA to find out why. Note that this is consistent with Dan's overall philosophy of making small incremental improvements with results made better over time (the underlying notion of Continual Service Improvement). He is also a believer in making problems visible, and as the example of the headsets demonstrates, he places great importance on mistake proofing.

Sometimes this approach leads to surprising observations. For example, they did RCA on processing time cards and it turned out there was a button that made it easy to delete all the timesheets. When talking to staff about how to mistake proof this so that it couldn't happen, it was discovered that some staff were resistant because they assumed the end result would be to identify people who "screwed up." From this, it was an important learning step to emphasize that this was about *error*-proofing, and not *fool*-proofing.

Application of Lean Thinking has been applied to the call center itself. Calls to the EPIC call center led to experimentation with Just-in-Time (JIT) notions and what it means to have a Lean Call Center. Calls would come in and one goal was to involve EPIC Subject Matter Experts (SME) early on in the call cycle. First, this was construed as a thought experiment, which began this way: Ten calls into the call center, with eight agents, means a backup of two calls. Building in extra capacity that could be deployed quickly to handle overflow was one way of making the call center Lean. Dan was able to make this work, although it was difficult. From a Lean perspective, calls in queue are WIP, so this is like reducing WIP/inventory through level production techniques. It is also an example of JIT operations.

Next, they analyzed calls, e.g., identifying problems with specific EPIC modules. Whereas the traditional approach is to hand off issues and have them sit in someone's queue; here, they wanted to enable support by pulling in experts to calls early on. To do this, they needed to categorize requests. If the customer needed education ("how to" information), they looked at ways of providing on-demand education. When the Help Desk was unable to resolve a call (causing WIP to go up and with backlogs), they would try to pull in the SME as JIT support. The SME staff had other support duties, so these would be interrupted when they were brought into a call. This was done as either a "warm transfer" or as a three-way call. Note in this approach the attention to customer value.

From a patient portal, calls could be made to the call center directly from patients. Here, they identified common problems, did RCA of calls, and then addressed underlying issues in order to reduce volume and encourage more self-service. Because the highest cost resource is the SME, the goal was to error proof processes so the customer didn't need to call in the first place. These are good examples of focusing on the "big picture" (avoid remediation by fixing the real problem).

Dan also has experimented with use of 5S. This proved to be challenging and it was sometimes difficult to get groups on board. They began with use of the tool for addressing use of headsets, but discovered that while they could do some initial cleanup, it was fairly easy for things to get messy again. They also experimented with use of this on cleaning up file shares ("virtual stuff"), but again, it proved difficult to keep people focused on the objective. Even exercising the philosophy of looking at pain points, and despite the fact that there are several examples where 5S has been used in the hospital itself, it has proved difficult to convince folks who don't think they need to share something (e.g., on their desktop) that they will benefit from going through this type of exercise. He is still working on this because he thinks it could be a useful tool.

Dan is in his fifth year of his Lean journey, and regards himself as just getting started. As he looks ahead, he asks himself what he has had success with (and why) and what he has not had success with (and why). A lot of potential opportunities are based just on simple process observations. This reinforces the notion of looking and seeing for oneself (*Going to Gemba*).

Summary

In this chapter, we introduced several enablers of success for Lean improvement initiatives, and also discussed some common obstacles that are faced by practitioners involved in any kind of improvement effort. We used this discussion as a springboard to present three different case experiences from individuals who have been involved in implementation of Lean IT solutions. Their experiences cover the spectrum of activities we have discussed throughout the book and also provide a reality check on how these activities are performed in real operational environments. It is our hope that their experiences will lend credibility to the value and utility of the Lean practices they describe.

References

1. Imai, M. *Gemba kaizen*. 1997. New York: McGraw-Hill.
2. Tapping, D. 2007. *The Lean pocket handbook for kaizen events*. Chelsea, MI: MCS Media.
3. Bodek, N. and B. Tozawa. 2001. *The idea generator: Quick and easy kaizen*. Vancouver, WA: PCS Press.
4. Saraph, J. V., P. G. Benson, and R. G. Schroeder. 1989. An instrument for measuring the critical factors of quality management. *Decision Sciences*, 20 (4): 810–929.
5. Kotter, J. 1996. *Leading change*. Boston: Harvard Business Review.
6. U.K. Office of Government Commerce. 2007. Continual service improvement. ITIL Version 3. Norwich, U.K.: TSO.
7. Rother, M. 2009. *Toyota data: Managing people for improvement, adaptiveness and superior results*. New York: McGraw-Hill.
8. U.K. Office of Government Commerce. 2007. Continual service improvement. ITIL Version 3. Norwich, U.K.: TSO.
9. Bodek, N. and B. Tozawa. 2001. *The idea generator: Quick and easy kaizen*. Vancouver, WA: PCS Press.

Chapter 9

Looking at Lean IT

Future Drivers of IT Work

In Chapter 2, we made some observations about the current landscape in which IT practitioners work, including brief mention of trends that help shape their environment and drive many of their priorities. These include technology and cost drivers, as well as new service paradigms that represent responses to these drivers and the strategic requirement to ensure Business–IT alignment. We also can look ahead and more clearly identify some of the trends that are likely to shape the landscape of IT work in the future, including the following:[1,2]

- Disruptive technologies with new supporting service models for, e.g., cloud computing, mobility, social media
- Continuing transformation of IT to a Service Management paradigm, with focus on end-to-end service definition and service portfolio management (versus project portfolio management)
- Corresponding shift in IT roles and skills portfolio, e.g., less traditional IT and more Service Management
- New supporting organizational models and shared service structures
- Externalized service delivery (more outsourcing to service providers)
- Business Process Management and Automation with increased focus on underlying data analytics and knowledge management
- Convergence of IT applications and infrastructure with business services (IT becomes embedded in business services)
- Stronger partnerships between IT and Business, with diminished long-term role for traditional IT roles and responsibilities

This certainly suggests a changing landscape, and there is a lot of incentive for IT to get in front of these trends, which suggests a strong need for planning and design activities and proactive attention to improvements that can help facilitate transition to a new Future State. There will be problems in this transition, just as there are problems in the Current State, and we know that Lean can make a contribution in addressing these problems. By the same token, Lean also has contributions in planning and design for the Future State, a point which we alluded to in the previous chapter. While we have not spent much time on Lean design, there are complementary resources that can help the reader gain an introduction to Lean design concepts and practices.[3,4] From this we can envision a Future State where infusion of Lean practices within IT and business processes parallels the integration of IT within business services.

The Role of Lean

Whether we are talking about Lean problem-solving or Lean design, we are using the same underlying notions of Lean Thinking that we have discussed throughout this book. In other words, regardless of our domain of inquiry, Lean Thinking serves us well in helping to clarify and understand work, especially in its focus on conceptualizing work as a value stream. This concept alone provides a unifying framework for representing Current State and/or visualizing Future State, regardless of the trend to which it pertains. The bottom line is that Lean accommodates new realities while maintaining its essential core.

Despite these trends, however, the current state for many organizations will remain tied up in problems for the foreseeable future. There is just too much going on in most IT environments to permit practitioners to focus entirely on the Future State, so really, the requirement is to focus on both the Current State (with urgency, in some cases) and the Future State (with increased planning focus) at the same time. The value stream orientation allows us to work on both together.

We believe that as IT practitioners come to realize the value of adopting a Lean orientation, this could become another trend that eventually characterizes how IT work is done on a routine basis. The ease with which it can be integrated within any methodological framework is a strong selling point for sure, and the degree to which it can be institutionalized (in practice, even if not by name) makes it almost on par with adopting "common sense" or "structured thinking" as part of good practice, regardless of what we are doing. Therefore, while we are not making a prediction, we are nevertheless promoting the widespread use of Lean in the context of any and all IT work.

How can you, the reader, become a part of this Lean Journey? Hopefully, throughout this book you have had a chance to experiment with Lean practices and, perhaps, you even have some activities or projects underway in your organization that leverage these. As we have tried to emphasize along the way, this is really a learning experience, so things you can do to promote your own knowledge and experience from this point forward will only add to your confidence in making Lean a part of your organization's set of best practices.

Some of the practical steps you can take to promote your learning include reading and onsite observation. We have included in our references many books that can start you off, and there are many more you easily can find. There also may be communities of Lean practice in which you can participate. Some are online, but some may be local groups in your area. These allow you to interact with Lean practitioners in other areas, and the message here is that Lean practitioners always have a lot they can learn from each other, even if their disciplines seem far apart. When an IT practitioner visits a Lean manufacturing facility, for instance, it's possible to focus on the IT component of the work being done there. But there are just as many lessons to be learned that pertain to non-IT practices, and these, in many cases, can be translated into IT practices through simple thought experiments. They may provide good analogies for analyzing IT-specific issues as well. It is this ongoing, active learning that characterizes the Lean community, and IT practitioners should feel right at home.

One of the things that we believe happens when you gain some traction on Lean improvements is a subtle but radical shift in thinking. This means looking at IT work differently, from a reactive to a proactive perspective, from a siloed component perspective to one that looks at the end-to-end view of processes, and from a traditional process perspective to one based on value stream concepts. Looking around our places of work, it also means seeing the difference between old trails ("cow paths") that have evolved over time and new roads and highways that we can visualize. In some respects, too, it's the difference between being kept up at night with vague notions of dread regarding problems in your organization versus getting up in the morning with some excitement to solve problems. Once the problem-solving orientation is viewed as "what it's all about," you can immediately adopt a strategic orientation toward addressing problems rather than being stuck in a reactive mode where you constantly struggle to keep up with things. So, not to sound too far-fetched, but Lean is really quite liberating, and its easy accessibility means that it can work with any process-based problems. We look at processes differently and, therefore, when we look at the work of IT, we can see Lean opportunities everywhere.

References

1. CIO Executive Board. 2010. The IT talent implications of the future of corporate IT. Information Technology Practice. Washington, D.C.: CIO Executive Board.
2. CIO Executive Board. 2011. The path to end-to-end IT services. Information Technology Practice. Washington, D.C.: CIO Executive Board.
3. Schipper, T. and M. Swets. 2009. *Innovative Lean development*. New York: Productivity Press.
4. Morgan, J. M., and J. K. Liker. 2006. *The Toyota product development system*. New York: Productivity Press

Index

A

accommodation of problems, 25, 82
accountability, *see* RACI chart
airport fast food restaurants example, 42
Analyze, *see* DMAIC approach
applications of Lean
    company maturity indicator, 3
    healthcare company, 191–196
    health insurance company, 196–200
    hospital system, 200–205
    IT Service Management, 166–168
    overview, 191
areas of potential, responses, 8
as-it-actually-is processes, 47–48
as-it-was-intended-to-be processes, 47
as-we-designed-it processes, 47
A3 report approach
    clarification of difficult-to-identify
        workflow, 121
    continuous improvement, 174
    5 Whys, 106
    Lean Improvement Model, 57
    learning, 64–66
    problem management, 154
    problem solving, 71
    root causes, 92–93
attention, lack of, 70
automation, 21, 140–141
availability management, 166
averaging processing time, 41

B

backlogs
    common in IT work, 2
    creating flow, 134
    Current *as-is* State, 14
    impact on process performance, 42
    IT Operations, 21
    Lean Service Desk, 165
    Service Desk queues, 162
    waiting in line, 43
    work-in-progress, 63
Back Office operations, 35–38, 156, 163
ball throwing example, 65–66
batches
    batch-and-queue, 135
    process type, 31
    vs. one-piece flow, 138
before-and-after data, 190
best practices framework, *see* IT
        Infrastructure Library (ITIL)
bottlenecks
    common in IT work, 2
    creating flow, 134
    Current *as-is* State, 14
    impact on process performance, 41
    IT Operations, 21
    Lean Service Desk, 165
    rapid improvement events, 143–144
bottom-up perspective, 19
brainstorming
    cause and effect diagram, 91
    solution identification, 125–127
    value stream mapping, 101
budget constraints, 184
business-IT alignment, 18–21, 59

C

call center example, 40
candidate root causes and solutions, 124, 126, 161
Capability Maturity Model Integration (CMMI), 64
capacity and capacity utilization, 44, 162
cause and effect diagram, 91–95
Center of Excellence, 199
champions, 199
Change Management
    IT Service Management, 167–168
    Requests for Change, 45
    value stream mapping, 100–101, 103
Change Review Board, 169
checklists
    healthcare company application, 200
    hospital application, 203–204
    planning, implementing, and improving solutions, 130–131
    surgery environments, 34
clarification of difficult-to-identify workflow
    A3 reports, 121
    5S approach, 117–119
    go-and-see approach, 109–113
    Lean Thinking, 70
    overview, 107–109, 113–114
    questions to ask, 50
    removal of work-in-progress, 114–117
    shine, 118
    sort, 118
    standardize, 118–119
    straighten, 118
    summary, 121–122
    surfacing waste and exposing problems, 113–121
    sustain, 119
    visual management tool, 120
COBIT, 64
co-location, 139
color use, 132
common sense, 208–209
communication, *see* RACI chart
company maturity indicator, 3
comparisons, ITIL versions, 148–149
complexity of work, 9, 80, 87

configurations, changing, 138–139
Continual Service Improvement (CSI), 53, 188, 192
continuous improvement
    Kaizen approach, 142–143
    Lean culture, 188
    Lean Thinking, 63
    overview, 141–142, 174–175
    quality, 54
    rapid improvement events, 143–144, 175–177
Control, *see* DMAIC approach
conventional IT lifecycle, 23
cookie example, 31
cost-cutting measures, 73
creating flow
    one-piece *vs.* batch flow, 138
    overview, 132–135
    pull *vs.* push, 135–138
    rapid changeover, 138–139
    work cell optimization, 139–140
Critical Success Factors (CSF), 74, 188–189
Critical-to-Quality (QTC) requirements, 54
CSI, *see* Continual Service Improvement (CSI)
culture, *see* Lean culture
Cunningham, Jeanne, 3
Current *as-designed* State
    overview, 13–14
    process mapping, 83
Current *as-is* State
    A3 reports, 65
    good faith representations, 19–20
    "How do you do...?", 50
    overview, 14
    processing times, 41
    process mapping, 83
    Value Stream Mapping, 61
Customer Contact Workflow Model, 37
customer contact workflow model, 35–38
customers
    IT as service provider, 18
    "picked the wrong line" feeling, 42
    value stream map, 97
customer value
    Lean Thinking, 59–60
    quality improvement, 54

tasks, contributing to, 70

D

data
before-and-after, 190
quantification and analysis, 193
day-to-day operational work of IT, 12
decentralized decision-making, 180
decomposition, 49
defects
common in IT work, 2
creating flow, 134
criterion, 76
Current *as-is* State, 14
IT Operations, 21
Lean Service Desk, 165
Six Sigma, 166
waste overview, 61
definable states, 13–14
Define, *see* DMAIC approach
delays
common in IT work, 2
creating flow, 134
Current *as-is* State, 14
hospital application, 201
IT Operations, 21
Lean Service Desk, 165
rapid improvement events, 143–144
value stream mapping, 102
difficult-to-identify workflow clarification
A3 reports, 121
5S approach, 117–119
go-and-see approach, 109–113
overview, 107–109, 113–114
questions to ask, 50
removal of work-in-progress, 114–117
shine, 118
sort, 118
standardize, 118–119
straighten, 118
summary, 121–122
surfacing waste and exposing problems, 113–121
sustain, 119
visual management tool, 120
distractions, 70

DMAIC (Define, Measure, Analyze, Improve, Control) approach, 54, 194
Do This Work, 4–6
downsizing, 73, 184
drivers, future, 207–208

E

education, 180
elimination of waste, 61–63, *see also* Waste
employee empowerment, 179
employee on-boarding, 198
Enable Everything, 4–6
enablers
decentralized decision-making, 180
education and training, 180
employee empowerment, 179
flexibly-deployed skills, 180
industry experience with Lean, 181
Lean Improvement Model, 73–74
management support, 179
overview, 178–179
positive communication, 180–181
process management, 181
product and service design, 181
project governance, 181
quality awareness, 180
quality data and reporting, 182
end-to-end transparency, 112–113
EPIC call center example, 203–204
error-proofing, 204, *see also* Mistake proofing
escalation procedures and processes, 34, 152
event management, 166–167
examples of waste, 74–77, *see also* Waste
Expanded Incident Life cycle, 159
exposing problems, 113–121
external view, Service Desk, 158–160

F

failure, process improvement efforts, 20
fast food restaurant examples, 42, 92
firewall IDs, 197
fishbone diagram, *see* Cause and effect diagram

5 Questions technique, 186–187
5S approach, 117–119, 205
5 Whys
   brainstorming, 126
   healthcare company application, 193
   problem management, 154
   waste in clearly identified workflows,
      104–106
flexibly-deployed skills, 180
flow
   creating, 132–140
   "factory" parallel, 45
   healthcare company application, 199
   jumbled flow, 30, 32–33, 110
   lines, 30–31
   low volumes, 29
   one-piece *vs.* batch flow, 138
   overview, 132–135
   pull *vs.* push, 135–138
   quality improvement, 54
   rapid changeover, 138–139
   repeatable batch linear flows, 35
   work cell optimization, 139–140
   workflow concepts, 41–42
focus, lack of, 70
fragmented information symptoms, 77
Front Office operations, 35–38, 156, 163
functions, of IT, 12
future drivers, 207–208
Future *to-be* State
   A3 reports, 65
   good faith representations, 20
   overview, 14
   Value Stream Mapping, 61

G

"Get IP address of devices to monitor"
      subactivity, 48
go-and-see approach (Gemba), 109–113, 205
grassroots efforts, 24, 25

H

haiku contest, 202
healthcare company application, 191–196

health insurance company application,
      196–200
Help Desks, *see also* Service Desks
   back office components, 38
   capacity, 44
   "factory" parallel, 45
   fast food restaurant comparison, 92
   front office components, 36, 38
   haiku contest, 202
   jumbled flow, 32–33
   pull *vs.* push, 136–137
   service request fulfillments, 156–157
   ticket system, 38–45
   waiting in line, 43
   workflow, 38
   work-in-progress, 63
"hidden" linear flow, 45
hidden processes, 113
high-level, server build process map, 83, 84
highly reactive culture, 182–183
historical developments, 3
hospital system application, 130, 200–205
"How do you do...?", 50
human error, 93–94
human potential, 62, 76–77

I

identification of waste, 79–80, *see also*
      Waste
identifying and managing solutions
   automation of operations, 140–141
   brainstorming, 125–127
   checklists, 130–131
   continuous improvement, 141–144
   flow, creating, 132–140
   Kaizen approach, 142–143
   mistake proofing, 131–132
   nonlinear processes, 141
   one-piece *vs.* batch flow, 138
   overview, 6, 123
   Plan-Do-Check-Act approach, 129–130
   planning, implementing, and improving
      solutions, 128–132
   pull *vs.* push, 135–138
   rapid changeover, 138–139
   rapid improvement events, 143–144

root cause analysis, 123–124
solution identification, 124–127
summary, 144
work cell optimization, 139–140
identifying and understanding problems
A3 reports, 121
cause and effect diagram, 91–95
Change Management interaction, 100–101
clarifying difficult-to-identify workflows, 107–113
exposing problems, 113–121
5S approach, 117–119
5 Whys, 104–106
go-and-see approach, 109–113
human resources interaction, 112
identifying waste, 79–80
Lean Improvement Model, 71, 72
overview, 79
pain points, stumbling on waste, 81–95
Pareto chart, 106–107
Patch management, 98–99
Patch management and teams, 102–103
Plan for Deployment, 99–110
process mapping, 83–90
RACI chart, 86
removal of work-in-progress, 114–117
root cause analysis, 90–91
shine, 118
sort, 118
standardize, 118–119
straighten, 118
summary, 121–122
surfacing waste, 113–121
sustain, 119
swim-lane diagram, 85–86
User Provisioning process map, 110–111
value stream maps, 97–104
visual management tool, 120
waste in clearly identified workflows, 95–107
implementation of Lean
IT Service Management, 168–171
mistake proofing, 131–132
Improve, *see* DMAIC approach
improvements, implementing and sustaining
applications, Lean IT, 191–205
continuous improvement, 174–177
decentralized decision-making, 180
difficulty of, 25
education and training, 180
employee empowerment, 179
enablers, 178–187
5 Questions technique, 186–187
flexibly-deployed skills, 180
healthcare company, 191–196
health insurance company, 196–200
hospital system, 200–205
industry experience with Lean, 181
Lean culture, 187–188
management support, 179
metrics and measurement, 188–191
obstacles, dealing with, 182–186
overview, 7, 173–174
positive communication, 180–181
process management, 181
product and service design, 181
project governance, 181
quality awareness, 180
quality data and reporting, 182
rapid improvement events, 175–177
summary, 205–206
improvements, opportunities for, 22
inaccurate information symptoms, 77
incidents and incident management
Expanded Incident Life cycle, 159
IT Service Management, 150–153
workflow, 38–45
work-in-progress, 63
incomplete information symptoms, 77
incremental, small improvements, 69
industry experience with Lean, 181
inefficiency, *see* Waste
information technology, *see* IT
informing others, *see* RACI chart
insufficient resources, 184
internal view, Service Desk, 160–163
inventory, *see also* Work-in-progress (WIP)
criterion, 75–76
reduction, 62
waste overview, 61
Ishikawa diagram, *see* Cause and effect diagram
ISO standards, 64
IT (information technology)

complexity of work, 9
day-to-day operational work, 12
domain, 22
"factory" workflow concepts, 45
functions, 12
future drivers, 207–208
Operations, 21–22
process type, 31–35
role of Lean, 208–210
view of itself, 11–13
IT Infrastructure Library (ITIL)
best practices framework, 21
checklists, 131
customer value, 60
overview, 147–148
processes, 149
value stream mapping, 103
Versions 2 & 3 comparisons, 148–149
waste, 150
IT Project Management, 23
IT Service Management (ITSM)
applications of Lean, 166–168
availability management, 166
change management, 167–168
comparisons, ITIL versions, 148–149
event management, 166–167
external view, 158–160
implementation of Lean, 168–171
incident management, 150–153
internal view, 160–163
IT Infrastructure Library, 147–150
Lean Service Desk, 164–166
overview, 6, 147
problem management, 154–155
processes, 149
Service Desk, 157–166
service request fulfillment, 155–157
summary, 141
waste, 150

J

job shops
jumbled flow characteristics, 32–34
process type, 30
treated as line processes, 33
journey, 9, 70

jumbled flow, *see also* Flow
creating linear from, 133–134
"factory" parallel, 45
going to Gemba, 110
internal view, Service Desk, 163
job shops, 30, 32–34
Just-in-Time (JIT), 204–205

K

Kaizen approach
continuous improvement, 63, 142–143,
174–175
healthcare company application, 194
hospital application, 201
Lean culture, 188
Key Performance Indicators (KPI), 188–189
knots example, 66

L

Lean
hybrid approach, 192–196
metrics comparison, 190
overview, 2–4, 6
role of, 208–210
Lean culture
continuous improvement, 63
foundation, 25
implementing and sustaining
improvements, 187–188
overview, 4
rapid improvement events, 177
Lean Improvement Model
A3 thinking, 64–66
continuous improvement, 63
customer value, 59–60
elimination of waste, 61–63
enablers, 73–74
examples of waste, 74–77
learning, 63–70
overview, 4–6, 57–58
Plan-Do-Check-Act cycle, 66–70
problem-solving, 71, 72
summary, 74
thinking, 59–63
tools, 71–73

value stream flow, 60–61
waste, 61–63, 74–77
Lean IT, work of, 22–23
Lean Learning
A3 thinking, 64–66
overview, 63–64
Plan-Do-Check-Act cycle, 66–70
Lean problem-solving, 6
Lean Six Sigma hybrid, 54, 192–196
Lean Thinking
clarifying objections, 70
continuous improvement, 63
customer value, 59–60
elimination of waste, 61–63
overview, 3–4, 59
value stream flow, 60–61
Learn to Improve, 4–6
legacy monitoring data, 48
linear flow, 30–31, 45, 151
line processes and characteristics
job shops treated as, 33
operation types, 31–32
overview, 30–31

M

making IT Lean, 24–26
management
as obstacle, 185
support, 179
matrix, People-Process-Technology, 16–17
Measure, *see* DMAIC approach
metrics and measurement, 188–191
mini-Kaizen events, 143, 175, 194
mistake proofing, 131–132
mistakes, applying Lean, 8
models
customer contact workflow, 35–38
Lean Improvement, 4–6
motion, 61, 75

N

narrative structure, 6–9
Network Management, 45–49
nonlinear processes, 141
nonvalue-added (NVA), 61, 97–100

O

obstacles, 182–186, 193
"one-off" projects, 35
one-piece *vs.* batch flow, 138
Operations Management (OM) perspective
batches, 31
capacity, 44
Change Management, 167
customer contact workflow model, 35–38
flow concepts, 41–42
IT "factory," 45
IT work, 31–35
job shops, 30
lines, 30–31
overview, 6, 27–28
process analysis, 45–51
process improvement, 51–53
process types, 28–35
projects, 29
quality improvement, 53–54
summary, 55
volume, variety, and variation, 38–41
waiting in line, 42–44
workflow concepts, 38–45
opportunities for improvement, 22, 121, 195
overprocessing and overproduction, 61,
75–76

P

pain points
cause and effect diagram, 91–95
as driver, 12, 80
hospital application, 200
overview, 81–83
process mapping, 83–90
putting in parking lot, 88
RACI chart, 86
root cause analysis, 90–91
swim-lane diagram, 85–86
value stream mapping, 98–99
Pareto chart, 106–107
patch management
Pareto chart, 106–107
process map, 96
teams, 103

value stream mapping, 98–99, 103
waste, clearly identified workflows, 95–97
People-Process-Technology perspective
cause and effect diagram, 93
IT Operations, 21
Lean enablers, 178
nondiscrimination between, 184
OM perspective, 27
work of IT, 14–17
phone tree interaction example, 33
pianist example, 70, 171
Plan-Do-Check-Act (PDCA) cycle
continuous improvement, 141–142, 174–175
Current-to-Future state, 66–67
hazards of, 68
incident management, 153
IT Service Management (ITSM), 168–169
lack of awareness of application, 24
Lean Improvement Model, 57
learning, 66–70, 71
metrics, 191
planning, implementing, and improving solutions, 68, 128, 129–130
problem management, 155
process improvement, 51–52
Plan-Do-Drift cycle, 67
Plan-Do-Stop cycle, 67
plan for deployment, 99–100
planning, implementing, and improving solutions
checklists, 130–131
mistake proofing, 131–132
overview, 128–129
Plan-Do-Check-Act cycle, 129–130
poka-yoke, *see* Mistake proofing
positive communication, 180–181
preoperative checklists, 34
prioritization, 123–124, 127
proactive problem management, 155
problem management
accommodation *vs.* solutions, 25, 82
IT Service Management, 154–155
problem-solving, identifying and understanding problems
A3 reports, 66, 121

cause and effect diagram, 91–95
Change Management interaction, 100–101
chart, 72
clarifying difficult-to-identify workflows, 107–113
exposing problems, 113–121
5S approach, 117–119
5 Whys, 104–106
go-and-see approach, 109–113
human resources interaction, 112
identifying waste, 79–80
Lean Improvement Model, 71, 72
overview, 79
pain points, stumbling on waste, 81–95
Pareto chart, 106–107
Patch management and teams, 98–99, 102–103
Plan for Deployment, 99–110
process mapping, 83–90
RACI chart, 86
removal of work-in-progress, 114–117
root cause analysis, 90–91
shine, 118
sort, 118
standardize, 118–119
straighten, 118
summary, 121–122
surfacing waste, 113–121
sustain, 119
swim-lane diagram, 85–86
User Provisioning process map, 110–111
value stream maps, 97–104
visual management tool, 120
waste in clearly identified workflows, 95–107
process-based work, 13–14
processes
abstraction, 48–50
analysis, 45–51
batches, 31
control, 52–53
definable states, 13–14
efforts failure, 20
enablers, 181
hidden, 113
IT Infrastructure Library, 149
IT work, 31–35

job shops, 30
lines, 30–31
mapping, 83–90, 111–112
Operations Management perspective,
    51–53
overview, 28–29
projects, 29
types, 29–35
product design, 181
productivity, creating flow, 135
projects
    enablers, 181
    process type, 29
pull *vs.* push systems, 135–138

Q

quality awareness, 180
quality data and reporting, 182
quality improvement, 53–54
Quality Management, 178
quality management maturity cycle, 24
queues, work-in-progress, 63

R

race car tires example, 173
RACI chart, 86, 87
rapid changeover, 138–139
rapid improvement events
    continuous improvement, 143–144,
        175–177
    hospital application, 201
RCA, *see* Root cause analysis (RCA)
reactive culture, 182–183
reactive proactive problem management,
    155
references, required reading, 9
removal of work-in-progress, 114–117
repeatable batch linear flows, 35
repeatable operations, 33–35
reporting, quality data, 182
request fulfillment, *see* Service Request
    Fulfillment
Requests for Change, 45
required reading, 9
resources, unplanned consumption, 40

responses, 8, 119, 121
responsibility, *see* RACI chart
role of Lean, 22, 208–210
root cause analysis (RCA)
    eliminating waste, 71
    5 Whys, 106
    going to Gemba, 110
    hospital application, 203
    identifying and managing solutions,
        123–124
    internal view, Service Desk, 161
    pain points, stumbling on waste, 90–91
    Pareto chart, 106
    problem management, 154
    value stream mapping, 102

S

scientific reasoning, 66
scope creep, 198–199
sequential and repeatable operations, 35,
    81–82, 102
server upgrades example, 35
service-based work
    customer value, 60
    ITIL, 147
    work of IT, 17–18
service design enablers, 181
Service Desks, *see also* Help Desks
    activities, 161
    external view, 158–160
    internal view, 160–163
    Lean perspective, 164–166
    overview, 157–158
Service Lifecycle, 22
Service Management, *see also* IT Service
        Management (ITSM)
    Customer Contact Workflow Model, 37
    OM perspective, 27
    overview, 23
service operations, *see* IT Infrastructure
        Library (ITIL)
service recovery, 158, 160
Service Request Fulfillment, 155–157
shine (5S), 118
silo organizational structure, 16, 8216
Single Minute Exchange of Die (SMED), 138

Six Sigma
  availability management, 166
  customer value, 60
  hybrid approach, 192–196
  Lean, broad definition, 3
  metrics comparison, 190
  process control, 53
  quality improvement, 54
small, incremental improvements, 69
solutions, identifying and managing
  automation of operations, 140–141
  brainstorming, 125–127
  checklists, 130–131
  continuous improvement, 141–144
  flow, creating, 132–140
  Kaizen approach, 142–143
  mistake proofing, 131–132
  nonlinear processes, 141
  one-piece *vs.* batch flow, 138
  overview, 6, 123
  Plan-Do-Check-Act approach, 68,
      129–130
  planning, implementing, and improving
      solutions, 128–132
  pull *vs.* push, 135–138
  rapid changeover, 138–139
  rapid improvement events, 143–144
  root cause analysis, 123–124
  solution identification, 124–127
  summary, 144
  work cell optimization, 139–140
sort (5S), 118
special orders, 31
stakeholders, not forthcoming, 90
standardized work
  created from jumbled flow, 34
  healthcare company application, 34199
  simplification, 68
  slight changes, 53
standardize (5S), 118–119
Statistical Process Control, 53
stitches example, 66
straighten (5S), 118
structured thinking, 209
stumbling on waste, pain points
  cause and effect diagram, 91–95
  overview, 81–83

process mapping, 83–90
  RACI chart, 86
  root cause analysis, 90–91
  swim-lane diagram, 85–86
Subway restaurants, 39
summaries
  clarification of difficult-to-identify
      workflow, 121–122
  identifying and managing solutions, 144
  implementing and sustaining
      improvements, 205–206
  IT Service Management, 141
  Lean Improvement Model, 74
  Operations Management perspective, 55
  work of IT, 26
surfacing waste and exposing problems,
      113–121
surgery environment preoperative
      checklists, 34
sustainability, 174, *see also* Improvements,
      implementing and sustaining
sustain (5S), 119
sweet spot, 135
swim-lane diagram, 85–86, 87
systems overview, 27

T

thinking
  continuous improvement, 63
  customer value, 59–60
  overview, 59
  value stream flow, 60–61
  waste, 61–63
Think This Way, 4–6
throughput, 41
throughput tine, 41
"tiger teams," 142
tools, *see also specific tool*
  A3 reports, 121
  brainstorming, 125–127
  cause and effect diagram, 91
  checklists, 130–131
  5 Questions, 186–187
  5 S, 117–119
  5 Whys, 104–106
  Go-and-See (Gemba), 109–113

Lean Improvement Model, 71–73
Lean overview, 71–73
mistake proofing, 131–132
one-piece flow (*vs.* batch), 138
Pareto chart, 106–107
Plan-Do-Check-Act cycle, 129–130
process mapping, 83–85, 86–90
pull (*vs.* push), 135–138
RACI chart, 86
rapid changeover, 138–139
rapid improvement events, 143–144
removal of Work-in-Progress, 114–117
root cause analysis, 90–91
swim-lane diagram, 85–86
using, 4–6
Value Stream Map, 97–104
visual management, 120
work cell optimization, 139–140
top-down perspective, 19, 46
Total Quality Management (TQM), 53
traffic jam example, 143–144
training enablers, 180
transportation, 61, 75

U

understanding problems, *see* Identifying
and understanding problems
unstable processes, 53
User Acceptance Testing, 200
User Provisioning, 108, 110–111
Use These Tools, 4–6

V

value-added (VA), 61
Value Chain, 19–20, 59
value stream flow, 54, 60–61
value stream maps/mapping (VSM)
Change Management interaction, 100–101
going to Gemba, 110–111
health insurance application, 197–198
incident management, 150
obstacles to, 186
overview, 61, 97–98
Pareto chart, 107

Patch management and teams, 98–99,
102–103
Plan-Do-Check-Act cycle, 129
Plan for Deployment, 99–110
waste in clearly identified workflows,
97–104
variability
arrival rate, 43
overview, 40
process control, 52–53
variety, process types, 28
version comparisons, ITIL, 148–149
visual management, 120
Voice of the Customer (VOC), 54, 60
volume, 28–29
volume, variety, and variation model, 38–41

W

waiting
criterion, 76
in line, 42–44
Service Desk queues, 162
waste overview, 61
workflow, 42–44
waste
awareness, 62
Change Management interaction,
100–101
clearly identified workflows, 80, 95–107
elimination, 61–63
enablers, 73–74
examples, 74–77
expected, 153
5 Whys, 104–106
identification, 11, 79–80
internal view, Service Desk, 161–163
IT Infrastructure Library, 150
IT operational work, 21–22
management interest, 1876
overview, 95–97
pain points, 12, 80–95
Pareto chart, 106–107
Patch management and teams, 98–99,
102–103
Plan for Deployment, 99–110
problems, seeing in different way, 25

service recovery, 158
surfacing, 113–121
tolerated, 153
types, 61–62
unLean approach, 4
value stream maps, 97–104
workflow problems, 41
"We already do that" response, 8
"We don't do that at all" response, 8
"We do some of this already" response, 119
"Well, we do that, but not very well"
    response, 8
"We will get back to you on this" response,
    121
"What's not working well here?", 16
wiring diagram example, 169–170
work cell optimization, 139–140
workflow, incident management
    capacity, 44
    flow concepts, 41–42
    IT "factory," 45
    overview, 38
    volume, variety, and variation, 38–41
    waiting in line, 42–44
workflows, clarifying difficult-to-identify
    A3 reports, 121
    5S approach, 117–119
    go-and-see approach, 109–113
    overview, 107–109, 113–114
    removal of work-in-progress, 114–117
    shine, 118
    sort, 118
    standardize, 118–119
    straighten, 118
    summary, 121–122

surfacing waste and exposing problems,
    113–121
sustain, 119
visual management tool, 120
workflows, waste in clearly identified
    Change Management interaction, 100–101
    5 Whys, 104–106
    overview, 95–97
    Pareto chart, 106–107
    Patch management and teams, 98–99,
        102–103
    Plan for Deployment, 99–110
    value stream maps, 97–104
workforce reductions, 73, 184
work-in-progress (WIP), *see also* Inventory
    hospital application, 201, 204–205
    Lean Service Desk, 165
    overview, 62–63
    removal, 114–117
    removal of, 114–117
work of IT
    business-IT alignment, 18–21
    IT view of itself, 11–13
    Lean IT, 22–23
    making IT Lean, 24–26
    Operations, 21–22
    overview, 1–2, 6, 11
    People-Process-Technology, 14–17
    process-based work, 13–14
    service-based work, 17–18
    summary, 26

Z

zero defects, 166